THE BATTLIN' BASTARDS OF BRAVO

Bravo Company, 1/506th, 101st Airborne, in Vietnam and Beyond

MELISSA ZIOBRO

Published in the United States of America and Great Britain in 2025 by
CASEMATE PUBLISHERS
1950 Lawrence Road, Havertown, PA 19083, USA
and
47 Church Street, Barnsley, S70 2AS, UK

Copyright © 2025 Melissa Ziobro

Hardcover Edition: ISBN 978-1-63624-483-9
Digital Edition: ISBN 978-1-63624-484-6

A CIP record for this book is available from the British Library

All rights reserved. No part of this book may be reproduced or transmitted in any form or by any means, electronic or mechanical including photocopying, recording or by any information storage and retrieval system, without permission from the publisher in writing.

Printed and bound in the United Kingdom by CPI Group (UK) Ltd, Croydon, CR0 4YY
Typeset in India by DiTech Publishing Services

For a complete list of Casemate titles, please contact:

CASEMATE PUBLISHERS (US)
Telephone (610) 853-9131
Fax (610) 853-9146
Email: casemate@casematepublishers.com
www.casematepublishers.com

CASEMATE PUBLISHERS (UK)
Telephone (0)1226 734350
Email: casemate@casemateuk.com
www.casemateuk.com

Cover images: (Front) Camp Evans, circa 1970. Left to right: Don Rollings, Tony Liguori, Roger Fitch, unidentified, and Wylie Glover. (Courtesy Don Rollings); and (Back) Near the Hue Citadel and military museum during a 2017 return trip to Vietnam. Left to right: Mike Smith, Jerry Hoffman, Pete Falco, Terry Ostendorf, and Steve Conroy. (Courtesy Steve Conroy)

The Publisher's authorised representative in the EU for product safety is Authorised Rep Compliance Ltd., Ground Floor, 71 Lower Baggot Street, Dublin D02 P593, Ireland.
http://www.arccompliance.com

Contents

Foreword

I have been retired from the Army for over thirty years. All vestiges of my military service and career had long since been packed away or discarded. I loved the Army and what I was able to do and experience (for the most part)—but it was eons ago. Other than an occasional salute from the gate guards at Fort Bragg (now Liberty)—no one except my family and a very few close friends know I ever even served. I sort of like it that way. After a post-Army career teaching high school history in public education, I retired in 2011 to the rural sandhills of North Carolina and live an intentionally isolated life of peace and relative quiet.

In the fall of 2013, I received a call from Pete Falco. He introduced himself as a former "member of Bravo Company, 1/506th" who had served with the unit in Vietnam. He told me that he was "studying the unit's history" and had learned I had also served in B Company. He asked if I would be willing to meet him for lunch in a nearby town and discuss my time with the unit. Initially cautious, I was admittedly curious and intrigued by his enthusiasm—I agreed to meet.

We met and discussed our experiences in B Company—we served at different times and our times did not overlap. After Vietnam, Pete became a teacher and administrator in the New Jersey school system and was (in his own words) an amateur historian. Pete also stayed in the Army Reserve and retired as a colonel. He had spent an extensive amount of time researching and compiling the history of B Company, 1/506th, during the Vietnam War. Pete was irrepressible in his enthusiasm for chronicling the history of B Company. Pete also told me that a "reunion group" of former B Company men had formed, was meeting annually, and invited me to come to the next one. Not one who normally attends reunions—family, school, or military—I gave it little thought. Pete and I talked often over the next few months, and after several requests, I agreed to attend the 2014 reunion in Myrtle Beach, South Carolina.

The "reunion" was a very well-organized, weeklong affair, families included. There were about thirty or so former B Company members in attendance. After the day's family activities—the former soldiers (and many family members) gathered to "socialize." There were lots of beverages, storytelling, laughter, and I am sure—discreetly—a few tears of sadness for fellow soldiers lost. What was most impressive was the final night's reunion dinner, where a solemn "Missing Man" ceremony was conducted to honor every soldier, by name, lost in Vietnam from April 1969 through September 1970—the period in which B Company experienced some of the most intense fighting in the war. I left humbled by the experience and significantly impressed by the reunion attendees—former soldiers and their families—who took the singular opportunity to honor the 44 fellow warriors lost in Vietnam, the "missing men."

Among these valiant former B Company warriors is a Medal of Honor recipient—Distinguished Service Cross, Silver Star, or Bronze Star for Valor awardees galore—the Purple Heart almost a rite of passage. Each has earned the right to wear the Combat Infantryman Badge. These men honestly and truly care for each other—a true Vietnam-era "Band of Brothers." At the 2014 reunion, I watched as Leon Heaton received the medals and awards he had earned in Vietnam but had never been given as his heroics went unrecognized due to the fog of war. Painstaking research, diligence, and hard work by Pete Falco corrected that oversight. Similarly, in 2023, I saw John Brown receive the medals he earned presented and pinned on by his family—through the work and perseverance of Chuck Choney along with Bob and Marilyn Harasick (Chuck and Bob are former B Company officers—Marilyn, a former Army nurse, served in Phu Bai, Vietnam).

Since 2014, I have attended two other reunions and remained in touch with many of the men, our common bond being our service in B Company, 1/506th, the "Currahees." During the reunions, I listened to countless stories—some about the "war," and others about survival after returning to grateful families but an ungrateful nation. Contained in this book are the recollections of just some of the men, representative of all who served in one of the most "storied" units that fought in Vietnam—fighting daily against an often numerically superior enemy, fighting for each other, and fighting to hopefully return safely home. Most did—but some carried with them the physical scars of battle and the mental anguish of fellow warriors lost. I know—I've heard their stories, seen the faraway look, the sadness, the momentary tears in their eyes.

Through diligent archival research, by 2009, Pete Falco and others identified 306 former B Company soldiers from Vietnam who served as "Battlin' Bastards" from late 1968 through to the fall of 1970. Of that number, 44 were killed in Vietnam—as of September 2023, 88 former troopers from B Company have died. Those who survive have stories that have never been told that should be, that need to be, recorded. Unfortunately, Pete died in December 2020 before we could collect and compile the stories. I contacted Steve Conroy, also a former platoon leader, and he agreed we should pursue publishing. Some of the stories from the B Company veterans are presented herein, compiled and lightly edited by Professor Melissa Ziobro, an eminent historian who truly loves history; loves, respects, and understands military veterans.

This is not just another "book about Vietnam." The stories herein are by young men sent to fight—and they did. They returned, ground in the crucibles of battles named and unnamed, hardened and tempered in the white-hot, unforgiving forge of combat. They asked nothing in return. For years, many never thought of, let alone spoke of, their experiences. This compilation is for those readers who appreciate military history and realize that real heroes walk amongst us.

James W. Tarleton III
LTC, U.S. Army (Ret.)
Second Platoon Leader, B Company, 1/506th (December 1968–May 1969)

Preface and Acknowledgements

I started my career as a professional historian in 2004 in the Command Historical Office of the United States Army Communications-Electronics Command at Fort Monmouth in Central New Jersey. The base started as an Army Signal Corps training camp during World War I. It outlived the conflict, and was for many decades known as the "Home of the Signal Corps." Until its closure in 2011, it trained scores of soldiers for war and contributed to the development of countless devices that saved lives on the battlefield. Many of these technologies made their way into civilian life, and probably impact the way you live today—for example, when you check the weather or use the GPS on your phone, get an alert from your doorbell camera, or when a police officer clocks you speeding on their radar (sorry about that one).[1]

I resigned from my position as a civilian historian for the Army in 2011, when Fort Monmouth closed and my job moved to Maryland. (This Jersey girl lives nowhere other than the Garden State.) I moved into teaching history full-time at my alma mater, Monmouth University. Still, military history remained a passion of mine. For example, I taught a Vietnam War class, and served on the board of the New Jersey Vietnam Veterans Memorial and Museum Foundation in Holmdel, New Jersey. I have always been particularly interested in humanizing the military. Part of this is, selfishly, because I personally find the stories of individual soldiers more engaging than statistics and strategy—and there are plenty of very talented military historians who enjoy tackling the past from that angle. I'm also always thinking of the general public, and students in particular. How can we as historians get them to care about military history? To be interested enough to extrapolate and implement lessons learned? Statistics can be so cold. And today, it's not unusual for me to stand in front of a class where not one student even knows a veteran. It makes it difficult to care; to relate. Yet, these students are the leaders of tomorrow, who will be voting for politicians who determine policies that impact our active-duty military and veterans. They may even serve in office themselves. It's imperative that they understand the sacrifices of those who serve. It can be difficult to get these students to relate to traditional "bullets and beans" military histories, but I have found, in my 17 years of teaching, that the soldier stories will make them sit up and listen every time.

But I was actually telling a story about New Jersey's dollar princesses—yes, princesses—when I met the man who would lead to me writing this book. The dollar princesses—"new money" American women who married often impoverished European men with titles during the Gilded Age—were a minor side project of mine; a fanciful distraction from the military history work I often focused on.[2] I was asked to give a lecture on the topic at a local library back when the original *Downton Abbey* series finale was airing in 2016. If you're not familiar with *Downton Abbey*, it's a series about the lives (and loves) of a wealthy, titled British family and their staff, set in the early twentieth century. The mother of the family just happens to be an American dollar princess. In any event, I received dozens of unsolicited requests to give the talk at different venues throughout the state for years. People just really enjoyed it, so I figured, why not? We all need a little escapism. By chance, veteran Jim Tarleton—once a member of Bravo Company, 1st Battalion, 506th Infantry Regiment, 101st Airborne Division, or, the "Battlin' Bastards" of Bravo—saw me deliver a dollar-princess lecture virtually for the Monmouth County Historical Association in January of 2023. Jim kindly and generously reached out afterwards to tell me how much he and his wife enjoyed the program. It turned out, Jim had once served at Fort Monmouth. Long story very short, he suggested I write a book about the experiences of Bravo Company during the Vietnam War. The inspiration for this book, he suggested, could be a painstakingly researched, self-published journal compiled by members of the unit, augmented by additional research and oral histories.

In the book that ultimately took shape, I endeavor to allow the Battlin' Bastards to speak as often as possible in their own words by presenting lightly edited transcripts of their oral histories and written accounts, in the spirit of earlier works like Studs Terkel's *The Good War: An Oral History of WWII* and Wallace Terry's *Bloods: An Oral History of the Vietnam War by Black Veterans.* As Terkel writes in the introduction to *The Good War*, "This is a memory book, rather than one of hard fact and precise statistic."

Why a book about these men, in particular? I believe every soldier's story is unique and deserves to be told, regardless of the conflict. And as Battlin' Bastard Jim Hartman notes, "If you get three different guys that were in Vietnam and … you listen to the three of us talk, it's three different guys with three completely different stories … it's just like you're in three different countries and the more people you talk to, I think, Vietnam vets, I don't think you'd get the same story from anybody."[3]

I also believe we owe a special debt to the men and women of the Vietnam War era, who were often treated with indifference or even outright hostility when they returned. Many of them struggle with post-traumatic stress disorder (PTSD), the impacts of chemical defoliants such as Agent Orange, and other lingering aftereffects of their service to this day, often without adequate support from the government. The 50th anniversary of the fall of Saigon on April 30, 2025, provides an opportunity to reflect on the sacrifices of the men and women who served during the war. Let us honor those who died. Let us say a hearty "Thank you for your service" and "Welcome home" to those who returned. And let us ponder the lessons we can learn from this fraught period in our nation's history.

Writing this book became a bit complicated when in August of 2023 I transitioned from my faculty role to serve as the curator of Monmouth University's Bruce Springsteen Archives & Center for American Music (BSACAM). Shortly after I started, Monmouth University announced that the BSACAM would be building a new, 30,000-square-foot museum building to open in the spring of 2026—just in time for the nation's 250th birthday! This exciting opportunity would allow me to teach United States history through the very accessible prism of music and reach far more people than I ever would in the classroom, but it also left far less time for my own personal scholarship pursuits. Still, I did not want to disappoint the Battlin' Bastards who had placed their trust in me. I mention this because I carved out time for this book on nights, weekends, and vacations, with the support of my husband and two sons. Thank you, John, JP, and Donovan!

But thanks are also due to Jim Tarleton, who has become a faithful friend, cheerleader, and true source of inspiration to me. Steve Conroy was enormously helpful herding the cats, so to speak, and keeping the project on task. Danny McNair generously documented the stories of men who were more comfortable speaking with a fellow veteran than a stranger. Christopher Pupillo and George Bogdanich shared interviews with veterans that they conducted at the Battlin' Bastards 2023 reunion. Matthew Seelinger, Chrissie Reilly, Rebecca Ashdot, Thy Cavagnaro, and Keri Giannotti provided helpful feedback on drafts. Lastly, thanks to all the men who trusted me to share their stories with the world. I recognize this may at times have felt a bit frightening, given you have not always been shown the respect you deserve. I am honored by your faith in me, and hope you are heartened by the impact your stories will make via this book, long after you and I are both gone. Any author royalties will be donated to the Vietnam Veterans Memorial Fund in your honor.

Currahee!

Introduction

This book addresses the personal experiences of a group of men from Bravo Company, 1st Battalion, 506th Infantry Regiment, 101st Airborne Division in the Vietnam War, primarily 1968–1971. It draws heavily upon archival records and, most importantly, the words of the Battlin' Bastards of Bravo themselves. Many of the men of Bravo Company who you will meet on these pages arrived in Vietnam, as they tell it, "green as green can be" to a place "they couldn't have found on a map." They were largely "transported to Vietnam as individuals, rather than as units," but, through intense fighting at places like "Hamburger Hill," "a trust was developed between the men." Decades after their service ended, many of them continue to meet. They share their stories still, seeking to "bring some closure to that chapter in their lives" and to honor those "who sacrificed for their country and their unit." This book, which is divided into three major parts, is your chance to join them on that journey.

As an educator, one learns providing proper context is key. Therefore, Part I of *Battlin' Bastards* seeks to provide that and ensure that the book is accessible to audiences who are not necessarily military history enthusiasts. It first provides a brief history of the 101st Airborne Division. For some, "101st Airborne" will ring no bells at all. But many may hear "101st Airborne" and think of *Band of Brothers*, the 2001 award-winning HBO miniseries created by Steven Spielberg and Tom Hanks and based on historian Stephen E. Ambrose's 1992 non-fiction book of the same name. That series dramatizes the World War II history of Easy Company, 2nd Battalion, 506th Parachute Infantry Regiment, 101st Airborne Division. However, the 101st Airborne has a long and proud history that continues to this day, and the "Band of Brothers" of Easy Company and the Battlin' Bastards of Bravo Company are but chapters in this expansive story.

The second half of Part I provides a brief overview of the Vietnam War. When asked when the Vietnam War started, most students will suggest it's somewhere in the 1960s. Yes, in 1965 U.S. President Lyndon B. Johnson ordered the sustained American bombing of North Vietnam and committed the first combat boots on the ground. But America had been sending military aid and "advisors" to Vietnam since the 1950s. Some of those advisors died there. And one can go back even further, to explore the impacts of decades of French occupation of Vietnam, beginning in the nineteenth century. There are also periods where the Japanese and the Chinese occupied Vietnam. How did those experiences shape the Vietnamese people, and influence wartime circumstances in both North and South Vietnam? What did it mean for America's ability to achieve its objectives in the war? What exactly were the Battlin' Bastards sent to do? Did their nation set them up for success?

Part II of the book presents select Battlin' Bastards' experiences before, during, and in the immediate aftermath of the war. These lightly edited first-hand accounts are the heart of the book. These self-selected veterans have bravely shared their stories to serve as stand-ins for the Battlin' Bastards more broadly. It is simply not possible here in this book to share the story of every single man who served in the unit during the entirety of the War, but the examples provided herein give readers a unique glimpse into types of situations the unit's men encountered.

Before the war, the Battlin' Bastards were brothers, sons, sweethearts, husbands, and fathers. Some were athletes, some musicians, some bookworms. Some were just out of high school, some already established in civilian careers. There is no monolithic American Vietnam War soldier, and there is no monolithic "Battlin' Bastard." These are human beings, from diverse backgrounds, being asked to cross the globe and do things those of us who have never served cannot completely fathom. Some were drafted; some enlisted voluntarily. Take Jerry Hoffman. He was a student at Illinois State University, Bloomington, when he left school to serve. He shared:

> I guess ... partly because of my dad, and knowing that he had served [in World War II], I kind of grew up with the idea that, kind of like John Kennedy said, "ask not what your country can do for you, but what you can do for your country?" And unlike the typical college person of that time, I kind of went to the other side of it and thought it was our responsibility to do something.
>
> I really didn't tell my dad and mom that I joined till after I had signed the papers. They weren't really happy with my decision. Not so much because they weren't in support of the country, but worried about what might happen [to me].[1]

Such concerns were justified. Once in-country, the Battlin' Bastards saw numerous engagements with the enemy, including at Hill 937, where, for almost 11 days in May of 1969, American troops famously waged a deadly battle for control of a three-thousand-foot-tall hill in a remote valley in South Vietnam. After nearly a dozen deadly assaults, the Americans finally captured the hill, known locally as Dong Ap Bia. Dong Ap Bia translates to "the mountain of the crouching beast." The Americans would give it another name: Hamburger Hill, because soldiers saw it as a human meat grinder. Sergeant James Spears, a 19-year-old who fought in the battle, told reporters, "Have you ever been inside a hamburger machine? We just got cut to pieces by extremely accurate machine-gun fire."[2] When the Americans abandoned the hill just days later, controversy erupted over what many saw as a senseless loss of lives—a debate that has continued in the decades since. As Bravo veteran Jim Tarleton wrote:

> From a purely strategic standpoint—the American military (in general) could argue that it "won the battle." True enough. The [enemy] forces were routed from the area (retreating into sanctuaries in Laos). There were an estimated 675 enemy killed. Tons of weapons and supplies were found and destroyed. Ultimately, although the American and South Vietnamese "conquered" the enemy forces, they gave up holding and occupying the "mountain," sparking outrage in the U.S.—especially in Congress. Within a month after the Americans left the area, the NVA and PAVN forces were again operating there with impunity—but certainly not at the strength they had maintained prior to the battle. If there is any better example of a Pyrrhic victory throughout American military history—I cannot think of one.[3]

It's difficult to put something like that behind you. Even for those lucky enough to return home from the war, the adjustment could be difficult. For many, there were injuries and traumas, seen and unseen. Bravo veteran Terry Taylor, for example, recalled:

> I learned at the age of 18 that you don't have to die to go to hell. Vietnam was hell on earth. If I had had any comprehension of what I was getting myself into, then I would have done everything I could to avoid it.
>
> For years after I came home from Vietnam, I had PTSD (post-traumatic stress syndrome). PTSD didn't have that name then and I didn't know this was any kind of mental health condition. It was just something I lived with. I thought about the people and my experiences in Vietnam every day. I would not sit with my back to a door or window. I startled easily from unexpected noises and resisted the sudden urge to seek cover. I had trouble speaking with authority figures. I also felt survivor's guilt. I came home alive and physically whole. Too many of the guys didn't.[4]

Despite the obstacles, many of these men built very successful lives post-war. Part III looks at the Battlin' Bastards' stateside reunions, which started decades after the war ended, as the men were ready to cautiously revisit their experiences. Some of the men even returned to Vietnam, to visit the exact sites of some of their fiercest fighting: sites where they were wounded; sites where they lost their brothers. The average reader might puzzle over what would have inspired these men to return to this period in time, to this place, that so many of them fought so long to forget? Their epic journey illustrates Jerry Hoffman's observation that "the average person doesn't understand what we went through, and it makes it really difficult to establish friendships afterwards and do the things that the average person does. A lot of us make the comment that the only friends we really have are the guys in the unit."[5] Now, some of those "guys in the unit" are ready to share their stories with the world, to honor, to educate, and to inspire.

PART I

The Screaming Eagles and the War in Southeast Asia

CHAPTER I

The Screaming Eagles

The 101st Airborne Division, nicknamed the "Screaming Eagles," have been called "an elite fighting force,"[1] "one of the most famous (and feared) in U.S. Armed Forces history,"[2] and "probably the best-known army division in the world."[3] But name recognition alone does mean the general public truly understands the long and proud history of this storied unit, so famously portrayed in the miniseries *Band of Brothers*. This is intended as the briefest of overviews, meant simply to help the uninitiated reader understand a bit about the place of the Battlin' Bastards within the broader tapestry of American military history. The author's suggestions for further reading are included at the end of the book.

The 101st was originally activated not for World War II, but in 1918 as part of the mobilization for World War I. As America's participation in The Great War was relatively brief, the 101st would never see combat in that conflict. After the war was over, the 101st demobilized. In 1921, the 101st was reconstituted as the 101st Division, headquartered in Milwaukee, Wisconsin. Again, though, it was largely a "paper division" with little activity—until the United States entered World War II in a bid to help stop the march of fascism around the globe.[4]

In 1940, as war raged in Europe, the Army began testing the viability of parachute infantry units. This was not a novel American concept. As Gordon L. Rottman notes in *US World War II Parachute Infantry Regiments*:

> The idea of parachute troops had been toyed with since World War I, but it was not until the 1930s that some countries undertook more ambitious trials and actually raised parachute units. The Soviet Union began forming units in 1931, followed by Germany and France in 1937, and Italy the following year. Britain waited until World War II had begun before raising its first units in 1940. Deployment concepts ranged from using paratroopers as small raiding detachments, to large strike units spearheading ground forces.[5]

The U.S. Army's experiments at Fort Benning, Georgia, were deemed successful. The Army authorized two airborne divisions: the 82nd and 101st. On August 15, 1942, the old 101st reserve unit was disbanded, and the next day, the 101st Airborne Division was activated at Camp Claiborne, Louisiana.[6]

Training for the new, elite parachute infantry units was intense. Soldiers not only needed to learn basic infantry skills, but they also had to prepare to jump from planes into combat. (Most Americans had never even been on an airplane at that point in America's history.) As World War II veteran Kurt Gabel noted in his memoir, he was told upon arriving at the reception station of parachute school:

> No one asked you to come here. You will not be welcome until we decide that you are fit to become one of us. You will have three days in which to make up your mind whether that is what you want. At any time during these three days you may quit and there will be no dishonor attached to your quitting. It would, in fact, be a sign of good sense because you have to be crazy to want to belong to us. Paratroops are the shock troops of the Army. They are employed only on the most dangerous missions. They are dropped behind enemy lines, are expected to fight against overwhelming odds, and are not expected to get back. No one in his right mind would want to join an outfit like that.[7]

The 101st trained primarily at Fort Bragg, North Carolina, and then in England, preparing to invade Europe.[8] Early on D-Day, paratroopers of the 101st Airborne parachuted into France to clear the way for units storming the beaches. By September, the paratroopers were fighting their way across Europe to liberate Holland. After rest in France, the 101st was abruptly returned to action in the Ardennes in December 1944. They were one of the units that held out at Bastogne, completely surrounded by German forces and under constant bombardment and sniper fire, until they were relieved by the 4th Armored Division on December 26.[9] The 101st Airborne fought on across Alsace and the Ruhr Valley. In Bavaria, the division liberated the Landsberg concentration camp. They reached Berchtesgaden and captured Hitler's mountain retreat, Eagle's Nest, on May 4, 1945, three days before Germany formally surrendered. The unit was preparing to be deployed in the Pacific when the war ended.[10] The division was deactivated on November 30, 1945.[11]

The 101st Airborne did not see significant military action again for 30 years.[12] On July 29, 1965, the 1st Brigade of the 101st landed at the American military base at Cam Ranh Bay. The rest of the division (including the 1/506th) deployed to Vietnam in December 1967.[13] The "Screaming Eagles" earned the nickname "the nomads of Vietnam" because they moved all across the country. Altogether, they fought in 45 operations.[14]

One of the most grueling fights the 101st participated in—to include the Battlin' Bastards—was the battle for Dong Ap Bia in May 1969. It would become controversial, as the hill had no clear strategic importance, but the fight for control over it dragged on for 10 days. The carnage earned the site the grim nickname "Hamburger Hill." After many brutal assaults, the 101st Airborne finally gained control of the hill, only to abandon it days later due to its relative lack of value.[15]

Despite the heroic efforts put forth by American fighting men—like those at Hamburger Hill—combat troops began to withdraw from Vietnam in 1969 as the American people increasingly turned against the conflict. By the beginning of 1972 the units that remained had less and less involvement in combat—though Americans continued to die. The 101st officially returned to Fort Campbell on April 6, 1972. According to the National Archives, 4,011 men of the 101st had been killed in action, and 18,259 were wounded, over twice the number of soldiers lost from the unit during WWII.[16]

Why the Screaming Eagles? The 101st Airborne Division's Screaming Eagles nickname originates from their insignia, which features a bald eagle (the national symbol of the United States) on a black shield. The eagle on the patch is named "Old Abe" in honor of President Abraham Lincoln and was originally the mascot of a Wisconsin regiment during the Civil War.[17] Somewhat humorously, the 101st Airborne Division earned some other nicknames during the Vietnam War. The enemy noticed the distinctive eagle patches on the 101st Airborne uniforms, and mistook the eagles for chickens or roosters. They often communicated to each other to avoid the "chicken men" or "rooster men" at all costs.[18]

Now this book is not about the 101st Airborne in Vietnam broadly speaking. It's about Bravo Company, 1/506th, 101st Airborne, specifically. During the Vietnam War, a company—like Bravo **Company**—comprised of roughly sixty to two hundred soldiers, generally led by a captain or 1st lieutenant. It was normally made up of three **platoons**. Each platoon, generally led by 2nd lieutenants, numbered eighteen to fifty soldiers, in three to four squads; while **squads**, consisting of six to ten soldiers, would be commanded by a staff sergeant or sergeant.[19]

The 506th Parachute Infantry Regiment was activated on July 20, 1942, at Mount Currahee, Camp Toccoa, Georgia, as part of the newly formed 101st Airborne Division. As 506th veteran Philip A. Russell recalled, "Mount Currahee is the Indian name meaning 'standing alone.' And we all said we stood alone together. But we would run that every day and then come back for two hours of calisthenics and then the obstacle course and that was our regular training."[20] The 506th was the first parachute infantry regiment to complete airborne training as a unit.

Their training continued in England until when on June 6, 1944, the 506th jumped with other elements of the 101st into the skies over France. Earl E. McClung, who, like Philip Russell, also served in the 506th, made his first combat jump into Normandy. He recalled, "it was bad for us. There was fire [gunfire] going all around us. It was really scary. If you saw the [series] *Band of Brothers*, it was close. Pretty close. That's the way it was."[21]

After 10 weeks of refitting and training, the 506th was once again called upon to parachute into combat, into Holland as part of Operation *Market Garden*. Philip Russell remembered it was "Not too much different. We were edgy about it. You know, we were a high-strung bunch anyway. We were ready. We knew we ha—we knew we had to go back in."[22]

The Regiment liberated the town of Eindhoven on September 18, and aided in the withdrawal of the British 1st Airborne from Arnhem on October 7. On December 18, the unit traveled by truck to Bastogne to stem a major German attack on the city. The mission of the 506th was to hold the town of Neville, four miles to the north. Successfully resisting the vicious German assaults, the 506th earned its second Presidential Unit Citation.[23] Earl McClung notes, "Bastogne—the weather I think was the worst. I think there were mornings we'd wished we get killed to get out of the misery of the cold and stuff.... When we were going in there were people running out telling us to get out; you can't stop these people and they'll have you overrun in two hours."[24] And yet they persevered.

For their bravery throughout "the Good War," as World War II is so often called, the regiment was decorated with two Presidential Unit Citations, with 25 men earning the Distinguished Service Cross for their actions in Normandy. In November 1945, the 506th Infantry was deactivated at Auxerre, France.[25]

The regiment was reactivated on August 25, 1950, as part of the Korean War buildup, but remained stateside as a training unit and was deactivated again on December 1, 1953. In 1957, the 506th was again reactivated, once again as part of the 101st Airborne Division at Fort Campbell, Kentucky. In addition to being an airborne unit, it tested new Army airmobile concepts, and was part of the Army's strategic reserve.[26]

In December 1967, battalions of the 506th began arriving in Vietnam. While in-country, the regiment was converted from airborne to airmobile infantry. (In the simplest possible terms, airborne meant jumping out of planes and using a parachute to get to the ground, while airmobile infantry would mean using helicopters to get from place to place.) The 506th battalions served in Vietnam for four years, with men fighting in the famed 1968 Tet Offensive—one of the largest military campaigns of the Vietnam War—and in 1969 at Dong Ap Bia (Hamburger Hill) in the A Shau Valley.[27]

As the war progressed, the battalions of the 506th then participated in numerous actions during the period of Vietnamization, or shifting of responsibility for fighting onto South Vietnamese forces. In December 1971, the three battalions of the 506th redeployed to Fort Campbell. It would later see service along the Korean Demilitarized Zone and in Iraq.[28]

The War in Southeast Asia

Any consideration of the history of the Vietnam War is irrevocably tied to the long national histories of both the United States and Vietnam. The text provided here is intended as the briefest of overviews of a very complicated situation, providing a modicum of geopolitical context for the situations in which the Battlin' Bastards found themselves.

First, the United States of America, which had declared its independence from Great Britain in 1776, was a relatively young country as it became more and more deeply enmeshed in the conflict in Southeast Asia in the mid-twentieth century. Initially a country with a tendency towards isolationism, it had been called upon to help "make the world safe for democracy" during World War I and II. Each war effort included the enormous mobilization of both the military and the home front, and a high cost in both blood and treasure.[29] Following World War II, America would not retreat behind her borders as she had during earlier crises. This time, there was a general consensus amongst most politicians, and the general public, that the United States had a responsibility to maintain a presence on the world stage for a number of reasons, including helping to rebuild war-torn corners of the globe, and keeping a third world war from erupting. The United States thus adopted a more interventionist stance in world affairs than ever before in its history following World War II.

In its new role as "the world's policeman," and sensitive to the ways in which the appeasement of Adolph Hitler and his Nazi regime in the lead-up to World War II had allowed fascism to devastate Europe, the United States took sometimes extreme measures in their initially well-intentioned desire to stop the spread of communism at all costs. This, most know, led to a protracted Cold War with the Communist Soviet Union (America's former wartime ally). The popular "domino theory" suggested that if one country turned communist, its neighbors would quickly do so as well. This was to be avoided at all costs, in part because communism was equated with totalitarianism, and seen as anti-democratic and antithetical to a flourishing global capitalist economy.

In 1949, Communist Mao Zedong assumed control of China—shocking the West. In 1950, war broke out between Communist North Korea and the South. NATO troops, led by the United States, fought side by side with their South Korean allies to a bloody stalemate. So, when in 1954, Vietnam—formerly a part of France's colonial holdings—was split into North and South, and North Vietnam wanted to reunite the country under communism—the U.S. government felt obligated to stop that from happening. The domino theory at that time warned that if one country fell to communism, its neighbors would soon follow. This was to be avoided at all costs. Towards that end, the United States started funneling millions of dollars in aid, and then advisors, and then active duty miliary personnel, to the country. But nothing seemed to stop the North Vietnamese and the communist factions in the South in their quest for a unified Vietnam. As the war dragged on, the American public turned firmly against the War. The U.S. government realized that they could not continue to try to prop up the South Vietnamese regime, that there was no viable path forward, and ultimately withdrew from the conflict. The Vietnam War had a huge cost in human lives. More than 1.3 million Vietnamese soldiers and about 58,000 U.S. troops were killed. More than two million civilians also died.

How did North Vietnam—a largely rural, agricultural nation roughly the size of California—withstand a bloody war with the wealthiest, most powerful country in the world for as long as it did? One cannot overstate the importance of the role of the Vietnamese people's desire for self-determination. From 111 BC to AD 939 much of the land we now call Vietnam was either a protectorate or colony of China. This loomed large in the Vietnamese psyche for generations. Then, jumping forward a bit, the French would invade the country in the mid-nineteenth century, only to be ousted by the Japanese during World War II. Once the Japanese occupation of Vietnam ended with their defeat in that war, France attempted to regain its colonial domination of Indochina (Vietnam, Cambodia, and Laos). This led, in 1946, to the outbreak of an insurgency against France by Vietnamese nationalists who wanted the ouster of the Japanese to mean self-governance. The United States, which initially actually favored Vietnamese independence, came to support France due to the aforementioned politics of the Cold War and American fears that an independent Vietnam would be dominated by communists. In March 1946, the French recognized Vietnamese nationalist leader Ho Chi Minh's government in North Vietnam as a "free state"; but they were determined to hold on to the South. Long story short, this would lead to a complicated war that would last for nearly three decades. As George C. Herring notes in *America's Longest War: The United States and Vietnam, 1950–1975*, "A localized rebellion against French colonialism … expanded into an international conflict of major proportions."[30]

As the outmanned, undersupplied Ho Chi Minh once noted, "If ever the tiger pauses, the elephant will impale him on his mighty tusks. But the tiger will not pause, and the elephant will die of exhaustion and loss of blood."[31]

PART II

The Battlin' Bastards of Bravo Speak

The accounts that follow take a number of different formats. Over a roughly eighteen-month period, Vietnam War-era members of Bravo Company, 1/506th, 101st Airborne were invited to share their stories for this book. In order to make them as comfortable as possible with the often-painful memories they were dredging up, they were given the option to do oral history interviews or submit written accounts. There were no strict guidelines on how they were to prepare these written submissions, so that they could tell their stories, their way. Some stories told here are more detailed than others; all are unique and important. All provide invaluable insights into what life was like for a combat soldier in the Vietnam War and help the reader ponder the lessons we can learn from their experiences. Although the author lightly edited for length, clarity, and context, each individual approved the final content of their story in the spirit of the public history best practice of "shared authority." At the end of the day, it is *their* story. They are for the most part presented in order of the month in which the veterans giving the accounts arrived in Vietnam. Part II concludes with a raw and moving account from a Gold-Star family member, to remind readers of the lasting impacts on those who lost loved ones in the war.

The men who share their stories here would like to recognize the leadership of several individuals who left Vietnam prior to Viking (Captain Harold Ericksen) taking over command of B 1/506th:

Company Commander
Michael Metzger

Platoon Leaders
Bryce Bickerton
David Brown
Terry Morgan
Michael Purdy
Artie Short
Herman Theeke

Battalion Artillery Liaison Officer
Joe Palagyi

Artillery Forward Observer
Artie Herbert (Phantom)

These men set a strong foundation for those who would carry the leadership of the Battlin' Bastards of Bravo forward into 1969 and beyond.

CHAPTER 2

Jim Hartman

In Vietnam August 1968–May 1969

> "They're going to put three stripes on your shoulder, and you're going to replace the guys getting killed in Vietnam."

The following is a summary, lightly edited by the author, of Jim's September 2023 interview with George Bogdanich, conducted at a Battlin' Bastards reunion for use in both this book and a documentary film project.

I was born in 1946, so I was 21 years old. I had just finished two years of schooling at a very well-known technical college in Minneapolis. And I graduated in April '67. I had my draft notice by May '67. One month after I got out, I got drafted, did my basic training, was assigned as infantry, and was sent out to Fort Lewis, Washington. I figured there's no jungle training out in Fort Lewis, Washington. Maybe I'm not going to Vietnam. And I kind of kept a low profile out there. I graduated from advanced individual training, they call it, the second phase of your training, and the whole company got orders to go to Korea for 13 months. I was happy—it was going to be cold, but I was happy. Nobody wanted to—you heard all the stories. Nobody wanted to go to Vietnam. So we were out the company area, it was raining like it always did, out in Fort Lewis, and we were going to go to Korea for 13 months. As we were just about to do that, and they handed a first sergeant a piece of paper. There were 18 names on it. He said, "Wait a minute." He said, "These guys ain't going." He rattled off the names. Mine was one of them. And I will say it politely, what he said. He said, "You lucky so-and-sos aren't going, you're going down to Fort Benning, Georgia. They're going to give you a crash course. They're going to put three stripes on your shoulder, and you're going to replace the guys getting killed in Vietnam."

So we went down to Fort Benning; great training, and it was almost fun. Almost fun. Got out of there, graduated from there as a buck sergeant. We went to Fort Gordon, Georgia, to get kind of on-the-job training, kind of almost like a pseudo drill sergeant. So you get used to pushing troops a little bit. I went through their advanced individual training cycle. And once I finished at Fort Gordon, I got orders to go to Vietnam. Went out there as infantry. I flew in-country and landed at Cam Rahn Bay, where everyone went. And I got put in the 101st next, then I joined B Company and … I made it nine months and two days before I got hit.

But let me back up. Once I got in the company, we'd do what I call minimal stuff, highway security. Bridge security. And we'd go out on a little reconnaissance once in a while. Pretty mundane except for the conditions. The mosquitoes are the one thing that always put me over the edge over there. So we did that for three months and then all of a sudden we were told that we were going up. They put us on a C-130 and we went up to Camp Eagle. Then we started getting a little more into the action.

At this point, I am 22 years old. I'm older than half the kids I'm with. I'm three, four years older. And of course Viking [company commander Harold J. Ericksen Jr.] was older than I was … he had guts. He wanted to stay out in the field. That was his thing—he was very comfortable being out there and not back in the rear where he had to deal with his superiors. And he pushed us hard, but I'm sure all the other guys will say the same thing, I'd go wherever he'd go and he'd stick up for his guys. Like, I got in a little trouble one time. We were in, I think it was China Beach, and I was the acting platoon leader because my lieutenant went on R&R. So I'm the acting platoon leader. We went in just for one day (24-hours). And at night, the three other lieutenants were going to the officers' club and they said, "Come on." I says, "Well, I can't go in there." And they said, "Oh, you're with us." So we get in there and we were overserved of course, right off the bat. And then this Marine colonel just comes over to our table and went ballistic on me. I mean, he went ballistic because all I had on was my olive-drab boxers and shower shoes. And I was a buck sergeant, but he didn't know that. But he was popping blood vessels, and he throws us out. He said, "You can't come in here dressed like that!" And then I made some crack about, "Well, I'm sorry sir, but I forgot my bleeping tuxedo at home." And then he really went over the edge, and as we're getting thrown out the door, Viking's coming in and he said, "What's the problem?" And I thought, "Oh, this is going to be interesting." And the colonel's still popping blood vessels and throwing us out. And he just looked at him, Viking—and this guy's two ranks ahead of him. He looked at him, he says, "Give me a fricking break." He says, "We've been out in the field for forty-five days. We're going to go out for another forty-five days. These guys were just blowing off a little steam!" It didn't do any good. We still got tossed. And then he come out and he says, "What were you doing in there!?" I said, "I'm just following your boys!" And all he said was, "Stay out of trouble for the next eight hours." So he'd stick up for you, but you didn't want to push him. When we went on that operation (Hamburger Hill) and I found out he wasn't going to be there, that was not good. The brass was forcing him to go on R&R.

So—everyone always asks about Hamburger Hill. It seemed to me about three days before May 17, two or three before the 17th, we ran into some stuff. And I don't know what it was because we weren't the lead platoon, but they called in artillery and had a little problem with that because the artillery got—the gun's barrel got hot and it got a little erratic, and landed above us. And the kid—I was laying right next to a Puerto Rican kid, who was a good soldier—that took half his butt off and fractured his pelvis and everything. That was the one thing I always remember. And so we lost a couple guys with our own friendly fire, not lost them, but got injured. Things start picking up the next day, the third platoon, the one that I was originally in, they ran into some stuff and I kind of got in the middle of that just to help out. And their lieutenant got shot, took a rifle and a bullet in the elbow and shattered his arm. And then about the third day, we had point and we lost our point guy. I can see—they were walking down this little swell in a knoll and they had a trail watcher and he got shot dead. Then we just opened fire on the top of the swell in the ridge line there. And while they're firing, I don't remember who the other guy was, but one of 'em was hit. And we went out and got him and dragged him back. And the thing I remember—after we're shooting and shooting—and we weren't shooting *at* anything. We were just shooting in the general direction. And then we stopped for a while and I saw the trail-watcher run. All I could see was a black shadow and he ran. And I knew, well, that then we started moving forward and I could see why we didn't get him.

I saw this shadow leave, and then we went farther up the ridge and we came up to this tree where I saw him run from, and it was a huge tree. We couldn't have got him out of there with a 500-pound bomb. He had dug a hole down in the root base of that tree and there's no way any small arms fire was going to get him out of there. He just waited until he picked his time, and knocked somebody off. They put a lot of planning into their defenses. And we were just grunts walking. We'd go from point A to point B, and then you never knew what the actual objective was.

So we finished that off. And then after the day ended, and then we started walking. The morning of the 17th, we had the lead again and we started up this trail. I was in the back again, I think there was only my radio operator and one soldier behind me. And I come across this log, which had to be five feet, four feet high across the trail. That just about everybody else had gone over. I'm in the back of the column and I was just about to go over that and all hell broke loose. So I dropped, and I couldn't see anything because the trail was very winding. Winding, and thick foliage. So for a second or two, I got my wits about me, so I dropped my gear and I was just about ready to get up, leaning on my right hand, and boost myself up to go over that log. And as I'm kind of leaning up, looking up to get up, a rocket-propelled grenade comes over that log and misses me. But it hit the tree in the back of me and it took me out and my participation was over.

I had a lot of holes in me, but it wasn't life-threatening and other guys were hurting and worse. In that particular instance, skirmish, seven guys were wounded and one killed. I was one of the wounded. It was a waste, but I never let it bother me. I don't know if that's callous. Maybe it helps you keep your sanity. Just when I came back, I never let it—I just had fun, carried on with my life. But first I spent two months in Japan. I got sprayed pretty good up both legs and it took off a piece of my hand there, and a shoulder. So after about a month I was starting to heal up, but my leg got infected, so they had to re-do that. I mean, they split it open, cleaned it up. So now I've been there six weeks. And the doctor comes, he says, "Well, you're looking pretty good. You can go back to your outfit." I said, "Well, doc," I says, "I don't want to sound like a chickenshit, but number one, I ain't got an outfit left." The numbers I had heard from guys following me to Japan in the hospital, of the hundred guys or so we went in with, we lost 65 of them one way or another. That's really simple math. I said, "Number one, I haven't got an outfit. Number two, I've been on my back for a month, six weeks. I can't go back in the field. I wouldn't last five minutes. I am not in shape. And number three, I only got forty-five days left." And the rule was, if you are under thirty days, they'll send you home. He looks at me, he says, "Yeah, I can understand. I see your point." So he disappeared. I said, "Okay." I didn't know what was going to happen. But ultimately he sent me home, which was nice.

I never really struggled with post-traumatic stress disorder when I got home. One thing that bothers me a little bit, now at this reunion that we have every year, some of these guys are real close because they fought together. For me, that first year in the States, I was in four different forts for training. You just get to know guys and boom, they're gone now. And then you start over at another place with a whole other batch. So I never got real tight with a lot of the guys. And I mean, I'm as outgoing as anybody, but it just didn't happen. And then when we got to Vietnam, I get into a company where most of them guys had been there nine months already. So they're real tight with each other. I'm a new guy and a couple of months later, they're all going home. And then we start getting new guys and then I get used to them. Terry Taylor was one of them. He was one of the—I was his first squad leader. And then all of a sudden, then they switched me from the third platoon to the first platoon. And that's like moving you from the State of Iowa to the State of Wisconsin. Because even though you're in the same company, it's too different—you don't see the other guys.

I came home and worked as a pipe fitter; loved it. When I retired, I ran a local VFW [Veterans of Foreign Wars] post for 12 years. I don't hold any grudges against the Vietnamese. Where I live, there's a huge Hmong population in the city of St. Paul in Minneapolis, Minnesota. But at the same time, I've been asked if I wanted—about going back to Vietnam, for these tours. I would never do that. It has nothing to do with the people. The country was so ungodly, hot, humid. It was not my favorite place, so I would never go back.

CHAPTER 3

Steve Conroy

In Vietnam August 1968–July 1969

> "There were twenty guys lying on tables, nurses were cutting our fatigues off, we were bald-ass naked."

Steve chose to share something he wrote for Bravo Company's private journal. It is largely focused around the events of June 4, 1969, and has been lightly edited by the author with Steve's permission. Though focused on one day of Steve's tour, it has much to tell us about the heroism and selflessness of the Battlin' Bastards.

This is the first time I have recorded in detail June 4, 1969. I have tried to capture the events from almost 43 years ago. If I left out an individual or mixed up names, I apologize. I did the best I could. From the 101st Purple Heart Orders, I was able to attach first names to members of the platoon who were wounded that day.

The action was not out of the ordinary. As a fighting unit we were doing our job. It was my last month in-country and I had not taken R&R. I was medevac'd on June 4, spent a week at the 95th Evacuation Hospital in Da Nang, and then came back to Camp Evans. I went to Sydney for R&R, and came back to Evans. It was a crazy month. I never had the opportunity to see "Viking," Captain Harold Ericksen, again in Vietnam. We did hook up in 1992 in Alabama. I looked up to him for he was like a big brother. I was not able to debrief him on these events. I felt bad that my final goodbye was from a radio in B Company, 1/506th Charge of Quarters (CQ) at Evans.

But let's back up a bit. I had rejoined Bravo, 1/506th, on May 27 after two months as the E 1/506th recon platoon leader. I took over second platoon, which I had earlier led from August '68 to January '69. It was a blessing to be back with "Viking." (Since leaving Bravo, I had also done a stint in operations but requested to go back out to a line unit in March of 1969. I ended up with recon platoon when their platoon leader was shot in the neck during an operation with D 1/506th.)

On June 3, from Firebase [FB] Currahee on the floor of the A Shau Valley, we helicoptered to grid 347991. From the landing zone, about three kilometers west of the A Shau, the mission was to move southwest to locate a weapons cache the

North Vietnamese had removed from Hamburger Hill (Dong Ap Bia) in the vicinity of 345987. It was also believed that the North Vietnamese had buried several of our men killed at Hamburger Hill in the area. We were supported by an aerial rocket artillery team until the combat assault was complete. The artillery was on frequency 67:45, call sign A23. The 81 mm were on 55:55, Rivet 43. The medevac was 66:80. I still have my topographical map in a plastic case with these frequencies written on the adhesive tape. We were in contact after being on the ground for a half hour. Second platoon was walking point. Since I cannot recall ranks and first names, I will use last names. Henderson was walking point. I was the fourth person back with my radio telephone operator, James Sherlock. We were moving up a very steep hill. About a half hour after our insertion, small arms fire broke out. A North Vietnamese, possibly a trail watcher, was coming down the hill towards us with his AK slung over his shoulder. This was a testament to the company's noise discipline. He never knew we were there. Henderson shot the North Vietnamese in the head. The lead element also wounded a second North Vietnamese who managed to flee back up the hill. We followed the blood trail. Viking halted the company and called in eight-inch artillery support and walked the rounds up the hill. The rounds were so close that we were receiving secondary shrapnel. The steepness of the terrain, however, protected us. No further contact this day. We continued our march and hunkered down for the night in the vicinity of 344982. The next morning, Viking had second platoon set up a stay-behind ambush. The North Vietnamese liked to scavenge our night defensive positions. Viking used this tactic with my platoon in the past with success, as in the case of the New Year's Eve, second platoon ambush in Quang Tri Province near the beach in Phong Dien. At dawn, the company began to move out, intentionally making noise, while second platoon dug in and set up an ambush. Henderson was in a listening post some forty–fifty meters down a trail leading to our night defensive position. Around 7:30 AM, small arms fire broke out. Apparently a North Vietnamese soldier got between the listening post and our position and Henderson shot him. He engaged several others and verbally alerted us that he was cut off from us. There seemed to be a squad-sized element between second platoon and Henderson. I feared he would be killed or if he survived, become a prisoner of war, based on our proximity to the Laotian border. I took several troops whose names I will try to recall: my radio telephone operator James Sherlock, M60 gunner Charles Martini, riflemen Sherman Newton, Servans, and Roser (aka Uncle Red; he was an African American with red hair). There may have been others and again, if I omitted them, I am sorry. We moved down the trail near Henderson. The dead North Vietnamese was on the trail. All hell broke loose and the volume of AK-47 fire was intense. The ground dirt from the impact of the bullets was flying around us. I recall being with Servans (I think so because I remember him being Hispanic) behind a tree and we were emptying our M16 magazines on full automatic. I firmly believed that the skinny tree would protect us. Martini was cranking the M60. An AK-47 round hit Servans in his steel pot and it spun him around in a split second as if he was a puppet on a string. Had he not been in front of me, that round would have got me. Miraculously, he wasn't even scratched. We tossed many grenades at the North Vietnamese element. Martini's M60 jammed allowing the North Vietnamese to use RPGs against us. Roser (Uncle Red), yelled over to me, "Hey 26, [my call sign] you're hit." I said "No way." He then said, "Look down at your pants, you're bleeding." Sure enough my fatigue pants had turned a black color as I checked my backside. I opened my fatigue jacket and the blood came out like a hose. The crazy thing was that Uncle Red and I started laughing in the middle of the firefight. We had been on an ambush together back on New Year's Eve. I chided him for being in the field when he was getting ready to go home. Sherlock, Martini, and Newton were also hit by RPGs [rocket-propelled grenades]. We continued to return fire, and thank God, the North Vietnamese element withdrew. I grabbed the radio and got on the horn with Viking. I remember telling him I had four wounded, including myself. We crawled back up the trail and rejoined the rest of the platoon at the night defensive-position site. Thank God no one was killed. The guy we went to help, Henderson, I remember him laughing at us for getting into such a pickle. The rest of the company was half a click away and they got back pronto. Doc Murray, second platoon medic, patched us up. Sherlock had a huge piece of the rocket-propelled grenade in his hand. I had three holes, and felt a little dizzy after Doc Murray told me I had a decent-sized wound in my armpit. I still have a piece of shrapnel in my rib cage today. I apologized to Viking for delaying his operation. I told Sergeant Barry Horn to take over the platoon as he had time in grade on Sergeant Robert Boulton. Viking called the medevac. They had to use jungle penetrators to extract the wounded. As an officer, I was the last one out. As the seat on the end of the penetrator cleared the jungle canopy, it was a beautiful sunny day. All I could think of was that one of those North Vietnamese was going to light us up during the extraction. They took us to a field hospital, whose name escapes me. There were twenty guys lying on tables, nurses were cutting our fatigues off, we were bald-ass naked. The nurses and doctors were shooting us up with Novocain (I think), removing the shrapnel and stitching us up. One of doctors made a joke, presenting me [with] a tray containing the shrapnel he removed, "Hey lieutenant, look what I pulled out of you." That afternoon, we were choppered to the 95th Evacuation Hospital in Da Nang. It was like a reunion there. I met wounded troops from other units in the 3rd Brigade who I got to know ordering choppers when I worked in operations.

So this concludes my little story. Anytime I think I am having a bad day, I take myself back to June 4, 1969. It really puts things in perspective. I thank God none of my men were killed. I thank God for looking over us. When I got home, I actually felt guilty and cried because my guys were still out there, and I was back home in New York, out of the Army.

From 1966 to 1969 Steve served in the United States Army as a commissioned officer. As a First Lieutenant, he was an infantry platoon leader with the 101st Airborne Division in Vietnam, 1968–1969. After the war, Steve taught high school on Long Island from 1970–1972. He would go on to spend 33 years in office automation and technology sales. Most of his career was with Xerox, from 1975–2003. After retiring from Xerox, Steve spent 18 years helping seniors as a reverse mortgage consultant, most recently with Longbridge Financial, LLC. Married and residing in Annapolis, Maryland, Steve and his wife Barbara have three grown children and five grandchildren.

CHAPTER 4

Warren Sutton

In Vietnam November 1968–November 1969

> "I got a letter from 'Uncle Sam' stating, 'Greetings, you will be at the Coral Gables Induction Station at 5:00 AM on June 27, 1968.' I was 19 years old."

The following was submitted in writing and lightly edited by the author with Warren's permission.

I got a letter from "Uncle Sam" stating, "Greetings, you will be at the Coral Gables Induction Station at 5:00 AM on June 27, 1968." I was 19 years old. I reported to the center as required and we all were assembled in a large hall. The officer in charge looked over the assembly and pointed out about twenty guys and said, "Move to the right side of the room. You're now in the Marines."

We were lined up and stripped down to our underwear for a medical exam. The guy next to me was asked if he had any problems. He stated he had flat feet. The doctor asked him if his feet caused suction on the floor when he walks. He replied "No," so the doctor said, "You are okay, continue on." We were each given a urine specimen collection cup and a paper with our personal information. We were instructed to fill in the information, fill up the cup, and put the cup on the counter on top of the information form. After most were on the counter some joker came over and swapped the cups all over the countertop.

We were then loaded onto buses and taken to Miami International Airport, where we boarded a plane. We were flown to Fort Jackson, South Carolina, where we were given buzz cuts and issued uniforms. We were then given 10 minutes to pack our belongings into a box and mail them home, before we were loaded onto buses and transported to Fort Gordon, Georgia, for basic training. Training there lasted about six weeks. The training consisted of a lot of physical training, basic hand-to-hand combat, and training with M14 rifles. After graduation from basic training I flew to Seattle, Washington, for advanced infantry training at Fort Lewis. This training again lasted approximately six weeks. This training included extensive use of M16 rifles, M79 grenade launchers, M60 machine guns, hand grenades, claymore mines, C-4 plastic explosives, .45-caliber pistols, light antiarmor weapon

(LAW; a single-shot rockets), etc. Among these exercises was an assault of a hill. We were loaded into armored personnel carriers and taken to the hill. Upon arriving at the hill the back of the ramp of the armored personnel carrier was dropped and we were to climb the hill in an assault manner. While we were ascending the hill, personnel on top started to lob tear gas grenades on us. We donned our gas masks. When I started running the hill, I tripped on a rock (vision is somewhat limited in a gas mask), and when I hit the ground my gas mask was pushed aside by a gas grenade, which squirted the gas directly into my mask. I was knocked out. When I came to, a lieutenant was sitting on my chest in his gas mask. All I could think of was a Martian or something and I started swinging. Later I heard some guys saying, "Did you see that poor guy on the hill heaving over and over?" Then I realized that was me. Not my best day.

After graduation from advanced individual training, I flew home for a 30-day vacation prior to deployment. When the 30 days were over I went to Miami International Airport for a flight to California. My family and girlfriend were there to see me off. I didn't know it at the time, but my pregnant sister collapsed at the airport and was transported to the hospital. I arrived in California and was given new uniforms, a duffle bag, and a slew of shots for Southeast Asia. The shots were given with an air gun. If they didn't hold the gun tight to your shoulder, it would rip your skin. Lots of us came out with fair-sized slits. After you got the shots you had to do push-ups.

After a few days in California we boarded a jet bound for Vietnam. It was a very long flight and stopped in Alaska and Japan. Our final destination was Bien Hoa. It was now November of 1968. In Bien Hoa, I was given an M16 and final orders assigning me to Company B, 1/506th Infantry, 101st Airborne Division. I soon left Bien Hoa and was flown to Camp Evans to join my company. Upon joining the unit, I was assigned as a rifleman in the fourth platoon.

When I got to my unit at Camp Evans, I was issued my combat gear. This consisted of a rucksack, entrenching tool, machete, canteens, ammo, grenades, multiple magazines of ammo, a bandolier of M16 rounds, a poncho, poncho liner, C-rations, etc. On resupply day with full loads of C-rations, water, and ammo, your combat load was around 105 pounds. Since I only weighed 129 pounds it was a challenge. You had to learn how to stand up and to walk with this load. The first thing you learned was to put a towel around your neck and shoulders, so the rucksack straps rode on the towel. If you didn't use the towel you would end up with "rucksackitis" where the straps cut off the circulation and you start to lose feeling in your arms and hands.

Life as an infantry soldier or "grunt" was fairly simple. You got two meals per day, a change of clothes once a month, and all the ammunition and explosives you could carry. Every soldier carried two hundred rounds of machine-gun ammo or a radio. Either way it added around thirty pounds to your load. My first mission with the company was in the rice paddies. Rice paddies are flooded areas with grids of dikes separating them. These dikes are made of sand and are about two feet wide. When walking on these dikes you have to only step in the center or the sand will give way, and you'll fall in the water. Learning to walk with this new combat load was a challenge, I kept stepping too close to the edge and into the water. Guys in my platoon were taking bets on how many steps I would get before I fell. Not fun. After a few days I learned how to remain upright with the rucksack.

On my second operation we were set up on a ridge line about two thousand meters outside of Camp Evans. During the night we were on three-man positions. Ours was a machine-gun position. One man remains awake at all times and the guard is rotated through the night. About 3:00 AM we were told to move out as an armored personal carrier not too far from us was hit by a rocket-propelled grenade. Unfortunately, I wasn't awakened until the other two guys were on the move with our machine gun. I got up and was moving up the trail to catch up while trying to get my gear on. When I was bumped into by two guys, they were evidently the guys that ambushed the armored-personnel carrier. Our two men saw them and started firing the M60. The rounds were going over my head and I hit the ground. As the level of fire was coming down I was yelling but they couldn't hear over the machine-gun fire. As the fire got just above me, the machine gun jammed. It was a very close call!

The next day we came across the torso of a Viet Cong soldier who snuck up on a tank. The main gun was loaded with a beehive round. The upper half of the body was completely gone but the bottom half was untouched. Death was everywhere. We did a lot of reconnaissance in the lowlands and would, on occasion, come across a grave. These graves were very recognizable as they were mounded on top of the dirt. We were instructed to dig them up as the North Vietnamese and the Viet Cong would sometimes bury caches of weapons in them in lieu of a body. When you got to a certain point a stench would come up which was extremely repulsive. We would then stop digging as an actual body was clearly there. We did, on several occasions, find weapon caches, though.

The lowlands in Vietnam were rough. Lots of the time we were walking through elephant grass. Elephant grass can grow up to around eleven feet tall and the edges are just like sawgrass and can really cut you up. The lowlands were also full of leeches. They look kind of like a worm but will sink their head under your skin and fill themselves with your blood. They particularly liked your underarms or belt line. You typically didn't know they were there until they dropped off full. You couldn't just pull them off because they would leave the head below the skin causing a quick infection. The only way to get rid of them was to hit them with a lit cigarette or put insect repellent on them. Either way they would pull their own head out. Snakes were also a problem, especially in the lowlands. One of our men got bitten by a highly venomous snake related to the cobra family. He was on the hospital ship for months.

Our company was moved out of Camp Evans to a northern location. To do this they sent some short takeoff, short landing aircraft. We were seated on the floor which was actually pallets. We took off, flew for a while, and landed. When we landed my butt was actually on a small crack between floor sections. As we braked, the entire floor moved forward. I thought I was going to lose my entire butt. I was okay but had problems walking and sitting for a few days. Our new location was in the mountains. You should try climbing a mountain with one hundred pounds on your back! As you are climbing you grab small trees to help pull yourself up. On occasion the tree comes out of the ground and you tumble fifty feet backwards and start over again. As you are walking in this terrain you get caught by a vine. These vines were called "wait-a-minute vines" because they had something like fishhooks that would catch your clothes or rucksack. Sometimes you would decide to overpower the vine, but always landed on your butt, as the vines were stronger than you. You would start pulling the little hooks out of the rucksack telling your comrades to wait a minute (thus the name wait-a-minute vines).

One afternoon we were setting up an ambush with half of the company in line, the other half in a L shape. As we were getting in position, we started to receive AK-47 fire. We returned fire and suddenly were in a major firefight. As it turned out there were a few North Vietnamese between the two lines and we were, in fact, in a fight with the other half of the company. Thankfully only one of our men was hit. He was hit in the leg and it broke the bone. He got what everyone called a "million-dollar wound" and was sent home. Later that week we were traveling along a trail when the point man was shot. We couldn't see where the point man was shot. We couldn't see where the fire came from but cautiously moved forward. The new point man was then hit. Turned out there was a North Vietnamese sniper in a spider hole. It took us about one hour to find the sniper and take him out.

After this incident the company again moved out, and very soon found ourselves in a major firefight. Since I was in a three-man machine-gun group, the three of us started running forward. The man carrying the machine gun turned around and handed the gun to George and ran toward the rear. George and I went forward, set up the gun, and returned fire. Meanwhile, the old gunner ran to the rear, helped a wounded soldier onto a medevac chopper, and was later awarded a medal for bravery. George and I never said anything, however he was very soon transferred to another company. Someone else must have seen the incident.

Several days later we were on a search-and-destroy mission. I was walking point, as I frequently did during my first four months. We were walking up a riverbed about waist deep which we had been doing for the past three days. After a while I slowed and spotted what looked like an active North Vietnamese base camp. We crept forward and entered the camp. Fires were still burning. We had obviously been detected and the North Vietnamese Army had quickly moved out. The first thing we noticed was their toilet, which emptied into the river upstream from where we came. We had been filling our canteens for days with their contamination. We went through their basecamp and encountered them in the jungle. This led to a very intense firefight. We took no prisoners. After we did our body count, medevac'd our wounded, and destroyed their basecamp, we moved out.

Several days later we were moving along a ridgeline in a fairly dense jungle when our medic, who was a conscientious objector and carried no weapon, was struck with a rock. He looked around and saw a kid running away. We then knew we were in trouble as we were a company of around one hundred men and the North Vietnamese Army would allow their battalion commanders and above to bring their families with them. Meaning, there was a minimum of a battalion force in the area. Later we encountered them. We were on high ground and they were all in the rocks and crevices just below us. It was almost impossible to hit them due to their cover. They kept creeping up toward us and we were by far outnumbered and outgunned. We had nowhere to go and they were pounding us with machine-gun fire and mortars.

Viking, our commanding officer, radioed the rear for air support. You could soon hear screaming and smell flesh burning as a helicopter arrived and engaged. The remainder of the North Vietnamese Army there broke off and retreated. We then moved out. The medic carried a .45-caliber pistol after that. A few days later we encountered them again. Very heavy fighting broke out. This time we had more available air support. Now, the Air Force was called in and jets rolled in on low strafing runs with their machine guns firing. The next wave came in with napalm. When the napalm ignited you could not breathe, as it sucked all of the oxygen out of the air. The smell of napalm and burning flesh is truly awful. This fight broke off about fifteen minutes later. I have to tell you, when these jets roll in at treetop level, even though they are yours, the scream of the engine and vibration still scares you to death! The jet jockeys were a story in themselves. We would begin heavy combat, they would come in on a strafing or bombing run, pull up, do some barrel rolls or other maneuvers, then leave the area. It was always a great feeling when they would show up as nasty things always happened to the enemy, which gave us a chance to regroup, reload, and relocate.

Everyone in our unit was issued a claymore mine. Each one was actually three pieces, the mine, an oval-shaped spool wrapped with about fifty feet of wire connected to a blasting cap, which was stored in the hollow center of the spool, and a hand detonator. On occasion you had to check the continuity of the system by plugging the detonator into one side of a test unit and the blasting-cap wire into the opposing side. When you squeezed the detonator, a test light would flash showing everything was ready to go.

Viking attached a newbie to me to watch and teach the ropes. The guy was actually a schoolteacher back home so you would figure he was reasonably intelligent. We were set up one night heating our C-rations when we heard a bang and our new guy screaming. He was lying on the ground writhing like he was shot. Found out he decided to check his claymore. When he set it up for the check, he neglected to put the test unit in line so when he squeezed the detonator, the blasting cap exploded and he had a very small burn mark on his stomach but nothing else. Of course, Viking had to read me the riot act for not watching him closer. Just glad he hadn't plugged the blasting cap into his claymore mine!

Being 129 pounds turned out to be not such a good thing and I ended up being the company tunnel rat. Anytime the company came across a tunnel, I went in to investigate. This was the scariest thing I ever had to do. You were given a flashlight with a red lens to retain your night vision, and either the lieutenant's .45 or just a knife. When you went in you were very aware that if anyone is there, only one of you is coming out alive. The tunnels were often booby trapped. They would often have a punji pit at the bottom of the entrance. A punji pit is a hole with sharpened bamboo covered in feces, concealed by foliage. They [the NVA] frequently hung pit vipers by their tails [in punji pits] so when you went in you would be face-to-face with this poisonous snake. They also liked to take a C-ration can, put a grenade in it with the pin removed, and tie a vine or trip wire to it, so when you caught the vine or wire, it would come out of the can and explode.

Typically when you went down, two guys would lower you by your ankles so you could remove any booby traps. After the booby traps were removed you would go back down. The first three times I went down I took the lieutenant's .45. After that I didn't trust myself and only took my knife. When I explored the first three tunnels I recovered all kinds of explosives. If you hit anything with a .45 round, the entire tunnel goes up and you have no chance for survival. I felt I had a better chance of living with my knife. Since there was no such thing as tunnel rat school in 1968, you had to come up with your own method.

When a new guy is sent to your company, regardless of rank, he was attached to a person with combat experience. I had a sergeant attached to me as I was a Spec 4. We were moving along a ridge line and he came across a tunnel. He immediately pulled the pin from a grenade. I asked him what he was doing. He said he was going to throw it into the tunnel. First, we were in an area where any explosion would give away our position and not knowing what was in the tunnel could be a disaster. I told him to replace the pin but he said he already threw it away. I took his grenade, unscrewed the primer, threw the grenade down the hill, and the primer into the tunnel. When I went into the tunnel we removed enough explosives to take the top of the hill, along with half of our company.

Life as a "grunt" was rough. Our commanding officer, Viking, was a very disciplined officer and had us moving until the sun went down and again moving as the sun rose in the morning. This angered a lot of the guys but really kept us alive. We were never hit in the middle of the night like some of the other companies. If the North Vietnamese didn't know exactly where you were set up, they couldn't attack.

When we set up at night, you first dug a foxhole and set up fields of fire, put out claymore mines, then started your dinner. Dinner consisted of C-rations which included a small can of spaghetti, ham and eggs, beans and franks, etc., also, small cans of peaches, fruit cocktail or apricots, and a small packet of cigarettes, a John Wayne Bar (a chocolate bar that is impossible to melt), salt, pepper, and a small packet of toilet paper. To heat the meals they had heat tabs which were like a small tab of Sterno in a foil packet. For some reason the heat tabs never made it out to us in the jungle. I guess people in the rear must have needed them more than us. So, instead of heat tabs, we would pinch off a piece of C-4 plastic explosive, light it, and cook our meal. The only problem with a C-4 is it burns hot. If you were heating say spaghetti, it would form an air pocket at the bottom of the can. If you didn't stick a knife down to release it, as soon as you turned your head it would pop out of the can and into the dirt. Since that's all you had to eat, it became a very crunchy meal.

A lot of the time in the mountains we were given long-range patrol rations in lieu of C-rations. Long-range patrol rations were dehydrated and required a lot of water to prepare. It always seemed to happen when there was very little water available (streams, rivers, etc.). When we needed water they would fill artillery canisters and drop them from helicopters. Whomever filled these canisters in the rear never bothered to rinse them out, so the water always tasted like gunpowder. Some of the long-range patrol rations would never soften. If you had, for instance, chili con carne, the chili beans would never soften and could literally take your teeth out when you bit one.

When the company moved out each day the lead platoon would be rotated. At the time we had four platoons. Then, someone had to walk point. The point man and slack man behind him were typically around one hundred yards ahead of the company. The point and slack men were essentially an early warning system for the company. If they tripped an ambush, the rest of the company would be alerted and could take defensive or offensive maneuvers. As I was walking point one day an order came down from battalion that we were in a police action and not a war, so if we saw the enemy we were not to shoot at them unless they shot at us first. Too bad the commander wasn't with me to be shot at first. Sometimes it seemed like we were our own worst enemy!

When you were on point you had to be very aware of booby traps, snipers, spider holes, and ambushes. With time and experience you became fairly adept at spotting this. On occasion you would find grenades stuffed into C-ration cans tied to vines, other times we found their homemade claymores consisting of like a garbage can lid filled with plastic explosives, embedded with rocks, broken glass, and anything they could use as a projectile. This was mounted in a tree, so had it gone off, a lot of guys would have been hit.

Our company very seldom got around any populated areas, however, on one mission we were in the lowlands and came upon a small village. We were ordered to cordon off the village and check for any Viet Cong or North Vietnamese soldiers. We had two Chieu Hoi Scouts with us who spoke Vietnamese and called all the people out of their huts. They all responded with "No problem," and we searched with negative results. After searching most of the huts, there was a noise coming from a barn. Since everyone was supposed to be out, our scout shouted for them to come out of the barn. When there was no response, our grenadier fired a round from his M79 grenade launcher. It was a beehive round (lots of small darts), almost like buckshot. When the round hit the barn there was a loud noise and the barn started to come down. It seems that there was a water buffalo inside and the round just made him mad. He came out and ran off as we all scattered out of his way. No one was hurt but the barn was destroyed. We completed our search, let the people return to their huts, and moved out without incident.

Shortly after this mission, we were loaded into helicopters for a combat assault into the mountains. We arrived on a mountain top and were directed to do a search-and-destroy mission of the area. Most of this area was triple-canopy jungle where even during the day it was hard to see. At night you couldn't see your hand in front of your face. Occasionally planes would fly overhead spraying Agent Orange to remove some of the foliage. This really did help, as when in an area which was previously sprayed you could see a little, possibly keeping us alive as snipers were frequently hiding there.

During this mission I was walking point, climbing up the mountainside, when I encountered a swarm of some type of yellow jacket or the like. We ran through the swarm, all of us getting stung, when a firefight broke out at the rear of the column. We had to run back through the swarm again, getting stung to help in the fight. After the fighting broke off, we headed back up the mountain, again through the swarm. I really don't know what the swarm was, only that they had to touch you to sting.

We continued up the mountain and came into a small clearing. It was dark but beautiful. There was a huge waterfall and all around there were what looked like black orchids growing along with other foliage that I had never seen before. It was kind of breathtaking to find this beauty in the middle of a war. But further up the mountain we encountered a very large unit of the North Vietnamese Army, with quite a fight ensuing. We were largely outnumbered and had to pull back, leaving one man reported as dead down the hill. After the fight ended, we went back down the hill to recover his body only to find his wrists were slit to make him bleed out. If any one of us had any idea he were still alive, there is no way he would have been left. His body was placed in a body bag and sent to the rear.

Several days later we were airlifted to a base near the beach. This was totally different than anything we had so far experienced. My first day on the base I had kitchen duty. This was really okay as all we had to date were C-rations and long-range patrol rations. While I was in the kitchen the cooks were making spice cake. I asked for some samples and the cook said sure, but be very careful as it can make you sick. The cake was great, so I had two more pieces, ignoring the cook's warning. About two hours later I was sick as a dog. Since C-rations and long-range patrol rations have no spices, your body becomes accustomed to the bland diet and seriously revolts when you introduce a bunch of spice.

The next morning found me on the perimeter of the base setting out trip flares inside the layers of concertina wire. This wire was similar to barbed wire, except that instead the barbs are actually small razor blades. While I was bending down setting a trip flare, a chinook came in to land. It blew the concertina wire all over me. It took thirty minutes for my comrades to extract me from that mess. The more you move the more entangled you get and the more sliced up you get. By the time I got out, my clothes were all cut up and I had slices everywhere. I guess it didn't really help our situation that as we worked, helicopters continued landing and taking off a very short distance away.

The next day our company moved out for a mission along the beach. Walking in beach sand with a combat load is every bit as exhausting as climbing mountains. A couple of days later, still on the beach, we set up early. Since you could see quite a distance, we were fairly safe, so we had a small football game using a canteen as the ball. While we were playing, one of our helicopters flew over, mistook us for North Vietnamese, and opened fire. No one was hit but I did get a hole in one of my canteens.

The next day we moved out and after several hours got into a fight with a small band of North Vietnamese. We took one prisoner. While he was being interrogated by our scouts, one of our men realized the prisoner wore the watch of our man who had had his wrists slit. The prisoner was picked up by helicopter and sent back to base came for further questioning, knowing he probably had pertinent information. Two days later found us right back up in the mountains.

At this time I was changed from rifleman/assistant machine gunner to fourth platoon radio-telephone operator. The duty was almost the same, only when a fight broke out I couldn't drop my rucksack as I had to maintain radio contact with the company commander and the other three platoons. As we were walking in the jungle at the base of a mountain, we came across a large cache of antiaircraft artillery rounds. The stack was approximately four feet tall and fifteen feet long. Three of us were left there to blow the ammunition. We were instructed to give the company one half hour to climb the mountain before setting off the charges. While the company climbed the mountain, we set up several C-4 charges, linked them with a det cord, and found cover. About twenty minutes later I called the commanding officer and he said to blow the charge as the rest of our troops were taking cover. We blew the charges and of course, the unexpected happened. The antiaircraft artillery blew up into the air and started exploding around our men on the mountainside. No one was hurt but it scared the hell out of all of us!

A couple of weeks later I was chosen to attend the Combat Leaders Course and sent to the rear for a week. This course was great and included slack jumping, repelling, quick kill, silent kill, and advanced explosives. At the school, they had a 10-story tower. One side was for repelling and the opposing side was for slack jumping. My first try at repelling was painful. The instructor told us to keep your feet perpendicular to your body as you descend. The first two drops were okay. I hit the wall, descended, hit the wall again, descended, and when I hit the third time my feet were not quite 90 degrees. This forced my nose right into the wall. The next time I listened more carefully.

Slack jumping was nerve wracking on the first jump. You made yourself a rope harness, tied around your waist and between your legs with a D ring connected to the front. The instructor had you tie your own harness because if you tie it wrong you could lose certain parts of your anatomy. After you tied the harness, a rope was coiled up on the top of the 10-story tower, possessed through the D ring, and the remainder of the rope tossed to the ground. You were instructed to hold the rope away from your face with your left hand, and bring the rope around to your back with your right hand as a brake. Next, you stood on top of the tower and jumped. It took all the guts you could conjure up the first time, but after that it was easy. Again, you could tell who didn't listen because by not holding your left hand out far enough the rope would leave a rope burn across your face. There were multiple burns in the group.

The Advanced Explosives Course was a ball. At the end of the course we formed a line. We were told to hold our arms out and proceed down the line. At each station they placed a different explosive in your arms. We were then told to go make a bomb. Our bombs created very impressive explosions complete with major craters in the ground and anything close blown over. After graduating the course I returned to Camp Evans to be re-deployed to my unit. Upon arrival at Camp Evans I was informed the company had been moved into the A Shau Valley, which was a major part of the Ho Chi Minh Trail. I was then asked to identify several bodies from our unit. Two of the men I knew very well but they were in other platoons from mine. The third man I was very close to as he was a sergeant attached to me when he came in-country. He and I had the same interests back home and had been in some very intense firefights together. He fought very well and learned fast. It was shocking to see him dead.

That afternoon I collected my gear and flew out to rejoin my unit. When I arrived things looked bad. Several more men from my platoon had been shot, including two different men carrying my radio. The other platoons had also taken losses. The next day we were attacked by a North Vietnamese force much larger than ours. We fought for some time, but had to pull back as we were being overrun. As we pulled back we took any wounded we could find and moved back to higher ground. We finally fought off the assault and things calmed down.

We were still receiving fire on occasion but had things under control enough to call in the medevac choppers.

The first chopper landed and was promptly loaded with the most severely wounded as it lifted off. The second chopper was being loaded when we again started taking ground fire. The chopper started lifting off when a wounded soldier we thought was dead came running through our perimeter, ran to the chopper and hooked his arm around the skid. The helicopter lifted off quickly with this man hanging while a wounded soldier in the chopper reached out and grabbed his shirt. The medevac was several hundred feet up when the shirt ripped and he grabbed a handful of hair. This too came out and the man fell. Our company searched for three days but never found the body. He was listed as missing in action. We never saw the trooper from inside the chopper again but were told when he reached the rear he went insane.

We didn't know at the time but this was all part of "Hamburger Hill." As a lower-ranking soldier you have no idea where you are going or what the mission is. Hamburger Hill was Hill 937, which meant it was 937 meters tall, about three thousand feet. This was a mission of the 3rd of the 187th. We, as the 1st of the 506th, were attacked. The 3rd of the 187th went up the face of the hill along with some South Vietnamese Army units. We as the 1st of the 506th were supposed to come up the back of the hill as a blocking force. As infantry soldiers, we had no idea what was going on, only we were being hit with far superior numbers than ours, including .51-caliber machine guns, RPGs, mortars, and small arms fire. From what we were told, over six hundred men went up the hill with fewer than two hundred returning. Our company started with around 126 men and 10 days later 28 of us were left.

Unless you have been in combat you don't realize what happens when the fighting breaks off. The first thing you do is find the wounded soldiers, bandage them, and get them to the medic or medevac. The second is getting the dead into a body bag, hopefully along with all of his parts. Thirdly, you find your expended magazines and reload them. Hopefully this all can happen before a counterattack.

The 101st Airborne at this point was a totally air mobile unit, meaning you would board a helicopter, be dispatched to whatever hotspot needed assistance, help with the fight, then do it again. Our company frequently went on these combat assaults. Prior to mounting the chopper, if it was probable that major fighting would ensue, a chaplain would hold a religious service, along with Communion. After the service we were put into formation. We were told to "Look at the man on your right, now look at the man on your left. Chances are one of them will not return. It's your job to make sure they return." Very inspiring prior to combat!

Combat assaults could be very hectic. Typically, six men would load into the helicopter. Two would sit on the floor in the center, two would sit in each door next to the door gunners. There was not too much room with all of our combat gear so only your butt was inside and your legs hung over the skids. The only problem was there was nothing to hang on to. On a lot of our assaults the Air Force would precede us with a pack of jets with 500-pound daisy cutters, [bombs] which would detonate above the ground on our landing zones, blowing the trees down. When we would come in, the choppers were not allowed to land. So as each soldier jumped out with combat gear, the weight was displaced. The chopper would rise a little so the two guys in the center could be jumping eight to ten feet. When you jump eight feet with a rucksack and land on a tree stump, it can be quite painful. Sometimes we would lose more people to injuries from the combat assault than the fight that ensued.

On the typical assault, we would be dropped off on a landing zone, given a specific pick-up point, and told to do a search-and-destroy mission of anything in between. Most of the time it was one or two mountains away. At the new pick-up point (typically a mountaintop or hilltop), we would blow a new landing zone. To do this we would place a C-4 charge at the bottom of the trees and at the top another charge to direct the way it would fall. All of the charges were linked with detcord [detonating cord]. Detcord blows very quick, faster than C-4, so when set off, all explosions would go off at the same time. This was quite a sight to see!

The 101st Airborne frequently used what we called a "Pink Team." This team consisted of a light observation helicopter (very small glass bubble helicopter) and a Cobra gunship, which was heavily armed. The small helicopter would drop down into the trees looking for enemy. If he took any ground fire, the Cobra would roll in and take out the area. On occasion, the light observation helicopter would pick up one of our officers to recon the area. Typically when the officer returned, he would be green from motion sickness. The light observation helicopter pilots took pride in providing rough rides!

During the fight at Hill 937 (Hamburger Hill), Viking, our commanding officer, was on R&R for most of the fight. When he returned I was moved from fourth platoon radio telephone operator to Viking's battalion radio operator. He had three radio telephone operators: one battalion radio telephone operator, one company radio telephone operator, and one headquarters radio telephone operator. I'm not sure what happened to his prior radio telephone operators, whether they were killed, wounded, or rotated out. I carried an AN/PRC-77 radio. Others used the AN/PRC-25 radio.

One of my duties with Viking was doing land navigation for the company. You always had to know exactly where you were. This was very difficult considering frequently we were in triple-canopy jungles. You couldn't see the sky much less other landmarks, so I was frequently climbing trees to locate landmarks. If you could find two landmarks you could shoot an azimuth with your compass, lay your map down, and line up the two azimuths. Where the two lines intersected was your location. There were many times when this was not possible so I would have to call for artillery. I would call a fire mission with white phosphorus rounds to explode five hundred feet above the group. I would give coordinates where I thought we were located. When the shell exploded we could then verify or correct our location.

Being in the mountains during this monsoon season is a real challenge. The rain comes down day and night. The temperature drops and the wind picks up. The coldest I have ever been was while being soaking wet with low temperatures and high winds blowing. All you have is a T-shirt and regular fatigue shirt. When you set up at night you have a choice. Do you sleep in your wet shirt while it dries overnight, or do you remove it and have to put on a sopping wet, cold shirt in the morning? There's no good choice. And climbing steep terrain is very tricky when it becomes mud. You can slip and go down fifty feet in just a few seconds. The weight of your rucksack doesn't help, although it can take the shock of hitting a rock or tree if it hits first.

During my year in Vietnam we were in the jungle almost all of the time. My fiancée, Janet (now my wife), would send me "care packages." They would generally consist of brownies, which she baked and placed in coffee cans, along with other things. Sometimes they would get there fast and sometimes weeks later. Although the brownies were usually covered with mildew, we would just scrape it off and eat what was left. After eating only C-rations there was no way they were going to waste. Sometimes two or three would come at the same time. The problem was how to carry the overage as there was not much excess space in your rucksack. Hardcore (our field first sergeant) would pack his rucksack with what would fit and when Viking put his rucksack down Hardcore would stick the remainder in his sack. Viking would always say, "Somehow my rucksack feels extra heavy today," but when we set up at night we all shared the goodies.

One day we were walking down a riverbed about waist deep. Hardcore, who was pretty short, was in front of me. I was looking around for North Vietnamese and when I looked forward again Hardcore was gone. I reached down in the water and found him. He had stepped into a hole and couldn't get back to the surface, but was now okay. Further down we came to an area and exited the water. We moved a little further and came upon a clearing which was at the base of a fairly large mountain. The mountain had stairs cut into it all the way up with bamboo covering each step. We had never seen anything like this but had to remember we were along the Ho Chi Minh Trail.

While at the base of this mountain, I looked over and saw a tree with "Viking" carved into it. I looked over at Viking who saw it at the same time. Neither of us said anything so as not to panic the troops, as this carving meant that they had someone who spoke and could read and write English, and worse they were monitoring my radio transmissions. To have this type of person would require at least a battalion-sized unit and we were only company-sized. We immediately moved out so as not to be trapped in this valley. We did encounter some North Vietnamese and had a firefight, but it was not near[ly] as bad as it could have been.

Several days later we were extracted from the jungle and relocated to the Firebase Berchtesgaden. Our job was perimeter defense for the artillery unit on top of the hill. I was located in the company command bunker about three-quarters of the way up the hill. On the top of the hill there was a bunch of artillery which fired across the A Shau Valley. The artillery included 105 mm, 155 mm, and 175 mm howitzers as well as their battalion headquarters. The headquarters had things that we lacked, including generators and electric lights. One day I saw a helicopter arrive which had their resupply. Among the things I saw being offloaded were porcelain light fixtures and light bulbs. I snuck over and grabbed a light socket and bulb. I set up the socket in our bunker, took claymore mine wire, and tied our light in hot to the generator line. I got zapped a couple of times, but we now had a light in the bunker. While on this firebase we set out trip flares, claymore mines, concertina wire, and 55-gallon drums of fougasse [flammable liquid]. At night I would fire a star cluster flare which would initiate what was called a "mad minute." During a mad minute everyone on the perimeter opens up with their M16s, machine guns, and grenade launchers. This goes on for around one minute until I fire a second star cluster signaling ceasefire. This was done to keep any enemy troops off guard as it was always at a different time.

On the night of June 14, I set off the mad minute as usual. A couple of hours later Hardcore came running into the bunker saying there are sappers everywhere. He had gone out to urinate and was going [urinating] on a man's head who was climbing up the hill. About two minutes later a rocket-propelled grenade aimed at our light came through our bunker and exploded. All I remember was fire all around my head, people screaming, and the next thing I was regaining consciousness. When I came to, I noticed Viking was in a firefight with a man at our ammo dump on the landing zone. My problem was he was using my rifle. I had to go out and defend our bunker, but was still armed as I slept with a knife. We fought all night, which seemed to go on forever. In the morning the fighting broke off. Viking had everyone remain in their bunkers and had me and one other guy go down to recon the area. The guy next to me saw an enemy soldier move and opened up on him. He hit his hand and leg, taking off several fingers. Shortly after our medic went to help him and the finger was already coagulating. I guess their diet must promote this as GIs bleed a lot more.

Our firebase had an awful stench for days after the assault as body components decomposed. Several days later we were flown to Eagle Beach for a stand-down, where you spend several days at the beach, have entertainment, and get new clothes as well as hot food. When we got there Viking walked up to the officer in charge and asked where our new clothes were. He responded that another captain had come over and claimed them. Viking picked up his M16 and left. Shortly thereafter, a jeep pulling a trailer with the uniforms appeared. Viking took no prisoners. Viking was a very serious person and rarely joked or attracted attention to himself. I came back from the beach and there was a band from Australia playing on the stage. I looked around and saw Viking dancing and asked, "What are you doing?" He responded, "I'm doing the Funky Chicken," which was totally out of character for him. He was having a good time for a change which was great to see.

Two days later found us back in the A Shau Valley. We were back in the mountains not too far from Hamburger Hill. Viking got a call from the battalion commander asking about Hill 996 (again around 3,200 feet tall). Lieutenant Colonel Hayward asked Viking how he would approach Hill 996 as Viking had taken the hill once before. It seemed that a lot of North Vietnamese Army from Hill 937 had relocated to Hill 996. Viking responded that if he attacked from a specific ridgeline the Hill could not be defended.

A couple of days later Viking got a call from Hayward that he was getting fire from the top of the hill and wanted Viking to bring some troops and help them out. Since the fighting at Hill 937 had taken a toll on our company, we were still very short of personnel. We had some replacements but were still nowhere near full strength and most of the replacements were lacking any combat experience. Our fourth platoon and third platoon had been so decimated that there was no longer a fourth platoon. Third and fourth platoons combined did not make anywhere near a full platoon. Viking took a partial platoon to help and left the remaining troops to defend the position. When we arrived at Hill 996 there was a fierce firefight taking place. We followed the ridgeline that Viking had referred to and added to the fight. One of our men, Gordon Roberts, saw an opening and ended up taking out four bunkers. How he got through the North Vietnamese Army fire and our cover fire without getting hit is beyond me. Roberts would later receive the Medal of Honor.

After taking the Hill we found out that 20 men had been killed, including Hayward. Later that night Viking walked up and put on his web gear and his M16 and started off. I asked him where he was going. He said he got a call from Command that Hayward had been killed and he was to retrieve the body. I asked who was going with him. He responded, "I'm going by myself. I can't ask anyone to risk it." I went and found four other volunteers to help. This was the only time I or others volunteered for what we considered a suicide mission. We figured we would have to breach North Vietnamese Army lines to find the colonel.

As it worked out we went down the Hill around five hundred meters and found him wrapped around a rock. Rigor mortis had set in so we had a very hard time getting him into a body bag. By now a *Spooky* (a C-47 with mini-guns hanging out of the windows and deploying parachute flares) was on location. As we were coming back up the Hill a depleted parachute flare landed right in front of us, nearing taking us out. We re-entered the perimeter without incident. We had one man killed on that Hill which I know must have weighed on Viking's heart forever, as when we were getting ready to move out he called over and said, "Grab you men and let's go." The sergeant responded, "Can you take someone else as I have a really bad feeling about this." Viking responded, "You'll be fine, get your men and let's go." That sergeant was killed and Viking never would speak about it. I believe it was too painful.

While maneuvering through the steep mountains one day I slipped and went down the side. I landed about thirty feet down and was okay. However, on the way down I broke one of my knives in half and tore the back of my left thigh from my butt to my knee. We were always getting minor injuries so I didn't think too much of it. About two weeks later the company was taken to an area where showers are set up and new clothes available. As you were walking out of the showers medics were stationed at the door. As we walked out they would direct any visibly injured personnel to a different location where we were transported back to Camp Evans for treatment. When I saw the medic there he said, "A few more days and you will have gangrene." He rubbed an antibiotic on my leg, then scraped the scab off with a razor. He then rubbed alcohol on the wound. After that I was more afraid of the medics than being shot with an AK-47. I spent three days recouping at Camp Evans, then returned to the field.

After I returned to the company we were maneuvering in the mountains when Viking got a call from base camp saying that there was a group of our men refusing to board helicopters to return to our area. Viking said to put them on the choppers at gunpoint if they had to and send them out. When they arrived at our location, they exited the choppers and told Viking that they were not moving. Viking looked at them and said, "Suit yourself," turned around to us and said, "move out." About ten minutes later you heard footsteps running toward us. They rejoined their units and were never a problem again. I think Viking handled the problem masterfully!

During one specific mission we had to move fairly far so a Chinook was sent to transport us. The helicopter arrived, lowered the rear ramp, and some of our troops loaded in. Very shortly the men all came out and the pilot said no one could enter his chopper with live arms. Viking stormed up to him and stated, "You are nothing but an overpaid bus driver, get your ass back in your seat and get this thing off the ground!" We all loaded the chopper with no further incident. It's strange how a pilot would think that active combat units could travel without live ammunition.

Once we moved to a forward area, we were working on a hill with an existing landing zone. One of the men walked across the landing zone and apparently the North Vietnamese had placed a 500-pound bomb beneath it. The bomb detonated and the soldier was evaporated. He was listed as missing in action as there was no body to recover. I always thought that would give their family false hope to list them as such.

Our company was in frequent firefights and went on many combat assaults. Viking liked to go in on the first chopper, being the leader he was. Since I was his radio telephone operator, I was always with him. We went on one combat assault where we jumped out of the chopper and as soon as the chopper took off we were in the middle of an ambush. The two of us got behind some rocks and started returning fire. As the next chopper came in, our machine gunner was sitting in the door. The sight at the end of his barrel was shot off and his eyes looked like saucers. Viking and I saw this and laughed, so there really can be some type of humor in combat. As the fight went on, I called in some air support. The jets came in and I could see the pilot's face and could see the nomenclature on the bombs as they came out. I carried an instamatic camera in my top pocket, so I started trying to jump between shots and snap some pictures. Viking said, "You're crazy, but I want some of those pictures." Unfortunately, when I had the pictures developed I got the back of Viking's head. Dodging too many bullets, I guess.

In late August we again found ourselves back at Firebase Berchtesgaden. We again had perimeter defense and everyone got set up. When Viking came into the bunker I said to him, "Last time we were here we had the sapper attack and ended up fighting all night. I know that they waited until our mad minute ended, then came up the hill to attack. If we throw in a second mad minute occasionally, it may throw them off guard." Viking said, "I like that, we'll try it." That night we tried it with no results. The next day there was a change of command. Viking was transferred and we got a new commanding officer. Viking told the new commanding officer about the extra mad minute so we again did it the next night. That night three of us were sitting on top of the command bunker, around 11:00 PM. I sent up a star cluster flare to initiate the mad minute. The firing began and after one minute I sent up the second star cluster to signal a ceasefire. The three of us remained on top of the bunker and started singing. I took the two expended flare tubes using them as drumsticks, the other two guys used them as microphones. This went on for a while, we were making the best of our time between mad minutes. About 1:00 AM I sent up another star cluster to initiate the second mad minute. When we began firing it became very apparent that we were completely surrounded by North Vietnamese sappers who had lost the element of surprise. The ensuing fight was more of a massacre as the North Vietnamese Army were unprepared to fight at this time. I got a call from the artillery commander asking for permission to use direct fire on a knoll a short distance from our firebase. The North Vietnamese were massing there. As I looked around for the knoll I saw one of our bunkers across the landing zone from me, three of our men were sitting on top [of it] and a mortar round landed right in the middle of them. All three were wounded and one man lost his leg.

I spotted the knoll the artillery commander referred to and since our new commanding officer had disappeared, I gave my initials to commence fire. The artillery destroyed the top of the hill and all of the North Vietnamese Army massing there. The next morning a cargo net was placed in the middle of the landing zone and the dead sappers were stacked into it. There was something like 28 or 29 bodies.

A helicopter came in, picked up the net and released it over the jungle. The bodies all fell from the sky.

It seems all the brass got awards for the action. I was promoted to sergeant. You would always think being promoted to sergeant was a good thing, however the battalion commander flew in and said, "We need someone like you for a special mission." I was then sent to a Special Forces Camp to run six-man teams. Each team carried one M60 machine gun, one M79 grenade launcher, two M16s, and two AK-47s. The reason for the different weapons is because each weapon when fired has a different rapport. When a firefight breaks out the different rapports can be confusing to the enemy. I spent two months running these teams. We would be dropped off in different locations and spend three days to a week before pick-up. The main problem with the insertion on the choppers was the North Vietnamese knew you were there and were looking for you as well as you watching them. It was like jumping out of the frying pan into the fire.

November finally came and my tour was over. I went back to Camp Evans and boarded a small plane to fly to Bien Hoa where passenger jets would fly back to the States. As we were flying on the small plane I looked out the window and one of the engines was on fire. No big deal as the pilot shut it down, extinguished the flame, and flew to Bien Hoa. In Bien Hoa I boarded a large jet for the flight home. We flew from Bien Hoa to Guam. On the way to Guam one of the engines flamed out. We flew into Guam, the engine was repaired, and we took off for Hawaii. On the way to Hawaii the same engine again flamed out. We flew into Hawaii on three engines and while in Hawaii it was again repaired. After several hours we again boarded the plane and took off for California. Shortly after we left Hawaii the engine again flamed out and then the second one flamed out. We returned to Hawaii and were told to get back any way you can. Several of us got tickets on a commercial airline and had to walk across the parking lot to the new terminal. We all had duffle bags and I also had a Russian SKS rifle. As we were walking across the parking lot, a small flatbed cart similar to the Army mule came driving by. The driver was looking behind him and ran right under the back of a flatbed truck. The driver was beheaded. Seems we couldn't escape the gore, even in Hawaii. We boarded the commercial airliner and flew back with no further incident. I spent two days in California getting a new dress uniform, then flew home to Miami International Airport.

Warren was stationed at Fort Hood until leaving the Army in June 1970. He became a sheet metal contractor, building and installing air-conditioning duct systems in hospitals and schools in South Florida. He married his fiancée, Janet. They were married for 54 years, until she died in December 2023. They have two daughters and five grandchildren.

CHAPTER 5

Terry Taylor

In Vietnam November 1968–November 1969

> "I learned at the age of 18 that you don't have to die to go to hell. Vietnam was hell on earth. If I had had any comprehension of what I was getting myself into, then I would have done everything I could to avoid it."

The following was submitted in writing and lightly edited by the author with Terry's permission.

I went over there when I was 18 years old. I volunteered for the draft because I thought it would be an adventure prior to college. It was more than I bargained for. We left for Vietnam on a chartered commercial airline. It flew out of Oakland, California, and on to Fairbanks, Alaska, then I think on to Vietnam (although we may have stopped somewhere else in the Pacific to refuel). We flew into Tan Son Nhat Airport and were transported to a base camp at Bien Hoa. We were at Bien Hoa for several days. We were put through an orientation and given time to acclimate. We lived outside the entire time. During the day we played war games with Vietnamese children. We were given wood guns for the games. In spite of all the training in the States, one day a little Vietnamese boy was able to sneak up behind me and say "bang-bang" while aiming his wood rifle at my back. I had an epiphany right then. In spite of all the indoctrination in the States, I finally comprehended fully that I could die there. It scared me.

In the evenings and at night we had our M16s and ammunition back. We were put on guard duty on the perimeter of the base. One day we stood in a line in the heat and got a thorough lecture about venereal diseases: the signs, the symptoms, and how to get medical attention if you even imagined you might have one. That same day we were given a toothbrush and a tube of paste. We were told this was fluoride treatment that would protect our teeth while we were there. We used the paste and brushed to very specific directions and for a specific length of time.

After three days in Bien Hoa, we were given orders. Me and my buddies were assigned to Bravo Company, 1/506th, 101st Airborne. We got on a C-130 transport plane and were flown to Camp Evans, the base camp for the 101st. Camp Evans was a sprawling, dusty place, barren of all vegetation. We were assigned barracks. This was just a long plywood enclosure with folding cots in it, nothing else. I was in third platoon. We claimed a cot by putting our duffle bags on it. We were called in to meet our captain in groups of about four. The captain was new to the company, too. His name was Harold Ericksen, and his radio call sign was Viking. He introduced himself and asked each of us something about ourselves. He mentioned that he selected us for his company because we were all volunteers. I did not know it then, but Harold Ericksen had played football at Georgia Tech. After college he played professional football for two years, as a backup quarterback for the Philadelphia Eagles. He got drafted into the Army and decided to make it his career. He was a fine leader; the best captain our company had while I was there.

After visiting the captain I walked back to my barracks. When I got there, other people were in the building that weren't part of the newly arrived group. These guys were the rest of our platoon—the veterans. When I walked in, the place was full of smoke. It didn't smell like tobacco smoke. It was different. I sat down on my cot across from one of the guys and saw he was smoking a strangely rolled cigarette. I asked him what it was. He told me it was marijuana.

By this time there was a group of us sitting together, talking. We, the replacements, learned that the 101st had just recently moved up to Evans from Cu Chi. The battalion (1/506th) had been in a human wave attack [wherein huge numbers of the enemy advance on a unit, like a human wave]. It had decimated the battalion. It had been declared combat ineffective due to its losses. They were rebuilding their manpower with all the replacements coming in. Replacements were referred to as "cherries" because they hadn't yet been in combat. The veterans told us stories that were hair-raising. I got scared when I was shot in the back by a Vietnamese child with a wood rifle in Bien Hoa, and I was scared again as I heard these stories.

After supper that evening at the mess hall we came back to the barracks and met our new platoon leadership, which included the platoon sergeant, Staff Sergeant Samuel Sparks. He was an Airborne Ranger and without a doubt the best combat non-commissioned officer I served under while in the Army. Each company had four infantry platoons, and each platoon had two squads. While we mostly operated as a company in the field, we lived and died in our platoons.

For a week or so we operated out of Camp Evans. We would walk outside the perimeter wire (rows and layers of concertina wire and barbed wire) and patrol the surrounding area. Camp Evans was within walking distance of a Vietnamese farming village. The district we were in was called Phong Dien, Hue. We referred to the village as Phong Dien. There was a vast area of rice paddies and a river. During the day young boys and women would work in the rice paddies. Boys would ride on the backs of the water buffalos used to till the paddies.

We actually learned a lot of very good useful tactics and practices in infantry school. One of the things we were taught was to never use trails. Trails could be ambushed, mined, and booby trapped. Around Phong Dien the area was pretty much open and we could see for good distances. There were civilians in the area. Also, many of the trails and paths were along rice paddy dikes. You could walk on the dikes or walk in the water. Later, when we started operating in the jungle, it exhausted the men trying to hack through the underbrush, made a lot of noise, and really slowed us down if we didn't use a trail. However, it was necessary because what we were taught was correct. The trails were sometimes mined and booby trapped. Snipers also set up in areas where they had clear views of trails. Trails were also great places to set up ambushes, for both us and the enemy.

It wasn't too long before we started living outside the wire. We would patrol all day, usually in either our platoons or our squads. At night we would set up a company night defensive position (NDPs). These night defensive positions were generally circular, with the riflemen on the perimeter. The men on the perimeter were generally in groups of three. We were to dig a foxhole that we could all fit in. We always had one man facing out guarding the perimeter while the other two worked, ate, or slept. My group was me, Joe Stafford, and Rodney Teats. Rodney had been in my infantry school company in Alabama. Joe had not. We would put listening posts (LPs) way out in front of the night defensive position. These were teams of three riflemen who found cover and sat out all night with a radio so that if the enemy starting coming toward the night defensive position for an attack, then they could radio in an advance warning. LPs could be deathtraps if an attack did occur. Some squads or a platoon sometimes went out after dark and set up ambushes around the village. There was a curfew for the Vietnamese. Anyone out at night who wasn't us was the enemy and we were to shoot them.

Actually, when I was there, Vietnam was a simple war. Except around Camp Evans, everywhere we operated was a free-fire zone all the time. If a person wasn't an American or allied soldier, we were to kill them. Our mission was to kill the enemy, nothing more. The hard part was that they didn't want to be killed and their mission mirrored ours. It was not a war for territory. It was a war of attrition.

A few times we were helicoptered out to a beach on the ocean. We would patrol and search for the enemy there. There was a destroyed village on the beach and we would sometimes set up a night defensive position in the ruins. When I was doing my turn on guard there, a big cat came up out of the ruins and started walking toward me. I decided to shoot it. As soon as I raised my rifle the cat took off and disappeared. Every time we set up a night defensive position in those ruins I would see the cat but I never managed to shoot him.

The reason there was a big, apparently well-nourished cat there was because there were lots of rats. The reason there were rats there was because there was a huge cache of hidden rice. We eventually found the cache of rice. It was buried and some of the guys were set to digging it up. One of the men was a red-haired fellow that had been in my training company. I don't remember his name. This was a sandy area.

He was scraping sand away from the bags of rice when a grenade showed and the handle popped off. He didn't react quickly enough. The grenade wounded three men. The red-haired fellow lost one of his eyes. This was the first booby trap we had encountered since I arrived in Vietnam. These were the first American casualties I saw.

We patrolled around Phong Dien for a few weeks. This was because they were rebuilding the battalion and trying to give us some confidence; building experience. In retrospect, I feel lucky to have come into the company at this time. Later, when we were in the A Shau Valley and were constantly engaging the enemy, I felt sorry for the replacements. They arrived freshly trained from the States and got thrown into combat very quickly, if not immediately.

Sometimes we worked with armored cavalry. These guys rode around in armored personnel carriers. These were large, tracked vehicles with machine guns mounted on the top. We followed these folks around periodically. We were never allowed to actually ride on the armored personnel carriers though. We were told it was too dangerous; one grenade or mortar would get us all. The crews sat on top and rode. They never seemed to worry about the danger. We walked in the sun and the heat.

One night we set up a night defensive position with the armored personnel carriers. My squad was sent out after dark to set up an ambush. We were getting accustomed to this now and had never [actually] ambushed anything. We had a lieutenant with us. We set the ambush up in some scrub trees along a well-used trail that bifurcated like a "Y." We could see the single trail and both trails that split off. Joe, Rod, and I were on the end right by the split. The rest of the platoon was spread out and hidden along the [part] of the Y.

While we were out there, the night defensive position got attacked. We could hear all the shooting and grenade explosions, and see flashes and tracer rounds way off in the distance where they were located. After a while all was quiet again. I was on guard while Joe and Rod slept. We did two-hour shifts on guard. I finished my two hours and woke Joe. It seemed like I had just fallen asleep when Joe shook me and whispered, "Somebody's coming down the trail." Rod and I got up and here came a squad of dark figures walking fast toward the split in the trail. We were not in contact with the rest of our platoon. They were positioned too far away from us for us to see or communicate. The squad walked right by us and kept moving on the upper part of the split. They were walking rapidly away from where the rest of the platoon was positioned. I told Joe we needed to fire on them. I carefully aimed my M16 rifle at the lead man, who was taller than the others, and fired. Almost immediately the rest of the platoon started firing. The enemy squad scattered and disappeared.

After we fired and received no incoming fire back, the lieutenant ordered us up and in a line to sweep the area. We found one dead uniformed enemy soldier. It was the tall fellow. It looked like he had one bullet wound through his torso. He did not look Vietnamese. An intelligence officer told me the next day that he was probably a Chinese military advisor. The lieutenant took the credit for the kill, though I'm sure I was the one who shot him. The lieutenant then asked me why I hadn't waited for his command to fire. I told him no one was in communication with us and the enemy was rapidly advancing on us. I didn't even know that he was aware the enemy was there. He seemed to accept that.

Normal procedure after springing an ambush is to move. Otherwise, the enemy knows where you are, and you become the target. I don't think we moved that night. The officers in charge thought there were probably still enemy in the area and decided it would be too risky to move around. Most of the area around Phong Dien was open and flat. The next day at first daylight we went out to retrieve the body of the dead soldier and it was gone.

Another time we set up a night defensive position with the armored personnel carriers and my squad went out on an ambush. A staff sergeant led the squad that night. The armored personnel carriers got attacked again. The enemy loved to kill machinery. The next morning when we got back to the night defensive position, the lieutenant was gone. We thought maybe he had been wounded. We had seen the medevac helicopters come in after the attack. One of the armored personnel carrier lieutenants told us the lieutenant had indeed been medevac'd but not due to a wound received by the enemy. He said that while everyone else was behind some cover and firing, the lieutenant was standing on top of an armored personnel carrier yelling at the enemy to "Identify yourselves." The armored personnel carrier lieutenant told us he got up on the armored personnel carrier and knocked our lieutenant off. When he fell, he hit his head and needed to be evacuated. This story will have more significance later on. It was a concrete example that something wasn't right with this particular lieutenant.

Another day we were patrolling by the river. It was a hot day, so we set up security and took turns filling our canteens, drinking lots of water to slake our thirst, and bathing and playing in the river. After we were done, we continued patrolling upstream. We didn't go more than a hundred yards when we found three dead, bloated North Vietnamese Army soldiers in the water just beyond the riverbank. A couple of guys dumped the water out of their canteens but most of us didn't. We had used iodine tablets in our canteens to purify the water, so what the heck.

The area around Phong Dien was the only field area where we ever encountered and interacted with civilians. Little Vietnamese girls in conical reed hats and brightly patterned clothing would approach us and try to sell us Cokes, food, and liquor. The Cokes were counterfeit and did not taste like real Coke, but they tasted better than the iodine water we were drinking. The liquor was counterfeit too but it sure worked like liquor was supposed to. I remember once going out patrolling so drunk it was all I could do to stand up and walk. I never ate the food. We were ordered not to buy anything from these girls, but when officers weren't around we did.

Phong Dien was physically strenuous because we lived outside, ate C-rations, and patrolled all day. We were usually sleep-deprived because of guard duty at night, LP duty, and setting ambushes. We occasionally would catch and engage small groups of Viet Cong or North Vietnamese. These fights were always one-sided as the enemy was outnumbered and outgunned. We had artillery if we needed it, and they didn't. Some of our people got wounded but I don't recall anyone in my company being killed during this time. Phong Dien was the easiest duty I had in Vietnam. I didn't know that everything was going to change.

About the middle of December we started working in the foothills further inland from the coast. This was more physically challenging. We were going up and down hills and we were in jungle. Then, in a brief reprieve, we were helicoptered back to Camp Evans just before Christmas. We were served a Christmas dinner in the mess hall. I think it was turkey. But the next day we were back in the hills. We set up a night defensive position on top of a high hill and stayed there for several days because there was a ceasefire agreed to for the holidays. While we were sitting up there doing nothing, though, the enemy was busy. We were sitting out in the jungle in the middle of nowhere and not moving. The North Vietnamese Army spent their time constructively by putting booby traps on the trails off the hilltop.

After New Year's Day, we packed up and began moving off the mountain. We didn't get very far when there was a huge explosion. We all felt the heat and blast wherever we were in the column. The point man had apparently stepped into a tripwire attached to an American dud 500-pound bomb (based on the crater size). Both the point man and his slack man were killed. Others were wounded. All that was ever found of the point man was the top of his skull inside his steel helmet. There was nothing else left of him.

Rainy season was in December, January, and February. We patrolled the hills. We were wet and in spite of being in the tropics, it was cold. We slept rolled up in our rubberized ponchos. They were the only thing we had. Each man carried a pack that contained rations, bandages, two spring-triggered injectors of atropine (to be used if we were attacked with nerve gas), ammunition, hand grenades, two colored smoke grenades, a gas grenade, a claymore, a trip flare, a mess kit, a poncho, and maybe a poncho liner. Most guys carried an extra pair of dry socks. We didn't wear underwear as it would always be wet and the wearer would develop a rash or infection (jungle rot). Sometimes we carried C-4 plastic explosives. Officers and non-commissioned officers carried flashlights with red-filtered lenses in order to read maps at night. Other equipment distributed throughout the platoon and squads were a starlight scope for seeing at night, extra ammunition for the M60 machine gun, and a couple of light antitank weapons. Each squad also had a machine gunner. An average pack weighed about seventy pounds. The machine gunner wore a .45-caliber pistol for self-defense. Each squad also had a person who carried an M79 grenade launcher (called a thumper because it made a thumping sound when fired). The grenadier also wore a pistol. We also had flak jackets, but most of us didn't wear them; too heavy and/or too hot. The radio telephone operators carried a radio and extra batteries for it.

We patrolled as a company, as individual platoons, and as squads. At least once a week one of the patrols would encounter the enemy. There would usually be a brief firefight and the enemy would disappear. Sometimes we would find bunker systems and tunnels. We would throw grenades or C-4 into the tunnel entrances and leave. We would report the find and location by radio and were usually told that engineers would come out and blow the tunnels.

On my 19th birthday, February 20, 1969, we were patrolling as a company. We were in the jungle, in the hills. My platoon was in the middle of the column. The point platoon was leading us up a hill. The column stopped and word passed back that there were enemies on the hill. They had not seen us, so we backed up and formed a semicircle around the bottom of the hill. We were told that helicopter gunships had been called to fire on the hilltop. As soon as the helicopters began their attack, we were to start running up the hill and attack.

We sat there waiting for the helicopters. The word got passed back that it had looked like a North Vietnamese Army base camp on the hilltop. I sat there hidden in the brush and trees and imagined the irony of my soon-to-be newly acquired tombstone reading born February 20, 1950, died February 20, 1969. Sitting and waiting was sometimes the hardest thing we did.

Finally, we got word that the helicopters were approaching. Word was passed down the line that every other man was to pop a colored smoke grenade so the helicopters would know our positions and not fire on us. When the command was given we popped our smoke and ... colored smoke started rising through the trees. At the same time the helicopters came out of the sun and started firing rockets and strafing the top of the hill with machine-gun fire. We charged up the hillside but when we got to the top all we saw were some backs of a few enemy running away from us down the other side.

It was very late in the afternoon when we made it to the hilltop. There were no dead enemy but we had obviously surprised them. Between seeing the smoke suddenly rising in a large arc from the base of their hill and the helicopter gunships swooping in and opening fire, we had scared them enough that they ran. The hilltop was a fairly large base camp. There were bunkers and tunnels between the bunkers. There was rice and other food cooking over small fires in some of the bunkers. There was a large kitchen bunker that had big cartons of canned foods. The cartons read, "CARE," and "Donated by the People of the United States of America." It really made us angry that a charity was letting food get into the hands of a military that was killing U.S. soldiers. To do this day I have never given any money to CARE, nor will I ever.

We spent the night in the North Vietnamese bunkers on the hilltop. In the morning we moved on. We were told that engineers would come out and blow the bunkers and tunnels. So we continued to live in the field and patrol. Sometime during this period Rodney Teats got sent off to sniper school. He came back after two weeks of training but didn't stay with us long. He got reassigned elsewhere. It was another company but I don't remember where or why. Joe Stafford and I had both grown up in Florida and had coon hunting in common. Joe was a couple years older than me. He had been a railroad clerk before being drafted. Joe walked point a lot and either I or Rodney would walk slack. After Rodney left, it was me.

Walking point was a high-risk job. Actually, we were all in a high-risk job. Walking point was just a higher risk. Not only might the point man step on a mine or trip a booby trap, but if the column was ambushed or you ran into the enemy, you were likely the first to be shot or blown up. Joe Stafford got wounded three times while walking point. None of the wounds were crippling nor were they bad enough that he was rotated back to the world, as we called the United States. Joe always spent some time in a hospital in-country, and when he was healed, he was always sent back to our company. After a soldier received three Purple Hearts, they could be removed from the field. I do not recall when Joe got wounded the third time, but afterwards he was assigned to a clerical job at Camp Evans.

By the end of March, the rainy season had ended and the 101st began to move into the A Shau Valley; the valley of death. The A Shau Valley was a dense jungle with monkeys, tigers, and snakes. I never saw any tigers but they were supposed to be there. I saw a few monkeys but they were afraid of people and always ran away. For the North Vietnamese Army this was a major staging area and route to the interior and coastal areas of South Vietnam.

At the beginning of April, we entered Firebase Veghel at the mouth of the A Shau. We spent a day filling sandbags and building bunkers. I hated filling sandbags. The next morning, we were sitting around eating a breakfast of various cans of C-rations. Our Kit Carson Scout (as we called Vietnamese guides), Hua, came by with a little monkey with a collar and a chain. Kenny Guilford was there and some others. We played with the monkey for a little while. A lieutenant came by and selected several of us to go on a patrol. I think he selected the people who had not been real productive filling sandbags the day before.

Staff Sergeant Sparks led the patrol. We were to go out from the firebase a few clicks (kilometers), reconnoiter a helicopter landing zone on top of a small hill, then return to the firebase. We figured we would be back by late morning. It was April 4, 1969. I did not know it at the time, but it was Good Friday. We hiked out into the jungle in a column. Infantry protocol was to keep 30 feet from anyone else when moving in the field. This was so one mine or one grenade or one mortar round would result in fewer casualties. We probably walked about an hour and moved up onto the landing zone on top of the hill. There was a trail up and a trail down the opposite side. We secured the landing zone and checked it out. It was a large bare spot on top of a hill, big enough for helicopters to bring in troops. There was no evidence of mines, booby traps, bunkers, spider holes, or trenches around it. We started to leave by the trail on the opposite side.

That particular day I was the last man in the column. I don't know how it happened but if I wasn't walking slack for Joe then I tended to gravitate to rear guard when we moved as a squad or a platoon. This seemed relatively safe to me. However, we later got a replacement who had been a computer programmer before being drafted. He was a college graduate so he was better educated and a little older than the rest of us. He wanted to do his two years in the Army and get out, so he didn't try to get a commission. He was a rifleman just like the rest of us. He liked to do rear guard too.

I don't remember this fellow's name and he disappeared after two or three months so I imagine he got wounded somewhere along the way. Whereas I operated by always trying never to lose sight of the person ahead of me in the column, this fellow would go find cover off the trail and watch the trail for fifteen minutes to a half hour. Then he would take off alone down the trail to catch up with us. No one told him to do this. He did it on his own. What we discovered by him doing this was that sometimes the enemy would follow us from a distance. This guy would spy a small group following us and would fire on them. Of course when we heard gunfire we would turn around go back to find and support him. This happened a couple of times. The first time we were all clueless about what was going on behind us because no one knew what he was doing and he had no radio.

Anyway, this day we were walking down the trail from the landing zone when all hell broke loose. There were gunfire and explosions. There was a bend in the trail in front of me and I had to work myself up to it to see what was happening. My platoon had walked into an ambush. The enemy was well camouflaged and well covered. I couldn't even see muzzle flashes or leaves and bushes vibrating from a muzzle source. There were claymores in the trees and along the trail that were being detonated. I had not walked into the kill zone and I watched this unfolding in front of me. After a time people started coming back up the trail with wounded. Someone was dragging Hua, our scout, up the trail by the arms. I went down to help and the other guy disappeared. Hua was dead. His fatigue blouse was open and there were three bullet holes in his upper chest that formed a perfect equilateral triangle. He was heavy too and hard to drag. Someone stopped and helped me and we got Hua's body up to the landing zone. I learned the meaning of dead weight that morning.

I was physically sick. I lost the contents of my stomach and between the heat and the massive amount of adrenalin in my system I could barely function. In retrospect, I believe I probably had heat stroke. I laid down on the landing zone with the wounded that were coming up. One of the guys was a recent replacement from Oklahoma. His lower jaw was gone. I don't know if it was a claymore or a large caliber round that did this, but his lower jaw was gone. It was an awful-looking wound and he was obviously in excruciating pain. I have always wondered what happened to him. I heard he lived, but what kind of life could he have had?

I was laying there in a state of semi-consciousness when someone started shaking me and asking where I was wounded. I realized there was a medevac helicopter in the landing zone and this was a medic from the chopper. I sat up and told him I wasn't wounded, just sick and went to be with my squad. Everyone was back up on the landing zone by this time except Walter Chase and our platoon medic, Mike Flood. More than half the guys who had come out on this patrol were casualties. Walter Chase was another relatively recent replacement who had been walking point. He was the first man shot. Mike Flood, dedicated and brave, ignored Sergeant Sparks' order to stay in place and ran to Walter's assistance. He was killed also.

The battalion recon platoon was in the area and was coming to our assistance. They arrived. I recognized some members as people that had been in my training company at Fort McClellan in Alabama. The lieutenant was Terry Ostendorf, who I had seen around but didn't know. We made a plan to go back down the trail and recover Chase and Flood. As it turned out the enemy was in an L-shaped bunker system built along the trail to the left of us as we descended the hill. The bottom of the L was angled perpendicular to the trail and came right up to it. The system was very well camouflaged and no one could see the bunkers unless they were right up on them. Walter Chase and Mike Flood were in the jungle down close to the angle of the L.

The remains of our platoon and the recon platoon were going to go down the trail and put down covering fire while Lieutenant Ostendorf crawled through the jungle to try to get to Chase and Flood. Our M60 machine gunner had been wounded so I inherited the machine gun. Staff Sergeant Sparks accompanied me down the trail and showed where to set up and where to fire. On the signal from Lieutenant Ostendorf we opened fire. The machine gun jammed after a short time and I was still too discombobulated and ill to get it going again. So we did our covering fire with the M16s.

During his effort to retrieve Chase and Flood, Lieutenant Ostendorf was wounded. His recon platoon was able to retrieve him. He reported that Walter and Mike were both dead. Lieutenant Ostendorf was wounded badly enough that he was evacuated out of the country. He never returned to Vietnam. To this day, he is one of my personal heroes. He could have ordered someone else to crawl down and retrieve Chase and Flood but he didn't. He went himself. He told me he couldn't order someone to do that if he wasn't willing to do it himself. I asked him how he felt and what he thought as he was crawling down there. He told me he kept his mind blank and tried not to think about anything. He told me that Chase was dead when he got to them, but Mike Flood was still alive. He told me that Mike died in his arms. He said he saw Mike's spirit leave his body. He was trying to drag Mike's body back up to the trail when there was an explosion and everything went black for him. He received a Purple Heart and a Silver Star for his actions that day.

At the end of this first day, I was cleaning my M16 rifle. I noticed there was a dent in the flash suppressor on the end of the barrel. It looked like a bullet had hit my flash suppressor. We stayed up on that landing zone for three days and two nights trying to recover Walter and Mike and rout the enemy. The first night Joe Stafford and I were asked to crawl down the hill in the dark and see if we could retrieve the bodies. This was one of the things I did over there which I had totally forgotten. Someone at a reunion told the story and I remembered it then. Joe and I weren't too keen on the idea, but well after dark we started down the trail and crept along quite a way. It was pitch black and we couldn't see anything. We were moving by feel and were concerned about blundering into a bunker. We crawled around in the dark for a time but we couldn't locate the bodies.

The next day Delta Company, 1/506th, came to help us. We assaulted the bunker system a couple of times that day but couldn't rout them. They were dug in well, hidden well, and they were fighting. The third morning we made one more unsuccessful attempt. After that we left and the place was bombarded by artillery. The remnants of our platoon walked back to Firebase Veghel. Mike's and Walter's bodies were recovered a few days later. A unit returned to the area. The bunkers were empty. Mike's and Walter's personal possessions were gone and Mike's medical pack was taken. Months later a North Vietnamese Army soldier was killed by an American unit of the 101st in the A Shau and he was wearing Mike Flood's watch. It was given to him by his grandfather and had an inscription on the back.

The A Shau Valley was bad. Combat assaults from helicopters became routine. I had been in helicopters during advanced infantry training in the States and at Fort Rucker, but they never left the ground. The Huey helicopters in Vietnam had a crew of four: a pilot, a co-pilot, and two door gunners. They hauled five infantry soldiers. One man sat well up in the chopper with his back against the pilot's and co-pilot's seats. Then two men sat in each of the doors with their feet dangling out of the doors above the skids.

The first time I got on a helicopter outside Camp Evans to be taken to the beach area of operation, I sat in the doorway with my pack on and my feet out the door and that helicopter went straight up. I felt a little panic. There wasn't a safety belt or harness and [there was] nothing to hold onto. The heavy pack on my back was firmly on the floor behind me and seemed to be holding me in. After we got up in the air and I saw I wasn't being blown out or slipping out, then I kind of enjoyed it. This first time though was still a little tense. When I got comfortable with this after multiple times, I enjoyed it. I also always wanted to sit in the door. A couple of reasons for this. First it was a beautiful view and fun to be zipping over that green landscape from high above in a Huey turbo-powered helicopter. Second, sitting in the door you could exit quickly. As I already said, the enemy loved to kill machinery.

Sometimes we took fire coming into a landing zone so you were a whole lot safer outside that helicopter than in it.

One Saturday morning we were informed that the recon platoon was missing. They had been inserted into an area by helicopter the previous day. That evening all radio communication had stopped. Two platoons from my company, one of which was my platoon, were helicoptered out to look for them. We were put down on a wide mountain ridge with few trees and a lot of high grass. We spread out across the ridge and began walking, looking for evidence of the lost recon platoon. We came to an area with a lot of huge boulders, several times our height. John Sasse carried the machine gun in the other platoon. They were on point. John climbed up on one of the boulders and saw a squad of six North Vietnamese Army walking on the other side. He opened up on them with the machine gun.

While we were down there exploring among the boulders, we found a large cave entrance. A couple of our people entered the cave a little way and called out for the recon platoon. They answered back and a few minutes later emerged from the cave. The recon platoon told us that they had been reconnoitering the area late the previous day and there were a lot of the enemy around. They found the cave and decided to hide in it. They were in the cave up on a ledge, hiding behind rocks. Their radio didn't work in the cave so they couldn't send sitreps [situation reports]. They said the enemy had been walking in and out of the cave early the previous evening.

After we found the recon platoon, helicopters came in and extracted us. I imagine some kind of action was taken to eliminate the enemy in the cave, but I don't know what it was. Our company was not a part of it. We went on, continuing to live in the jungle and do daily patrols. We were constantly running into the enemy. Generally, there would a brief firefight, usually a few minutes to a half an hour, but they seemed like eternity sometimes. Then the enemy would fade away into the jungle. We also set up ambushes on larger, well-used trails. The North Vietnamese Army would sometimes walk into the ambushes. Our ambushes never seemed real effective. As soon as we opened fire, the North Vietnamese Army would scatter and run away from the gunfire into the jungle. On rare occasions we managed to kill one or two this way. At night we would come back together in the company and set up a night defensive position on the highest point in the area. The reason we always tried to be on the highest ground at night was so that enemy mortars couldn't reach us. Also, it's somewhat easier to defend high ground if attacked. We always sent out listening posts in different directions after dark. Sometimes we would send out a platoon for a night ambush. We never stayed in the same place two nights in a row.

There was one hill above the A Shau that we sat atop several times, which apparently had a mass grave on it. I have no idea what the history of the hill was. When we would dig foxholes at night, a good many of the guys would uncover skeletons. Some of the guys would keep a skull and say they were taking it as a war souvenir. They had to hide them in their rucksacks because we were forbidden to treat the enemy dead with disrespect. This included taking their body parts. In retrospect this seems odd since we called them "gooks" and "slants" in order to dehumanize them and make killing them easier than killing a human being.[1]

One day we were patrolling in our platoon. We came up a little hill and surprised a platoon of the North Vietnamese Army. It's probably more correct to say we surprised each other. We started maneuvering forward and shooting at them. They did the same to us. Kenny Guilford was down in a prone position in some brush firing. When the enemy dispersed and faded away, we took stock; looked to account for all our people and find out if anyone was hurt. We heard Kenny yell out from somewhere in the bush, "I think I'm wounded." Turns out he was. A bullet had gone right through both cheeks of his ass. It turned out to be what we called a million-dollar wound. It was bad enough to keep him out of the field for a long time, maybe permanently, but not crippling or life threatening. We called in a medevac helicopter. They lowered a basket through the treetops, we strapped Kenny in, and they winched him up onto the helicopter skid and left.

As it turned out Kenny got evacuated to a hospital in Japan. He healed and was given the choice of coming back to Vietnam to rejoin us or finishing his tour in Korea. Kenny did the wise thing and went to Korea. I think it's the choice most of us would have made. You have to realize our guys were routinely wounded. Sometimes our guys were killed. I am told that during 1969 Bravo Company had five wounded to every soldier killed. Needless to say, we had a lot of attrition and were constantly receiving replacements. Your odds were much better in Korea.

We got resupplied in the field. Helicopters would come out to cleared areas or landing zones we cut ourselves. They brought mail, ammunition, sundry packs, and rations. We had two types of rations. One was the classic C-ration; the canned rations. They had a can of some type of meat. Everyone's least favorite was the pork patties. They had ham patties and beef patties, and canned spaghetti. They had some kind of starch; potatoes and beans are what I remember. They had a can of fruit, either peaches, pears, apricots, or fruit cocktail. Everyone's favorite was peaches. Some had little cans of peanut butter or yellow cheese, and little cans of crackers. Some had a can of date bread and a little can of creamed cheese. The all-time favorite C-ration of everyone were the little cans of pound cake. Pound cake and peaches were a divine meal for us. Some had bars of tropical chocolate. This chocolate had some additive that made it really hard, but it didn't melt. It wasn't the best chocolate, but it was chocolate. Some contained a package of cocoa. There was also a foil package with each individual box of rations that contained a one-serving package of coffee, sugar, salt, pepper, dry creamer, a folded package of toilet paper, matches, and a little box with three cigarettes. One individual box of rations was intended to last us the entire day. If we ran out before resupply or didn't get resupplied, we went hungry.

The second type of ration that we got was dehydrated food. There was more of this toward the end of my tour than the beginning. The dehydrated rations had to have water added and had to be heated. Some of the dehydrated meals were good and they were a change from the C-rations. We got the runs a lot with these rations. Maybe it was just the change in diet. While we heated our rations when we could, we often would open a can of something and eat it cold while on patrol. Breakfast, too, might be eaten cold. We usually didn't have a lot of time in the morning. We had to eat, retrieve our claymores and trip flares, and pack up, and we were supposed to cover up our foxholes. Some guys would fix themselves hot coffee in the morning. I never did. At this point in my life, I didn't like coffee and wouldn't drink it. It was especially bad when made with our iodine-treated water. If it was a cold morning and there was time, then I might make hot cocoa, if I had any.

We were issued heating tabs to cook with. They were little squares of material that you could light and hold your opened can or canteen cup over and heat your food. We used to make little camp stoves out of old C-ration cans, put the heat tab inside, and set the container to be heated on top. The tabs took a long time to heat anything and never heated thoroughly or well. When officers and some of the senior non-commissioned officers weren't around, we cooked with C-4 plastic explosive. A little ball of C-4 burned bright, hot, and fast. Your food would be thoroughly cooked in practically no time. We would dig a little hole to put the C-4 in or shield it with a poncho so no one could see the light. We carried bars of C-4 explosive, but when we ran out, we would take the backs off our claymore mines and use the C-4 in them. When your claymore was about half empty, then you had to come up with an excuse to blow it during the night so that you could get a replacement. "I heard something" or "I saw something moving on the perimeter last night" were always acceptable excuses.

The sundry packs that came to us on resupply were big, three-foot square (or maybe bigger) cardboard cartons. They contained candy bars and cartons of cigarettes. The cigarettes were not the popular brands like Marlboro, Winston, Salem, Lucky Strikes, or Old Gold. The only brand I remember were Chesterfields, but there were others. I would always take a carton or two of cigarettes. We never seemed to be short of cigarettes. Usually after resupply, when everyone had all the cigarettes they wanted there would still be cartons of cigarettes left over. We would dig a hole, chop up the leftover cigarettes with entrenching tools, and bury them. This was so the enemy wouldn't get them. In retrospect we didn't know about the ill health effects of cigarettes. We probably should have just left them there with matches so the enemy could have them.

When we were in the rear, rear being Camp Evans, we would go to the PX [post exchange] and buy cigarette brands that we liked. My favorite was Old Gold. When we were in the field at night then we would cup our lit cigarettes and hold them in the foxhole or behind something that would shield them. Oftentimes we would put a poncho over our heads and smoke under it. We had a saying that "Three on a match was bad luck." It didn't take me long after I arrived in-country to figure out this saying. If you lit a match at night, it flared and burned producing a light that an enemy sniper could see from a long distance. If you lit one person's cigarette on the match or maybe two, then an enemy sniper would not have time to zero his aim in on the light. Three people on a match gave him time and the third person might get shot.

Speaking of snipers—these guys were plentiful. They would sit in trees and watch open areas in a trail from a distance. They would shoot the point man or someone near the front of the column, then run away before we could get artillery called in on them. Men in open areas in a night defensive position were also targets. One time the battalion commander and his retinue were out with our company. As we were setting up a night defensive position, a sniper shot at one of our troops from down the hill. This lieutenant colonel pulls out his .45 pistol, commands the men around him to "Come with me," and goes running down the hill. It was twilight and it was dark by the time he finished his run through the jungle and came back into the night defensive position. Our company commander, Captain Ericksen, wrote him up for a Bronze Star for his bravery. It seemed unfair to me and my comrades as we did something like that at least on a weekly basis and never got a medal for it. He didn't even find the sniper.

Sometime before Hamburger Hill, I took an R&R. R&R was rest and relaxation for seven days outside Vietnam. Every soldier was supposed to get one during their year-long tour of duty. I got mine unexpectedly. The guy who was scheduled to go had been wounded and there was an open slot. A lieutenant asked if anyone wanted it. It was to Hong Kong. I said I would go if my platoon mates would loan me some money. I borrowed a little bit from everybody who had some and left on a helicopter before sundown.

Hong Kong was an interesting place. At the airport in Vietnam someone who was returning from there gave me and another fellow his two unused tickets for a day-long guided tour of Hong Kong that he hadn't used. I really enjoyed learning about the place, its geography, and history. I thought it was wonderful to be able to sleep in a bed in a nice hotel and take a shower every day. It was a feeling beyond description to feel safe. I had some first-time adventures in Hong Kong that I don't need to go into here.

When I got back to my unit I repaid all the money I had borrowed with my next paycheck. All except Willard Palmer. Willard was a Georgia boy who had been a mail carrier when he got drafted. I had borrowed $75 from him. He got wounded while I was on R&R and was sent back to the States for treatment. I never have repaid Willard. I heard at one of our reunions that he still lives in the Atlanta area and retired from the Post Office. He has never come to a reunion. I would still like to see him and pay him back. Even after fifty years, I feel guilty that I was never able to.

In May we got picked up by helicopters one afternoon and inserted onto a ridgeline above the A Shau Valley near the Laotian border. To me and the others in my platoon it was just another combat assault. The lower-ranking men were generally never told what was going on. Anyway, this was not just a routine combat assault. We were inserted onto a wide spot on a ridge and began to move out in a column along the ridgetop toward a mountain way off in the distance. First platoon had the point. We had not gone far when we starting hearing the "Pop, pop, pop" of automatic weapons fire from up front.

I have not yet described the feeling that this sound nearly always gave me. When we heard it, we were trained to run and maneuver toward it to support our people and engage the enemy. It often made my stomach feel like I was on a falling elevator, and gave me an adrenaline rush. Many times I felt terrified and if it were not for my training I would not have been able to react at all. What generally happened though was that once I began to move and act in accordance with my training, it was actually alright.

Before we could move up toward the head of the column, our people began coming back to us. We regrouped and my platoon, third platoon, took the point. That day I was carrying ammunition for the M60 machine gun and was the assistant machine gunner. That just means that I hauled the ammo and fed the belts of ammunition into the gun while the machine gunner was firing it. The machine gunner was a big red-haired fellow named Harvey. I think Harvey was his last name.

We moved up the trail on the ridgetop and came to an area where all the vegetation for about forty feet had been cut. It was an absolutely bare area perpendicular to the trail from one side of the ridge to the other. We lined up in the trees and brush on our side of this bare area, then our new lieutenant gave us the order to charge across. As soon as guys started to run across the bare area, gunfire began from the opposite side. Harvey hesitated and I stayed in the prone position. Fourth platoon's new lieutenant, Lieutenant Jones, was behind me. He nudged me with his boot and commanded, "Taylor, get going." I jumped up and started running across that area with the intention of going all the way across into the trees on the other side. Our guys started dropping in the bare area. I don't know if what happened first was that someone got shot and fell, then others went down into the prone position and started firing, or whether they just went down and started firing. Anyway, we were about halfway across when Harvey dove down into the prone position and started firing the machine gun. I was surprised and wanted to keep going and try to get some cover, but I had to support the machine gun. Harvey was lying there in this open, barren area spraying machine-gun fire into the opposite tree line and I was feeding belts of ammo into the machine gun.

I don't think I knew the word back then, but the term for what was happening was "surreal." I was lying there in the dust. The gunfire was deafening. I watched as little puffs of dust kept popping up in front of and around me and Harvey. Harvey was to my right and over beyond him was our new lieutenant writhing on the ground. There was a lot of blood on his fatigue blouse and it looked as though he had been shot in the chest. He was moaning and making noise. We had a new platoon medic too. I don't remember the names of the lieutenant or the medic. Further off to the right behind a fallen tree on the edge of the opposite tree line, I watched a North Vietnamese soldier rise up into a kneeling position with a rocket-propelled grenade launcher on his shoulder. Before he could fire it, the rocket-propelled grenade exploded. I guess a bullet must have hit the grenade or it malfunctioned. As I watched, the headless body of the North Vietnamese soldier fell back behind the fallen tree. Our platoon medic ran out and starting giving aid to the lieutenant. He was kneeling over the wounded man when I heard him exclaim "Ow." I could see he had been shot in the upper part of his leg just below the thigh. Suddenly, he exclaimed "Ow" again and I saw he had been shot in the opposite leg in about the same place. I can't recall how we managed it, but we retreated back to the trees and bush on our side of the kill zone. We got all our people back also. We had a number of wounded but I don't think anyone got killed that day. We went back to the landing zone and set up a night defensive position. We called in medevacs to extract the wounded. Harvey was among them. I don't recall what became of the machine gun, but I functioned as an ordinary M16-toting rifleman from this point forward. This was our day one of the battle for Hill 937 (Dong Ap Bia; Hamburger Hill).

I need to explain how tours worked. In the Army, soldiers had a 12-month tour of duty in Vietnam. Marines did a 13-month tour because they needed to prove they were tougher and better. Enlisted men in the infantry were expected to spend that 12 months in the field. Commissioned officers did six months of combat duty in the field and then were reassigned to a rear job. We had a name for personnel who stayed in the rear. It was REMF (rear-echelon motherfucker). What I learned in later years was that in Vietnam there were 10 support troops for every soldier in combat arms (infantry, artillery). Not all of these people were always safe behind a secure perimeter, though. Helicopter crews and engineers were among those in the Army who worked in the field. Anyway, by mid-May when we were inserted onto a ridge of Dong Ap Bia, Lieutenant Robinson had done his six months in the field and been given an assignment elsewhere. The new platoon leader was a college graduate who had been in ROTC during his schooling. Captain Ericksen had requested to stay in the field longer than six months, but was sent on R&R. He went to Hawaii and met his pregnant wife there. So, in addition to a new platoon leader, we had a substitute company commander. I can't tell you either man's name.

According to the history I have read, the battle for Hill 937 began on May 10, 1969. The first element of the 101st Airborne to begin the attack was the 3/187th Battalion. We were inserted on May 15 on a ridge about one hundred and twenty degrees around the mountain from the 3/187th. I believe Bravo Company, 1/506th, were working our way up a southwestern ridgeline. The 3/187th was fighting up a northern ridgeline. Charlie Company, 1/506th, was on a ridgeline approximately parallel to ours and to our east. The second morning on the ridgeline, dawn broke and we again prepared to move up the ridgeline. Fourth platoon took point, third platoon was behind them, and first platoon was to be in the rear. Fourth platoon had not gone far when we started to hear gunfire. We moved forward to support them and I saw the wounded coming back. When we got up to where fourth platoon was, I saw Sergeant Pedue stand up, yell, "You son of a bitch," and throw a hand grenade. The grenade dislodged the fellows who were shooting at us. Unfortunately, when Sergeant Pedue stood up he was shot and killed. Third platoon moved past fourth and took up point.

We moved down the ridgeline into a saddle. As we started up the other side of the saddle we came under intense gunfire. We didn't know it, but at the same time the platoon in our rear was being attacked.

Here we were on a narrow ridgeline with steep sides with the enemy in front of us and behind us. About this time we heard mortars popping. Short moments later they began to fall in our midst. I managed to crawl under a large fallen tree. It was a tight fit. After the mortars fell we took stock. I spent the next three days lying in a prone position facing the enemy who was in a bunker-and-trench system in thick jungle undergrowth not too many yards in front of us. It was the most retched, stressful, and hopeless time of my short life. I don't think I was alone in thinking that I wasn't going to live through this fight. Sergeant First Class Angel Rosado was our field first sergeant (senior sergeant in the company in the field). He moved around to our positions and gave us encouragement. I have always appreciated those efforts of his and remember him as a decent person.

I learned that first platoon had been attacked up on the higher ground that we had come from and that the second platoon leader, Lieutenant Joe Conkle, had been killed. First platoon had been run off the high ground. At some point, the Army dropped gas masks. We were issued gas masks, but few people actually carried them into the field due to the weight and unlikeliness that they would ever be needed. Anyway, artillery fired gas onto the bunkers to try to dislodge the North Vietnamese. It didn't work. Some of them just charged through the gas at us. On the morning of our day three, a medevac came in to pick up our wounded. It never touched down as we started receiving gunfire. Wounded were loaded on and as the helicopter was lifting off someone from first platoon came running down the ridge and grabbed the skid. I didn't see him do this. He came from up the ridgeline where first platoon had been attacked the day before. People speculated that he had been hiding up there or playing dead. There were still enemy fighters up there. Anyway, the helicopter went straight up in the air about three hundred feet and began moving to the west. I was looking to see the helicopter and I saw a man falling. I was told later that the crew knew he was there but couldn't get him inside. He was a wounded man trying to hold onto a helicopter skid. It was inevitable that he should fall. His body was never found—but there is no way he could have survived that fall.

It was very hot and dry on the ridge. We ran out of water. We had no food. The Marines sent a helicopter that was supposed to bring water and ammunition. They had a different type of helicopter than us so it was obvious this was theirs. The helicopter came in and hovered so high up in the sky that it was barely recognizable. Soon we saw things falling that had been pushed out of the chopper. All our ammo and presumably food and water fell so far out in the jungle that it was impossible to retrieve.

I don't know which day it was but we tried moving forward with a night attack. Third platoon was sent to do this. We were repelled. Sergeant Shray was badly wounded. He was a paratrooper from New York. He wanted to make a career of the Army. We got him a medevac. He survived, and I was told that he is now a Baptist minister in New York State.

On the morning of our final day in the saddle, I was told to take what was left of our platoon and go down on the side of the ridge to get past the North Vietnamese Army in front of us. We worked our way down on an angle that moved us forward. It was very steep and rocky. We started working our way forward. There were big boulders on the side of the ridge above us. I looked up and saw a North Vietnamese soldier duck behind one. We reported this on the radio and were told to come back.

I don't know why that guy didn't shoot at us or fire a rocket-propelled grenade. We were below him on a steep, rocky ridge. We were totally exposed. He had cover behind large stones. We didn't. Maybe he was just a lookout and by the time he reported us, we were gone. Sometime near the end of our stay in the saddle, Lieutenant Robinson appeared. I had no idea where he came from. I had not been aware of a helicopter coming in. I had not liked Robinson much, but I was never so glad to see someone.

About mid-morning we were told that we were going to go down our ridge and up the eastern ridge to join up with Charlie Company. We started down the ridge and due to the steepness, we couldn't stay in a column. We got spread out and scattered. When we finally got down into the draw between the ridges, Lieutenant Robinson took our platoon and started up the draw toward the mountain, probably to provide flank security. The jungle disappeared. It was grassy and there were some large trees here and there. We looked up the mountain and there were North Vietnamese everywhere, coming down the mountainside. I knew they were North Vietnamese from their helmets and weapons. They were retreating through this draw. I was with Robinson. I don't recall that we even had a radio man; maybe we did, maybe we didn't. Robinson headed for a large tree and took cover behind it. I had no cover. Our few remaining platoon members spread out in front of the North Vietnamese. I got up in a kneeling position and raised my rifle to begin shooting. Before I could get off the first shot, Robinson pushed my rifle down with his left arm, stood up and started yelling, "Who are you? Identify yourselves." They shot him. He was hit in the leg.

I really cannot remember what happened from this point on. I have tried to remember but I can't. I have decided not to try too hard because if I've repressed these memories there is probably good reason to leave them repressed. I cannot tell you how we extracted ourselves from that situation. I know that the North Vietnamese were running through us and more soldiers in the company were wounded. I recall sitting in some high grass later and someone told me Charlie Pearce was dead. That was a tragedy because Charlie was past his DEROS date. He couldn't be evacuated to go home due to the ongoing battle.

The only other thing I remember from that day was us struggling up the eastern ridge in the dark to reach Charlie Company. When we got up there, I saw a pallet of C-rations. I asked someone for some food and was told they would be distributed tomorrow. We were taken around by a sergeant and put on a perimeter. I was miserably hungry and thirsty, probably very dehydrated. I don't think I had eaten for quite some time. We had dropped our rucksacks when we encountered the bunker system on the upward slope of the saddle and started getting mortared. All the rucksacks had been gathered and taken into the captain's command post. The radio telephone operators and others in the command post scavenged the food and water from them.

As soon as we were settled in with Charlie Company, I crawled through the undergrowth to the pallet of C-rations, cut a hole in a carton, and took some rations. When I got back to my position, the two guys I was with and I drank all the juice out of the canned fruits and had the first food we had eaten in days. The next morning water and rations were distributed and we got ready for our final assault on the mountain. The 3/187th had gotten to the top the previous day from their ridge on the opposite side of the mountain. We heard later that the South Vietnamese Army had beat the 3/187th to the top.

We spread out and started our assault up the ridge. As we approached the top, the landscape was barren, devoid of vegetation from all the American artillery and airstrikes. It was barren but cluttered. There were big, jagged tree stumps and fallen trees everywhere. The underbrush was pretty much gone. There was shredded plant matter everywhere. The bunkers were exposed. It appeared there were a lot of the enemy facing us. They were behind stumps and fallen trees with raised rifles. When we would come up on them, though, most were dead. It looked as if the dead had been positioned to make us think we were facing live soldiers. One dead North Vietnamese soldier was positioned in a kneeling, shooting position behind a tree with a rifle to his shoulder. The barrel of the rifle was tied to the tree. There were a few alive among them who would fire and retreat. These must have been the really hardcore North Vietnamese because most had fled the previous afternoon and night. When we reached the top there were dead North Vietnamese everywhere. I have never in my life seen so many dead people as I saw there.

When we got to the summit we were put to work clearing bunkers. This just involved dropping down into them with a flashlight and making sure there were no live enemy inside. I was part of a three-man team. I do not remember who the other two guys were. We came to one bunker and found a wounded North Vietnamese soldier inside. We pulled him out and captured him. A Vietnamese translator from one of our companies came and questioned him. They were speaking Vietnamese so we couldn't understand what was being said. A helicopter was sent out with two intelligence officers on board to fetch him. I like to think that he made it back to a medical facility and was treated. Maybe that happened. Maybe the intelligence officers questioned him roughly and threw him off the helicopter. The translator told me that the fellow was only 14 years old.

That night we went back to the same night defensive position as the previous night. We had 124 Bravo Company soldiers inserted on the ridgeline on May 15. At the end of this day, we had 24 soldiers from Bravo left in the field. Six of our guys were killed. The rest were wounded, thus "Hamburger Hill." There were only three of us left from third platoon. We were placed in fourth platoon. (Note: From this point until after I rotated home, there were only three platoons in Bravo Company. I never thought of fourth platoon as third, but to the replacements that came in, it was third platoon.)

The next day we parted with Charlie Company and went back to the place on the ridge where we had been inserted. We found Lieutenant Joe Conkle's body buried in one of our old foxholes. He was laid in a poncho and four soldiers including me were tagged to hold a corner and carry the body down the mountain to a clear area where we could be extracted. The whole situation was stressful. I think we got extracted that afternoon. I don't remember where we went, most likely back to Camp Evans for a shower, change of clothes, and a hot meal. The usual drill was we got picked up from several continual weeks in the field and helicoptered back to Evans. We got off the helicopters, dropped our rucksacks and weapons, stripped, threw away our clothes, and walked through a large tent with showers. When we came out clean on the other side we were given brand new uniforms, socks, and new boots if we needed new boots. We would then proceed to get drunk or high or both, eat a hot meal in the chow hall, wander around Evans in the night drinking more and/or smoking more dope. The next morning we would get on a helicopter and go to the field again.

After our day of recuperation in the rear we were flown back out to the area around Hamburger Hill. We patrolled some of the ridges. We were walking up one and for some reason Sergeant Anderson, one of our platoon's squad leaders, was up on point. He spied a North Vietnamese lookout sitting on top of a bunker. I guess they saw each other about the same time. Andy dropped to a kneeling firing position and fired one shot from his M16. Then we continued walking up the ridge. When I got to the body of the lookout he was lying on his side. He had a small bullet hole right in the middle of his forehead. Andy had been my squad leader the day third platoon was ambushed outside Firebase Veghel. Squad leaders not only seemed to come and go, but they occasionally got moved around within the company. Andy was a postal service employee from Utah who had been drafted but then elected to go to non-commissioned officer (NCO) school before he was sent to Vietnam. NCO school was made up of promising people selected by the advanced infantry school trainers. I think it was a six-month course. Candidates were promoted to E-5 after completion and sent to us as squad leaders. The top person in the class was promoted to E-6 (staff sergeant; the platoon sergeant). We called these people "shake and bakes." There was a definite difference between them and people who had made E-5 or E-6 by coming up through the ranks. Andy was a really decent guy. He was competent. He was good-natured. He got along well with all of us and seemed interested in us. He was fair. He explained his actions.

We continued to live and patrol in the A Shau. We started spending time as perimeter guards at Firebase Berchtesgaden. It was on a high mountain peak overlooking the A Shau Valley. We were on the perimeter at night. We patrolled around the mountain during the day. We were in and out of FB Berchtesgaden multiple times while in the A Shau. Again, I do not recall the chronology of everything that happened and probably have it messed up. I was acting squad leader for a while after Hamburger Hill. Unfortunately, I had lost my gung-ho attitude and was developing a really bad attitude. I was realizing at this point that infantry and rifleman were just the expendable pawns on a chess board. It wasn't universally so, but most times the platoon leaders were behind us when the shooting started. This didn't help my attitude as all the lieutenants wore patches that read, "Follow Me" or "Lead from the Front." Viking would many times come up to where the action was, but here again, I am not sure he always comprehended how close to the enemy he was.

We got a new lieutenant. He was a West Point graduate. His name was Bowen or Bowman or something. He was an absolutely outstanding platoon leader. He made it a point to get to know each soldier in his platoon. He treated us like we mattered. In the evenings he would circulate around our positions and talk to us. We wanted to know our backgrounds and our hopes and dreams about when we returned to the world. He made each of us feel important and that he cared about what happened to us.

Lieutenant B had not been with us long when we were one day patrolling as a platoon. We were walking along the edge of an open area between two tree lines. The walking was easier here than in the underbrush in the trees. Suddenly we started taking gunfire from the opposite tree line. This was Lieutenant B's first time under fire. We turned toward the gunfire. We started firing back and maneuvering toward the enemy in the trees. No one had given us an order to do anything. It was our automatic response. I looked behind me and saw the lieutenant not quite in a prone position just watching with his mouth open and a surprised look on his face. I think we impressed him with our response. The enemy faded away as we approached them. None of us got hurt. Lieutenant B didn't stay with us long. After just a few weeks he was given a staff assignment back in the rear. He was a smart guy and a good leader. We all missed him.

One time at Berchtesgaden, I was told to take my squad out and reconnoiter five clicks (kilometers) out a certain direction from the firebase. We went out through the wire and started heading out a gentle slope down the mountain. We got well out of sight of the firebase. We were under large trees in high grass. We spread out and sat down. We decided this was as far as we wanted to go. It had nothing to do with us being afraid of anything. We were just tired, worn down, sleep-deprived, and demoralized. Sitting there in silence, separated by several feet, doing nothing, we went to sleep. I woke up, sat up, and saw a column of North Vietnamese right in front of me. The point man was looking at those of us he could see with a puzzled expression. He was studying us. I looked around and everybody I could see was asleep. I started feeling for my rifle and couldn't find it in the grass. The point man must have realized we were not North Vietnamese, or dead, and began raising his AK-47 right at me. The fellow next to me had a thumper (M79 grenade launcher). I lunged for it, grabbed it, sat up, and fired at the point man.

The M79 grenade launcher fires either a canister of ball shot or a grenade. It was a single-shot weapon and had to be reloaded after each firing. I don't think anybody in our company used the shot canisters. That would put you just too darn close to the enemy. The grenadiers wore a .45-caliber pistol for personal protection. As a safety measure, the grenades were designed so that they would only detonate if they had travelled thirty feet or more.

Fortunately, I was faster and more accurate than the North Vietnamese point man. I fired the grenade launcher directly at him and it did not explode, meaning he was less than thirty feet from me. The grenade hit him right in the chest. I saw him kind of go "Whoff" and fold up around the impact. At this point I saw my rifle in the grass and went for it. I started yelling, "Gooks, gooks, gooks," trying to wake my guys up. At the same time I started firing at the North Vietnamese Army. They sprayed some automatic weapons fire in our direction and took off running the way they had come. We weren't that far from Berchtesgaden so the radio activity started with Viking wanting to know what was going on. The radio man briefed him that we were in contact with the enemy while the rest of us began to chase them. We got a little bit of a slow start because all my guys were still a little groggy with sleep.

There was a narrow, overgrown trail through the brush and it was obvious this was the way the North Vietnamese Army had fled. Not only were there broken branches and disturbed earth but there was a blood trail. After a while we found a pile of bloody bandages. We went on for a little bit longer but the enemy was gone. We turned around and headed back into the firebase. None of our own people had been hurt.

When we got back inside the wire at Berchtesgaden, I was told to report to Viking. I was thinking, "Shit, now I'm going to get it. I wasn't where I was supposed to be and I wasn't doing what I was supposed to be doing." When I got to the command bunker, Captain Ericksen asked me how many of the enemy we encountered. I told him it looked like a squad. I told him I had shot at least one. I told him we had pursued them and about the blood trail and bandages. He just listened and nodded.

It was a very short report and when I was through, he asked me if I had applied for Warrant Officer Flight School before I came to Vietnam. This was an abrupt change from the chewing out I was expecting and it threw me mentally off-balance a little bit. I told him yes. He asked if I still wanted to go. He told me there was an opening in the next school and I had been accepted. I asked him, "If I say, yes, then what happens?" He said, "We'll get a helicopter in here before dark and get you out of here." I asked him if I could sleep on it tonight and give him an answer tomorrow. He told me no, that I had to make a decision right then.

I wanted out of Vietnam. I mean I *really* wanted out of Vietnam. My dilemma was that I had been there a little over seven months and had less than five months to go. Because it was late in the afternoon, I would not have time to say goodbye to any of my friends. I would feel like I was deserting them. I would just go; disappear. I would have to extend my time in the Army, which my girlfriend back home wouldn't like. Then after my flight training, I would be sent back to Vietnam. It never occurred to me that this war was going to wind down or end. After all it had been going on seven years. At the time, I thought it would go on forever. I told Viking no; I would stay with the company. Now, when I look back on my life, I wish I had made a different decision. I would have loved to have learned to fly. If I had gone to flight school, my life probably would have taken a much different path than it has. For better or worse though, it didn't happen.

In the coming weeks we were in and out of FB Berchtesgaden. I think at one point I was being considered for promotion to E-5, but my bad and bordering-on-insubordinate attitude made those in charge change their mind. That was alright with me. I was not at a place in my life where I wanted to be responsible for other people. Especially in a combat situation. The few weeks I was an acting squad leader, none of my men got wounded or killed.

At this point in my tour of duty, we were always running into the enemy in the field. At one point we were in our night defensive position somewhere in the A Shau and it was not quite dark. My pants leg was torn and there was blood on the cloth. I rolled up my pants leg and was examining a cut across the front of my lower left leg. Sergeant Woods from San Antonio, Texas was my squad leader. He asked what happened. I told him I cut myself. I had a cut. I didn't know where it came from or when it happened. My leg from the knee down swelled up and I got sick. I had a fever and I felt absolutely awful. It was all I could do to patrol and keep going. The field medic started feeding me penicillin pills, but he didn't deem me sick enough for a medevac. I got a big boil on the back of my calf. It ruptured and a little bitty fold of silver-looking metal came out with the pus. It was smaller than a BB. I tried to save it but it disappeared inside my clothes somewhere.

We were extracted and taken back to Camp Evans. We were told to stay in the company area and not go anywhere. We were told not to go on sick call either. But I was sick. I went to the aid station which was right next to our company. The medic there cleaned the hole in the back of my leg and packed it with gauze. He then sent me to the field hospital. The field hospital was up on a small hill in the center of Camp Evans. It was just above graves registration where the dead were processed before being shipped home. The doctors looked at my leg. They gave me an injection and a bottle of pills. They wrote me a profile for three days' light duty and sent me off.

I was walking down the hill to return to my company when I heard a bunch of screaming and yelling. I turned around and looked and saw a tracked, armored vehicle rolling down the hill. Right in its path was the officers' latrine for the hospital. All of a sudden captains, majors, and a lieutenant colonel poured out of the latrine with their pants around their ankles. The armored vehicle crashed into the side of the latrine, crushing the side it hit and knocking it several feet down the hill. The vehicle stopped after it hit the latrine. Seeing this really lifted my spirits. I think it was the funniest thing I ever witnessed in the Army.

But the reality of the war was never out of mind for long. Soon, we were headed to Hill 996, a rescue mission. Delta Company, 1/506th, was on this hill and was surrounded by North Vietnamese Army. Hill 996 was in the vicinity of Hamburger Hill. We were being sent to help. We did not get inserted into one location. Our company's platoons were inserted at different locations around the mountain. My platoon went in and we started patrolling around the mountain. I was last man in the column. We were up on a high area and I could see a large grassy area way below us. It had a huge pile of old, dead grey trees in the center of it. As I watched, three North Vietnamese appeared from the trees walked across the grassy area and crawled into the pile of trees. They were too far away to shoot at and I didn't report it to the lieutenant because the column was way ahead of me. By the time I caught up with them the North Vietnamese had disappeared. In retrospect, they probably had a bunker or tunnel complex under those trees and we could have called in artillery on it. I don't believe I even thought about that at the time.

We continued patrolling and were on a ridge line adjacent to the main part of Hill 996. I was still at the back of the column. I was one of the few experienced people in the platoon at this time. There was a break in the trees and I could see the side of 996. Between the trees I could clearly see a North Vietnamese soldier creeping up the mountainside. I passed word up to the platoon leader, Lieutenant Molyneaux. He sent Staff Sergeant Hensley back to me with a radio. He reported to the lieutenant over the radio saying, "He's one of our reliables." I told Hensley what I saw. We discussed it. He went forward again to report to the lieutenant, then came back. He told me I didn't see anything. I didn't really want to engage any North Vietnamese. I was still not feeling well and was pissed off that I was even in the field since I had been given a medical profile. I told Staff Sergeant Hensley, "You're right, I was mistaken."

I didn't know it but the battalion commander had been killed elsewhere on 996 that day. Also, Gordon Roberts, in a different platoon in Bravo Company, was singlehandedly attacking North Vietnamese bunkers on still-another area of the mountain. He would win a Medal of Honor for his actions this day.

Mid- to late afternoon our platoon walked up a ridge line to the summit of Hill 996. As we came up the ridgeline we encountered a column of dead North Vietnamese. They were lined up one behind the other as if they had been coming up the same ridgeline. After the dead North Vietnamese, there were three dead Delta Company soldiers still lying where they died facing the North Vietnamese. One of them was a blond fellow with a gold wedding band. I recall thinking some poor young wife back home is going to be devastated. I stopped and cut the belt buckle off the lead North Vietnamese guy. The North Vietnamese hardcore belts were coveted souvenirs. This was not the typical buckle. It was smaller and chrome plated. He was probably some officer. I still have the buckle.

When we got to the top, I learned the battalion commander had been killed by the North Vietnamese. A Delta Company officer was describing to us how Delta originally attacked and ran the North Vietnamese off the hilltop. Then before they could get organized and secure the hill the North Vietnamese counterattacked. This was a classic enemy maneuver that we learned about in infantry training, but it was the first time I knew of it happening to our battalion.

The battalion commander was in the field with us during the fighting on Hill 996. During the assault, the wounded were gathered in an area below the summit. The battalion commander and his retinue stayed with the wounded to provide security while the fighting was going on. The North Vietnamese came up the hill behind our troops. They encountered the wounded and their guards and killed them all.

Instead of being assigned a position on the perimeter, I (along with some other men) was told to reconnoiter a certain distance in a certain direction down the mountain. We went out as directed and did a proper reconnoiter. We were in a gently sloping area with high grass and trees that were not thick. There was no canopy. You could see the sky between the trees. The grass was high enough that when we crouched or sat down, it was above our heads. We radioed the lieutenant that we were coming back to the summit. It was twilight. The lieutenant responded negative. He told us it was too dangerous to try to return in the dark. We were ordered to stay where we were until morning.

So, we are three people sitting on a hill that is still crawling with North Vietnamese soldiers. We're about two clicks from the rest of our company. We're sitting there hiding in the grass. It's now deep twilight and suddenly we're lit up as if by a flare.

Someone had lit a little ball of C-4 to cook a can of C-ration. I hissed at him and started throwing dirt on the C-4. I got it put out and got all over the guy. "What the hell are you doing! There are gooks all over this mountain and we're sitting here practically defenseless. Eat those rations cold." The guy didn't take it well. He reached down, grabbed his open can, and threw it out over the grass as hard as he could. This elicited another less than complimentary verbal response from me. The third guy and I ate something cold. We sat back-to-back in that grass all night long. Occasionally we could hear something moving through the area. Our company had our coordinates so we hoped they didn't drop any artillery on us if they were attacked during the night. We also hoped no North Vietnamese were going to stumble onto us in the grass. We had no claymores, no trip flares, nothing. It was just us and our rifles, and a radio. I don't think I slept at all that night.

In the morning we went back up the hillside and rejoined our company. Bravo Company's battle on Hill 996 occurred on July 11, 1969. Our company had five soldiers killed in action that day. I don't recall that fourth platoon ever fired a shot. Delta Company was extracted. We stayed in the area and continued to search for the enemy. About a week later while patrolling, our platoon heard gunfire not too far away. It was another Bravo platoon. We went to their aid. When we got there, they had some wounded.

I had heard from someone that even if we had had our R&R, we could request a seven-day leave while in Vietnam. I tried it. I went to my platoon leader and requested a seven-day leave. To my surprise it was granted and I was given the chance to go to Bangkok, Thailand. I went. Bangkok was an interesting place. It was very Southeast Asia but not at war. It impressed me as an ancient place, yet still had a lot of the grandeur of European colonialism. Hong Kong on the other hand had been a big, flashy, bright modern city with a lot of British color and pageantry. I went to Bangkok with a guy from our company. He was a big, loud, dark-complexioned, black-curly-haired Italian from New York City. He and I had never been friends and weren't after this trip, but we hung together in Bangkok. He and I were definitely from different cultural backgrounds.

When I got back to the company, we were still working in the A Shau Valley and the mountains around it. We often would come into FB Berchtesgaden and do security for several days, then leave again back to the valley. In Berchtesgaden, we had a practice that we called a mad minute. Sometime during the night, and it wasn't every night, one of the non-commissioned officers would come around and tell us we were going to do a mad minute at a certain time. The practice of a mad minute was that the entire perimeter started firing their weapons into the jungle outside their positions at the same time. After one minute we stopped.

Near the end of August we were at Berchtesgaden. I was in the bunker I liked to occupy on the south side of the perimeter. Beside the bunker was a large foxhole. When we did a mad minute or needed to defend the perimeter, our locations were in the foxhole or behind the bunker. I can't tell you why now. I don't recall, but we didn't stay in the bunkers. They probably limited our vision and ability to cover as much of the perimeter. We slept in the bunkers except for the guard. The bunkers were also to hunker in when the enemy mortared us or shot rockets into the perimeter. They did this periodically. I am told that the date was August 24, 1969. Very early in the morning, sometime after 3:00 AM, we were notified we would do a mad minute. We did. It was always fun. We fired our M16s as we saw fit, on automatic or semi-automatic, shot or threw grenades, fired our M60 machine guns. It made a lot of noise. We had tracer rounds that we would load into the ammunition clips of our M16s. Every few rounds would be a red tracer. The M60 machine guns had every tenth round a tracer. So, when the shooting started at night it was a neat light show with all the red tracer rounds. The North Vietnamese sometimes used tracers but theirs were green. So, in a firefight at night, it could look like Christmas.

After the mad minute, I went back into the bunker and went to sleep. When I woke up the sky was just starting to lighten as dawn approached. There was obviously a fight on. I looked up the hill to the artillery position above us and saw dead American artillery men. There were also dead enemy here and there. I checked the perimeter in front of me and saw nothing. I moved over to an adjacent bunker to find out what was going on. About half an hour after the mad minute the North Vietnamese had attacked our firebase. The first indication was when a guy came out of the command bunker and was relieving himself into the perimeter wire. While he was standing there in the dark a figure rose up from just inside the wire and spoke to him in Vietnamese. He immediately realized this was a North Vietnamese soldier. He grabbed him by the lapels and threw him into the concertina wire. He then realized there were North Vietnamese sappers working their way through the wire. He began to raise the alarm.

Sappers carried explosive charges. Their job that night was probably to crawl through the wire and knock out the bunkers. There were assault troops behind them and the North Vietnamese began dropping mortars on Berchtesgaden. The North Vietnamese did get inside our perimeter and were shooting artillery men and soldiers on the perimeter from behind. I had blissfully slept through almost all of this. Yes, God must really watch out for fools and drunks as I've heard he does. No one ever threw a sapper charge into the bunker where I was sleeping. By the time I came out of my bunker the Americans were doing clean up. There were still some enemy inside the wire. Several in Bravo Company had been killed. Those of us who weren't wounded were formed up and put to chasing the enemy. We spent several hours trying to follow them but the group I was with didn't catch any enemy. We came back into Berchtesgaden sometime in the early afternoon.

We continued living and fighting in the A Shau. I recall one morning I woke up and was getting my gear together to move out. I heard something and went to investigate. My position was on a little rocky prominence, maybe ten feet high.

I went to the edge and looked down. There were three North Vietnamese soldiers huddled next to the rock whispering to each other. I was directly above them and could have easily sprayed them with automatic fire and killed all three. While I considered that, they suddenly took off back into the jungle. Nobody attacked us that day so the three North Vietnamese were not an immediate threat. I don't know why I didn't shoot them. I was not doing my duty as an American soldier in that place and time. They weren't threatening me and I just didn't want to shoot them. In retrospect though, I was wrong. By letting them go, I could possibly have let them live to do future harm to Americans or South Vietnamese.

Sometime in October, we were sent further north into the Marines' area of operation to cover the withdrawal of the 3rd Marine Division. I thought this was going to be absolute hell. We were to be a blocking force to keep the enemy away from the Marines while they began their withdrawal. As it turned out, we put ourselves in all the right places and positions to be between the North Vietnamese and the Marines, but the North Vietnamese hated the Marines so much that they would go around us and attack them. When we tried to engage the enemy, they didn't want to fight us. They wanted the Marines. So, my last two or three weeks in Vietnam were not all that bad. We were still living in the field, eating C-rations, but it was easier than the A Shau had been. In November 1969, I was still alive, physically intact, and due to be rotated back to the world. I was extracted from the field and sent down to Bien Hoa. They replaced our fatigues with new ones and we processed out.

Before we boarded the chartered commercial plane to return home, we did pre-clearance with customs. We were all sitting in a room and the customs people came in and tried to put the fear of God into us about all the things we were not allowed to take home. They then said they were going to leave the room for a period of time. We were given time to go up to the front of the room and place any contraband or forbidden items or materials into a large cardboard carton. It was a really big box. I didn't have anything to put in the box but I walked up just to see what was in it. There were a lot of the Vietnamese rolled marijuana cigarettes. I saw several hand grenades and a human skull. This was all scare tactics because we never saw customs again. We boarded the plane.

I watched out the window as the plane taxied and took off. I watched until I saw the green coast of Vietnam fade behind us as we flew out over the water. I felt a great sense of relief. We landed in Hawaii to refuel. I slept most of the way back to the United States.

Terry Taylor came home and attended The Ohio State University. He has a Bachelor of Science and a Doctor of Veterinary Medicine degree. He is married to Diane Hanna, a nurse practitioner, and has two adult sons.

CHAPTER 6

Jim Tarleton

In Vietnam December 1968–12 May 1969

"I was going to a 'fine unit' with a 'great combat history.'"

The following, concerning Jim's first tour in Vietnam, was submitted in writing and lightly edited by the author with Jim's permission.

Flights to Vietnam from the United States took a variety of routes depending on the carrier. Military flights were circuitous depending on what was being carried. Charter flights flew routes that were the most expedient. The Flying Tiger flight I took left Travis AFB and landed in Honolulu to refuel. We got off only long enough for the plane to be refueled. We got back on and flew to Wake Island. Another refueling stop—many of us didn't even get off the plane. The next leg would take us directly to Vietnam, landing near Saigon at Tan Son Nhut Airbase. All told, the journey there would take us about twenty-four hours. There was absolutely no in-flight entertainment other than if you had a book to read. The only meal served on the plane was during the last leg—a box lunch that had one piece of cold fried chicken, a bag of chips, a pickle, and a dried-up cookie. The only beverages were Coke or water. Smoking was permitted on the plane then—and it stunk to high heaven. I was traveling in "tans"—lightweight worsted fabric—and I was permeated with stale cigarette smoke and sweat. There were two complete fight crews for the trip including four female stewardesses. The civilian flight crews received extra compensation for flying into a "combat zone" and they were all about business. No frills, no extras—just the mission of flying soldiers to a specified destination and flying back out with a load of returning soldiers.

About an hour out of Tan Son Nhut, the plane's captain came on the intercom to tell us what to prepare for on the approach to the airfield. I can still hear his words. "Gentlemen. We will be making an approach in a combat zone—different than landing at a normal civilian airport. We be executing approach maneuvers that are designed to ensure your safety. Do not be alarmed. Please make sure your seat belt is secured and remain in your seat until you are told to disembark. In the event of an emergency, follow the directions of the flight crew." Soon thereafter we began a rapid, zig-zagging descent towards Tan Son Nhut Air Base. The fact that the stewardesses donned flak jackets before buckling into their seats was not lost on me—the passengers did not have them. The approach and landing were something I had not experienced before—the captain literally flew the plane in a rapid, random zigzag, up-and-down pattern onto the runway at a speed much faster than would have been normal. The captain touched down, screeched to a halt and parked immediately in front of a huge hangar. We were quickly deplaned, the crew bidding us goodbye and good luck—they were all standing—they did not take off their flak jackets. It was early in the morning of December 15, 1968. We had crossed the international date line enroute—I had already "lost" one day in my life.

The first things that struck me when I deplaned were the heat and the smell. Though it was early morning, the heat and humidity were already oppressive, and the air reeked of smoke, jet-fuel exhaust, and raw sewage. The sewage smell is unforgettable and would be ever-present in both populated and rural areas. The Vietnamese (like most Asian cultures) use animal and human waste for crop fertilization. The odor permeates everything—but you get used to it.

Most of the passengers on the flight were enlisted—they were gathered into a large hangar for in-processing. The few officers on board were separated from the group and taken to a small Quonset hut adjacent to the hangar. Our officer in-processing was not any different from the enlisted men, just quicker. I handed the in-processing non-commissioned officer in charge (NCOIC) a copy of my orders, which read essentially: "Assigned to USARV. Further assignment as determined by Commander, USARV. Priority to 101st ABN DIV". The NCOIC made annotations on a clipboard and told me to wait. In about ten minutes, I was directed outside to a military jeep with a driver. A placard on the jeep's windshield had a 101st Airborne eagle's head logo on it. I was the only passenger. The driver told me he was taking me to the "replacement center." We headed out, leaving the airbase proper, heading north for about five miles, still on what was obviously a U.S. military base. We arrived at the SERTS—Screaming Eagle Replacement Training School—where I would process into the 101st Airborne and receive about a week's worth of acclimation and orientation before being assigned to a unit operating further "up country." Taken into a small wooden building, a clerk assigned me a bunk in a small officer's quarters, told me where the mess hall and shower facility were, and suggested I "get some rest"—orientation and training would begin the next day. I went to the officer's quarters, changed into one of the two sets of jungle fatigues I had brought, then laid down and slept until the late evening. After getting something to eat, I went back to my bunk and slept until the next morning. At 0500, a clerk woke me, I had breakfast, and the "in-country orientation" began.

The next five or six days were a blur; a small group (I was the only officer) of about fifteen soldiers received training and orientation relative to our ultimate destination. We were all going the 3rd Brigade of the 101st Airborne Division, then conducting combat operations in the very northernmost geographic area of South Vietnam. We received information on the area of operations and were issued two pairs of jungle fatigues (no patches, name tags, or rank—just a U.S. Army tag sewn on above the right breast pocket). I was given a set of rank and infantry branch insignia to pin on the collar. No other identification would be worn. I was also issued a CAR-15 rifle—standard for an infantry platoon leader. Similar to the AR-15, it has a much shorter stock, larger ammo clips (30 rounds per clip vs. 15). I also was issued a .45-caliber personal pistol. We all got rucksacks, steel helmets, sleeping bags (I never used mine), LBE (Load-Bearing Equipment), collapsible canteens, gas masks (never used), flashlights, and myriad other field "necessities." The days were filled with all sorts of information briefings, some limited PT (in the heat), weapons firing, throwing live hand grenades and for me—using a combat radio to call and adjust mortar and artillery fire. The orientation was fast and furious—all designed to acclimate us for our onward assignment.

We finished the "formal" orientation on December 21. Now we had to wait for "final" orders and the transportation to our destination unit. That evening, a clerk brought me my orders. I was being assigned to the 101st Airborne's 3rd Brigade, 1st Battalion, 506th Infantry, B (Bravo) Company. (I had absolutely no idea at the time of the unit's storied history—I would come to realize that much later.) At the bottom of my orders was the mimeographed signature of the division adjutant. On the side of my orders was a handwritten note that read "Good luck LT. Lead your men well." It was signed "S. Berry." Brigadier General Sydney Berry was now the ADC (Assistant Division Commander) of the 101st Airborne and had personally written that note and directed my assignment to B Company, 1/506th. Transport to the unit up country was a rather haphazard undertaking. The were no scheduled flights, obviously no guarded ground transport. Often, officers were given their orders and told to arrange their own transport and means of getting to their unit.

Because of the tactical situation in Vietnam in '68, transport of soldiers to the final unit of assignment was somewhat chaotic. Isolated travel in individual vehicles was simply not feasible. Because of the potential for ambush, travel in individual, unprotected vehicles over the local roads was not done. Soldiers were transported by whatever means was most expedient. Mostly, groups of soldiers would move in trucks in a convoy—guarded by military police escorts, armored vehicles, or tanks. More often, officers were left to their ingenuity to figure out a way to their unit—and from the unit's forward location back to the rear when leaving. It's not a crazy at it sounds. There was a tremendous amount of military aviation assets in-country at the time. Most larger Army units (like the 101st Airborne Division) had their own aviation unit with an array of large (Chinook), medium (Huey), and small (Hughes light-observation helicopter or Bell Ranger) helicopters used for combat missions and transport. Most aviation unit pilots were quite willing to fly soldiers almost anywhere, and sometimes pilots would be "creative" in their missions—going out of their way to fly soldiers to even the most remote locations. Additionally, the Central Intelligence Agency ran air services (called Air America) all over Southeast Asia, using everything from small helos to large, fixed-wing planes—you could always count on "hitching a ride" with Air America if there was room on board. Figuring out how to get from point A to point B was simply a matter of knowing where you wanted to go, persistence, timing, and a little bit of luck.

During January 1968, the Communist North Vietnamese Army conducted a devasting and well-coordinated offensive against American forces, particularly in large cities where there were large concentrations of troops. The Americans were now wary of the potential for these types of attacks, especially around traditional "holidays"—like Christmas, New Year, and the like. It was now December '68, and American military forces and large garrisons were on alert. Units in the field were hunkered down but there was no real combat or contact occurring—there was also no real effort to get newly assigned personnel out to their respective units. In short, the was a lull, and no push to get us newbies to our final destinations from shortly before Christmas until after the New Year. I had already been in contact with my unit headquarters, and I expected to get up country to it sometime after January 1, 1969. Until then, I was pretty much on my own, in the 101st Airborne Division garrison located in Bien Hoa, about twenty-five miles north of Saigon.

I lollygagged around, going to the division tactical ops center, looking at maps, reading after-action reports and scrounging for "essentials" to pack in my rucksack that I thought a platoon leader would need. I talked to a couple of lieutenants who were heading home, trying to get a feel for my unit. I didn't get a lot. Mostly I was told to just relax, and I would get up country shortly—soon enough. I spent Christmas Eve '68 having dinner at the "O" Club in Saigon—a multi-service officers' club run by the Air Force. On December 26, I was told the commanding general of the division was flying up to the division headquarters at Hue/Phu Bai, and I was going to ride as a passenger with him, getting me one step closer to my final destination. In the early morning of December 27, I grabbed my gear and headed to the division helipad. I boarded a fully decked-out command and control helicopter specifically outfitted for the 101st Airborne Division commanding general, Major General Melvin Zais. He and a couple of his senior staff were going back to Camp Eagle (near Hue), having been in Saigon at the U.S. Army headquarters over Christmas.

I was already in the helicopter when Major General Zais boarded, He welcomed me to Vietnam, wished me luck, then settled back in silence for the ride north. The flight took about six and a half hours, with three refueling stops along the way. We flew from Bien Hoa east out to the coast, then north to Cam Ranh Bay, to Qui Nhon, to Chu Lai, to Da Nang, then finally to our destination near Hue/Phu Bai—Camp Eagle. Each time we refueled or stopped, Zais got out and went inside a building to chat or get status briefings. By the time we got to Camp Eagle, it was very late in the day. I was directed to the mess hall and then a transient hut.

I was told to be back at the helipad ops center early the next morning for further transport out to Camp Evans, where the 1/506th Battalion was located.

I was back at the helipad the next morning, December 28, by 7:00 AM. The ops sergeant told me the 3rd Brigade commander, Colonel Joseph Conmy, was coming in from Camp Evans to meet with Major General Zais and that I would be going back with him. Colonel Conmy was a veteran of WWII and the Korean War and already a legend. He would continue to lead soldiers in Vietnam—highly decorated for valor many times over. Conmy flew in around 10:00 AM, spent a couple of hours with Major General Zais, and re-boarded his "bird" for Camp Evans shortly after lunch—I was already on board. I introduced myself—Conmy was pleasant, telling me I was going to a "fine unit" with a "great combat history." We arrived at Camp Evans around 2:00 PM, where I was picked up by a driver from the 1/506th and delivered to the orderly room of B Company. I walked in and was greeted by the company first sergeant, Angel Rosado, aka "Hardcore."

Rosado took my orders, handed them to the company clerk, and then walked me over to the company's operational map posted in the orderly room. He gave me a quick briefing on the company, its past couple of weeks' activity, and general staffing and composition. He told me I would be replacing a platoon leader scheduled to rotate stateside in early January, and that I would be going out to "the field" in a few days. The company commander was Captain Harold J. Ericksen, aka Viking—the name the troops called him as well as his radio call sign. I was told that there was "no hurry" to get me out to the field, and that I would be spending the next few days getting "oriented," packing my gear, and "hanging around the orderly room"—seeing how things "worked." He then took me back to the supply room, gave me a 1:50000 color terrain map of the operational area, another flashlight, a gas mask (which I never used), a box of 5.56 mm ammo for my rifle (500 rounds) and six 30-round banana clips, a box of .45-caliber shells, and a new, lightweight nylon backpack. He then showed me to the "officer's hooch." The "hooch" (rarely used) was nothing more than a small wooden-framed structure with a tin roof, built upon sandbag walls about head high. It was screened, with a dirt floor and had a couple of bare lights hanging with pull chains. The hooch was partitioned in half with a plywood wall in the center—the other half was used by NCOs. There were six bare canvas cots, each with a footlocker at its foot. Four of the footlockers were locked with combination padlocks; mine was open, empty, with an unlocked combination padlock for me to use. Hardcore told me to put my personal stuff in the locker and change into field BDUs (battle dress uniform)—he had brought me two pair from the company supply room. (In the field, no one wore uniforms with name tags, rank, etc. The only emblems on the field uniforms were an Army patch and an olive-drab 101st Airborne patch.) He told me to start packing my rucksack for the field, leave it on the cot, and return to the orderly room when I was ready. He said we'd go to dinner together. I put everything personal into the footlocker, changed into the field fatigues, packed the rucksack with ammo, extra pants, shirt, and socks and left it on the cot. When I went back to the orderly room, I passed the four communal "outhouses"—essentially port-a-potties with 50-gallon drums cut crosswise underneath to hold waste. (Whenever the drums got full, they were dragged out to a remote location on the base, filled with diesel fuel, and burned.)

Camp Evans was a firebase (technically a fire support base—FSB) that was located northwest of Hue/Phu Bai about twenty miles towards and about ten miles from the Laotian border. Its purpose was to provide a base of operations and combat and service support for all the Army units operating in the general area. At the time, the base probably housed ten to fifteen different Army units, the infantry units using it as a base to come back to (infrequently) for hot food, showers, clean clothes, and (maybe) an overnight respite. The combat support units—artillery, armored, and aviation units—provided support to engaged infantry units operating near the base. Combat engineers, military police, a hospital, a PX, laundry, mess halls, an ammunition dump, a fuel storage depot, a chapel, and various other service and support elements were also located and operated at Camp Evans. The airfield was large enough to handle large Air Force transport aircraft (C-130s) and house a large Army aviation unit. Essentially a small "city," the base had been established originally by Marines as a forward support base and now by the Army. It enabled the Army to conduct and sustain combat operations in the northern part of "I Corps" from the Vietnam eastern coast west to the Laotian border. (At the time, the Army partitioned Vietnam into four corps areas, I–IV, north to south for both simplicity and control of combat forces. The 101st Airborne Division operated in I Corps.) Camp Evans was an impressive base capable of supporting a full infantry combat brigade (up to four thousand soldiers). The base had been the target of an enemy rocket attack in May of '68 where the fuel and ammo dump had been hit by rockets, destroying both. Since then, the Army went to considerable effort to preclude that from happening again. Artillery fired "harassment and interdiction missions" 24/7 to suspected enemy locations. No one ever got used to the sporadic artillery fire, the constant sound of aircraft coming and going, and the ever-present smell of diesel smoke burning human waste.

The evening of December 28, First Sergeant Rosado (aka Hardcore) and I went to one of the nearby mess halls. The mess hall was a combined facility, operated by several units together. Then smaller combat units did not run individual dining facilities (they were in the field most of the time)—so several units would combine resources and operate a single mess hall that served food 24 hours a day. Whenever a combat unit came in from the field—it was easy to beef up any given mess hall to serve those troops for whatever time they were on the base. Rosado was a veritable font of information, and he spent the evening catching me up on all the company's operations for the previous six months. I was slated to replace one of the platoon leaders (second platoon) who was due to depart in early January. We spent the evening going over the platoon's manning (there were only 21 men in the platoon as opposed to the normal 28–32), then he helped me pack/repack my rucksack for the field. We prepared my operational map, putting it inside the plastic gas mask bag for waterproofing. He got me a lightweight poncho and poncho liner, a towel, a machete, a couple of waterproof plastic bags for my extra clothing, an emergency strobe light—and a host of other small things needed for field operations (bug repellent, matches, a small round mirror, a box cutter, 25 feet of nylon rope, smoke grenades, one pound of C-4 explosive, a spare battery and handset for the radio). He checked my bag again and again, adding little things he thought might be useful. By the time he was done, my rucksack bag was full. He then went and got me another (empty) rucksack bag which he rolled up and attached to the bottom of the carrier (this would come in very handy later). I went to the hooch to sleep—my head spinning from all the info and stuff packed into both my head and rucksack. I didn't get much sleep that night due to the constant outgoing artillery and helicopters flying in and out of the nearby airfield.

The next morning (December 29), Hardcore Rosado and I again ate together and then he took me to the 1/506th Battalion tactical operations center (TOC) for a briefing on the operations for the day so I could familiarize myself with both the geographical area and how the battalion staff managed and reported the daily activities of its combat units in the field. After that, we took a ride around the entire camp so I would be familiar with all the facilities. All the roads were hard-packed clay—we kicked up dust everywhere we drove. The dust was always a constant and it permeated everything in the camp. Although it was Sunday, there did not seem to be any lack of activity. There was lots of vehicle traffic, helicopters were flying in and out, artillery was being fired. There seemed to be no end to the constant activity and noise.

We got back to the B Company orderly room around noon and ate C-rations for lunch. I had nothing to do for the rest of the day, so I went over to the battalion tactical operations center. In the operations center, the officers and men running the show were all too happy to show me what they did, where the battalion was in the field, and what had happened over the previous couple of weeks. There had been relatively little activity. It appeared that both the Army and enemy forces had both decided to avoid contact as much as possible over the period from about mid-December until after January 1st. That did mean the American forces weren't alert. In early January of '68, the North Vietnamese Army and Viet Cong had launched a major offensive attack (Tet offensive) lasting over a month against American and South Vietnamese forces, concentrating on major cities and installations like Saigon, Pleiku, and the northern provincial capital of Hue—surprising and catching them off guard. The American and South Vietnamese armies had no intention of that happening again. Though the forces were on alert, there was no concerted effort to search and destroy and so the daily activities went on, even on Sunday.

Around 3:00 PM, I went out to a crude wooden picnic table set up just outside the company orderly room and joined a couple of soldiers who were cleaning their weapons. This was a routine activity, done daily. I hadn't been at the table for more than fifteen minutes when a clerk came running out and summoned me to the orderly room. He said the company was in contact, and I might want to listen to the activity over the radio. I went inside, and for the first time, heard transmissions back and forth between the company commander, the platoon leaders, and the FO (forward observer—mortar and artillery fire coordinator). I could hear the gunfire and explosions in the background. It was sporadic, fast, and confusing. It was real and certainly no simulated training activity like those at Benning. After about fifteen minutes, it became apparent that this contact was not going to end quickly—the company had located an enemy encampment and was engaged in heavy contact.

There were several radios in the company orderly room, tuned to various frequencies—the company command net, the mortar platoon, the artillery net, air support, the battalion command net. The soldiers monitoring the nets in the orderly room were busy logging the many conversations on clipboards (the daily activity journal) and making grease pencil marks on the large, acetate-covered wall map showing company element locations, contact, and other data. It was hard for me to concentrate and make sense in the midst of the cacophony—but to the soldiers in the company command center it seemed to be a well-rehearsed routine, and they went about their business in a measured and well-orchestrated, methodical and business-as-usual manner.

The company's contact went on sporadically for the next two hours. I just sat and listened. Around 5:00 PM, an element of the company made enemy contact again. I was listening when I heard the call for a medevac. These unarmed helicopters are flown by specially trained pilots and crewed by medical personnel trained to treat combat injuries until the wounded can be transported to a field hospital. B Company now had three wounded who needed immediate evacuation. One of the wounded was the lieutenant I was scheduled to replace in early January. The company orderly room became a beehive of activity. Amidst all the radio noise, I heard Hardcore holler at me: "EL TEE," (or "LT"—lieutenant) "Grab your gear, you're headed out." I ran to the hooch, grabbed my LBE (load-bearing equipment) harness and my ruck and ran back to the orderly room. Hardcore was grabbing stuff for me and jamming it into my rucksack—extra radio batteries, a complete medic bag, six hand grenades, a claymore mine with detonator, and a roll of green duct tape. He opened two C-ration boxes, extracted only the cans, and tossed them into my ruck—he threw the other stuff from the box in a trash can. Two other enlisted soldiers were also being prepped to leave—it was frantic to say the least. Out of nowhere appeared one of the company's medics. He was calm (not anxious), fully ready to go—a seasoned veteran who had obviously done this before.

We loaded up in the waiting jeep and headed out to the airfield. At one of the side helipads sat a UH-1 (Huey), engine running, blades rotating, no side doors on it. Most of the Hueys in Vietnam used to transport combat troops were configured this way—no doors, seats, or safety belts. The Huey weighed about five thousand pounds empty and could easily carry about four thousand pounds of cargo (men, equipment, supplies). With the doors off, it's loud inside. Flying in one thus configured meant business. We headed over to it—the crew had just returned from the B Company area having already taken out four other soldiers who had been in the rear for a little break from the field. The aircraft was being refueled and loaded with all sorts of gear. I saw boxed ammo being loaded by the case, several cases of C-rations, wooden boxes of mortar shells, boxes of hand and smoke grenades, radio batteries, and other unmarked boxes. While refueling was underway, the pilot and copilot each got out, walked over to the edge of the refueling, and relieved themselves in a "piss tube," conveniently stuck in the ground at the edge of the pad. The two door gunners were reloading the ammo boxes on the side-mounted M60 machine guns. This practice was called a "hot rearm and refuel"—done over and over daily in combat operations—not practiced at the infantry school. A hot refuel could be done in about ten minutes—as turn-around time was critical when units were in contact.

With the chopper reloaded we were directed to load. I noticed the pilots pulling and locking the side protective armored steel plates into place. This was no practice—no drill. It was (all of a sudden) deadly serious. Hardcore yelled at me to load and chamber my weapon once in flight and keep the barrel pointed towards the floor of the chopper. I shouted to him "Who do I report to?" He yelled back, "Your radio telephone operator [RTO] will find you. Keep your head down and eyes peeled. I don't need another lieutenant screwed up today." (Very comforting.) There were no seats or safety belts on the aircraft, we sat on the boxes of ammo. As we lifted off the pad, I noticed the door gunners charging their guns. The gunner on my side yelled at me to "lock and load, the landing zone is hot"—meaning we would be landing where there was combat action on-going.

The bird took off, not the gentle easy takeoff I had experienced before on stateside exercises. Immediately, the pilot lifted off about ten feet, pointed the nose down, tail up, and rapidly accelerated—turning west towards where the company was. We didn't climb much, only to about two hundred feet. I looked at the instrument panel and saw that we were flying about one hundred knots. Four Huey Cobras (gunships), two on each side, joined us, lights blinking in the twilight—it was about thirty minutes until it would be totally dark. B Company was located about ten miles west of Camp Evans and still in contact. Flight time to the landing zone should have been about eight minutes, but the pilot took a circuitous route, flying low and fast to avoid enemy fire. I could see out the front of the chopper as we approached the low foothills that paralleled the mountains running north–south along the A Shau Valley. As the pilot zig-zagged towards the landing zone, the door gunner tapped me on my helmet, pointed at his watch, and held up two fingers—indicating two minutes to touchdown. He turned back to his M60, fired a couple of test bursts, and then focused his attention on the horizon scanning for enemy gunfire. About one mile out, we suddenly dropped to treetop level approaching the landing zône. The door gunners started firing and the escort Cobras started firing rockets into the areas near the landing zone to suppress enemy fire. And then—bam—we're on the ground. This was no gentle hover and land—the pilot dove into the landing zone fast, flaring the chopper to a halt with the skids on the ground immediately. I jumped off and looked around in the waning light—it was almost dark. The landing zone was about twice the size of an average backyard, cut into the side of a hill, trees all around. The door gunners were intermittently firing into the wood line. The Cobras were making passes overhead, firing their rockets into suspected enemy locations. The noise was deafening, and the air reeked of expended gunpowder and turbine exhaust gas. Out of the wood line came two soldiers who quickly started offloading the cargo, right onto the ground. Bullets were flying all around. I started to help offload when one of the soldiers grabbed my harness, spun me around, pointed, and yelled, "Get to the wood line. Your radio telephone operator is there." The chopper was already lifting off (total ground time less than a minute) as I started running towards the wood line and saw a soldier, on his knees, waving at me. I ran to him and got down on the ground beside him. He handed me the radio handset and yelled "Viking is on the horn. Your call sign is Bravo Two-Six." I put the handset to my ear, keyed the "push to talk" switch and said, "Bravo Six, this is Two-Six." The voice that responded was gravelly, distinct, clear, crisp. "Two-Six, this is Viking. There are two more ships inbound. Secure the landing zone until they are gone. When the second ship departs, move your platoon west two hundred meters and set up a night defensive line. Tie in with One-Six and Three-Six. Post two LPs [listening posts]. Over." I looked at my radio telephone operator quizzically—he just said, "Say Roger." I did—that's it. No formality, no introductions. I had just survived a tactical assault landing, in a live contact situation. I was now in charge of twenty-one soldiers, two machine guns and crews, protecting a "hot" landing zone—and I hadn't been on the ground for over five minutes. I had received my first set of orders in combat and had yet to meet my platoon sergeant (call sign Bravo Two-Five) let alone the company commander, Viking. Things were moving a tad faster than I learned at Benning.

The next two choppers were in and out in under ten minutes. Each dropped off four soldiers and another load of cargo. The landing zone was cleared in about fifteen minutes and then it got quiet. By then, I had become oriented to the terrain and situation—the radio telephone operator marked our location for me on my map. In the rapidly approaching darkness, I went around quickly noting the position of my men relative to the landing zone, making plans in my head on how to move them. The men were all in positions in a fan-shaped pattern guarding the western edge of the landing zone. None questioned me—they all accepted immediately that I was now in charge of the platoon. About halfway through this process, I met up with my platoon sergeant, Sergeant First Class Sam Sparks ("Bravo Two-Five"). Sparks was a Black man who had been the platoon sergeant for four months—battle-tested. We had no time for small talk—it was all business. It was immediately clear he accepted my authority as the platoon leader. We shook hands silently, then he was off to check the rest of the platoon. He simply stated that if I needed help, I should ask—otherwise, I was in charge, and he was there to support me see that my orders were executed. Simple, short, and to the point. I knew instinctively that he would accept my authority unless I showed I did not deserve it.

In fifteen minutes, the landing zone was cleared, and the din of the "battle" subsided. Suddenly it got quiet, really quiet. The radio cracked—"Two-six, this is Two-five. Time to move." I told the radio telephone operator to get the men up, he passed the word to the soldiers to our left and right and we started moving out. It would take about two hours in the darkness to move the men into night defensive positions on the western side of the company perimeter. My platoon would be guarding an arc of approximately one hundred meters, securing one third of the company's perimeter. Positioning of the machine guns was critical—Sparks took care of that. My radio telephone operator and I positioned ourselves in the middle of our fan so I could get to any of the manned positions easily. Tying in with One-Six and Three-Six meant linking my flanks with the first and third platoons, ensuring no gaps existed. This was done quickly by the men on each flank—I did not have to see the adjacent platoon leaders or sergeants. Sergeant First Class Sparks came to me, and together we plotted locations on our maps in case we needed to call for mortar or artillery fire. Each of the platoon's positions had two men; one would sleep, the other awake, alternating every two hours on guard—all night. Sparks and I (and his radio telephone operator) would be together—getting what little rest we could. Radio checks and situation reports to the company command post were every 30 minutes. The men did not dig foxholes. They slept on the ground, covering themselves with a poncho and liner. They were practiced and needed no guidance to prep their respective positions. I tried to ask the right questions about fields of fire, claymore positioning, rally points, etc. The men had answers to all the questions, and I wondered whether I was actually doing the right thing or whether I was trying to show the men that I actually knew what I was doing. I discovered I had an assigned medic (Specialist Four Mike "Doc" Flood) and after he checked on the men he came to the platoon command post for the remainder of the night. I had not eaten since breakfast earlier that morning—around midnight I opened a can of boned chicken while I was on watch and ate it with some dried crackers (also out of a can). Though we were supposed to rotate on watch, I did not sleep at all—there were too many things going through my head. It would not be the last time I spent a sleepless night in Vietnam.

About an hour before dawn, Sparks and I made another check on the men. Typically, North Vietnamese Army/Viet Cong forces would conduct surprise attacks on U.S. positions in the early morning trying to catch the men sleeping or not alert. To my surprise, all the men were awake—no one was sleeping—we called this "stand-to." They were wide awake, literally cocked and ready to go. It was a welcome surprise. It appeared that the men were seasoned, well-trained, and jungle combat savvy. Thirty minutes after sunrise, the men had eaten (cold C-rations), cleaned, and packed up, and were ready for the day's mission—whatever that would be. The radio crackled shortly thereafter, and I received the day's instructions for the platoon. We were to patrol an area west of our location about one thousand meters square—looking for any signs of enemy. The idea was to seek, find, engage, and destroy enemy personnel/units in the area of operations—simple as that. Just before the men formed up to move out, the first platoon leader (First Lieutenant Larry Jones) came into my command post. During that brief conversation, he indicated he would be working an area adjacent to mine—and we would be mutually supporting should the situation dictate. It was obvious the men knew him and respected him—and I think he was simply assessing me. We checked our maps, positions, and a few other things to make sure we were on the same sheet of music. Apparently satisfied, Jones departed, and I was on my own—my first full day of leading a platoon of men, in combat, in Vietnam.

The platoon moved out soon thereafter and thus began my tour in Vietnam—a daily routine of small unit activity, almost always the same. Go on patrol, seek, engage, destroy, set up ambushes, wait, secure position overnight, get up, go on patrol, and repeat. On the face of it—a rather simple task. In reality, a very complicated set of tasks, differentiated and determined daily by the enemy situation, terrain, time of day/night, weather, and a host of other things that materially (and often significantly) affected the day-to-day combat operations of any-sized unit—especially at the platoon level.

Fortunately, my first full day of combat operations was uneventful—our patrolling yielded nothing significant. Around 4:00 PM, the first platoon leader radioed me to say he would marry up with my platoon and we would then set up for the night. The other two platoons would be with the company headquarters, located about two kilometers from us. We did just that, setting up a perimeter about dark, grabbing a quick bite and setting up our positions for the night. Shortly after dark, the platoon sergeant (Sparks) told me that we would be moving to a different location about one kilometer from where we had initially set up. This was standard operating procedure to keep the enemy off guard, so we moved and reset—taking about two hours to do so. Using this procedure kept the North Vietnamese Army/Viet Cong from marking our exact position, provided an element of surprise, and (for the most part) kept us from being attacked by surprise overnight. By the time this was done, platoons weren't fully settled into their night positions until shortly before midnight, permitting only about four hours of rest before stand-to—when everybody was awake and alert. The requirement was always for at least one member of any position to be awake and alert—the best one could expect was to get maybe two hours of sleep—something that kept you tired most of the time.

It was now December 31. How quickly the day had gone by, and the platoon's daily regimen become routine. That evening, the company commander directed all four platoons to gather and set up a night defensive perimeter. Collectively, that meant about one hundred and twenty men would be setting up around the company command post. We got into position just before dark, being told we would not move that night. I also was told that I would be meeting the company commander (Captain Ericksen—Viking) at the command post the next morning.

Shortly after dawn, I made my way to the company command post. The other platoon leaders were already there, gathered around Viking. I was surprised to see Hardcore, the company first sergeant, in the group—I thought he would be at the company's rear area at the firebase. Viking was sitting, cross-legged, no shirt, shaving with cold, dirty water in an upturned steel pot held between his legs. Simultaneously he was eating cold spaghetti from a C-ration can—and seemed to enjoy it. Viking was a little over six feet in height, weighed about one hundred and eighty pounds, scruffy looking. He had been in command of B Company for about six months then, and the wear was palpable. He had piercing, steel-blue eyes that belied his mischievous nature. Viking finished his ablutions, laid out his map on the ground, using it to lay out the next week's mission—essentially to search and destroy a specified area around our current position. Asking if there were any questions (there were none) he dismissed us, but told me, "Two-Six, stay for a moment." I was immediately nervous, thinking I was in trouble (or had already done something wrong). Ericksen then went on to say, "Glad you're here Tarleton. You come well-recommended and you're replacing a damned fine lieutenant. You have a good platoon, and the men already respect you. Don't lose that respect, don't be a hero, and don't do any stupid shit. Any questions?" I replied, "No sir." Hardcore immediately spoke and said: "Two-Six—we don't use 'sir' out here—only call signs." I acknowledged that and then said, "I do have one question—what exactly is my mission?" Viking looked at me with a grin and slight twinkle in his eyes and said, "Two-Six—your mission is to find gooks and kill as many of those fuckers as you can." With that, he dismissed me and told me to get my platoon moving. Short, simple, and to the point—Viking's way. As I departed, he ironically added, "Happy New Year, Two-Six."

Thus began my "real" journey on January 1, 1969, as an infantry platoon leader in B Company, 1/506th Infantry. Our operational area was in and around about a fifty-square-mile area, in the foothills east of the mountains that borders the A Shau Valley, mountains running north–south along the Vietnam–Laos border. The area was heavily vegetated, and not very populated. The indigenous people (Montagnards) were mostly farmers, living in small villages comprising ten or so families, working the land, hunting whatever game was available, maybe with a cow or couple of pigs and chickens—eking out a hardscrabble life. There was no electricity, no telephones, very little running water, and (at best) rudimentary sanitation. Movement and/or transportation by locals was usually on foot or by two-wheeled ox-drawn cart. The largest major city (Phu Bai) was twenty-five miles away. Most local villagers had never been farther than the next village from where they were born. Vegetables (if any) and rice were grown in little paddies cut into the sides of the hills. Many of the locals gathered roots and herbs from the jungle and hunted deer, rabbits, wild pigs, and small game with traps and crossbows. Fish were abundant in the many of the area's streams. It was a simple agrarian life. Most of the local population were uneducated—there was no formal education system. The few locals (mostly children) who could read or write had learned from Catholic nuns who set up temporary, small, one-room schools scattered sparsely throughout the area—and that "education" was elementary at best. The was no real monetary system—that was used only in and around larger cities. Barter was the "legal" tender. Though Buddhism was the foremost practiced religion in Vietnam, Catholicism had been introduced in the late 1800s by French Catholics—but most of the population in our area still worshiped whatever god they thought brought them the best harvest—little attention was given to organized religion. Most of the villagers were fluent in both Vietnamese and French, and some even spoke a little English. The villages were connected by a very rudimentary system of footpaths and trails. Tribal chiefs controlled these villages and inhabitants, and though by American standards very primitive, for the most part the locals were content, and just wanted to be left alone—as they had been for almost two hundred years.

Our job (mission) was to protect the Montagnards from the ravages of the North Vietnamese Army/Viet Cong. The North Vietnamese Army brought supplies and weapons from North Vietnam into South Vietnam along a well-designed system of trails (known collectively as the Ho Chi Minh Trail) that traversed our operational area. One of our missions were to interdict these supply routes, and in the process eliminate as many enemy soldiers as we could. Part of our problem was that often, the enemy would integrate themselves into the local village, posing as locals—using fear, intimidation, and threats to force the villagers to permit them to stay and pretend they were actually "locals." Sorting out the wheat from the chaff often proved to be a difficult, almost-impossible task. Many times, what appeared to be a simple rice farmer by day would turn out to be a very effective guerilla fighter by night—only to be discovered when he was killed or captured by U.S. military.

So, for the next four months (January–April '69), my platoon conducted daily operations, 24/7 in this jungle area. It could be boring or exhilarating—depending on what occurred. We averaged a contact situation every other day or so. Contacts could be momentary and fleeting. Sometimes there would be an extended firefight lasting two to three hours. I learned to maneuver my men, how to call for mortar, artillery, and helicopter gunship support. We used UH-1 helicopters to move the platoon quickly from one location to another as the situation dictated. The disconcerting noise and confusion of battle I had experienced on day one gave way to begrudging acceptance—and became the norm. Though certainly not routine, I came to understand and realize that the gut feeling of uneasiness and fear I initially experienced from the sound of nearby exploding ordnance (or the sound of bullets whizzing close by) could be controlled (and indeed must be) if I were to be an effective platoon leader. To that end, I did my very best—and I think I was successful. To be sure, I also tried my best to follow Viking's admonition to "not do stupid shit." Inevitably, I'm sure I did my fair share.

The four months from early January through late April '69 were a great learning experience for me, and regardless of my youth I had become a competent platoon leader. I knew the men respected me and I had proven myself capable. There were a couple of incidents along the way though, that indeed showed that I was quite capable of "doing stupid shit"—one in particular stands out. Under the theory that a leader should not ask his men to do something he can't (or wouldn't) do, I decided one morning to walk point. The point man in any platoon is usually a very seasoned veteran, skilled in not only tactics, but one who has the experience to lead the unit through the jungle, on trails or not—keeping a wary eye out for enemy. The enemy combatants could be anywhere, from hiding in trees as snipers, to hiding in spider holes along the trails to anywhere to surprise a unit, ambush it, or otherwise wreak havoc. Point man is a highly skilled position, as is the slack man who walks directly behind him to take up the slack (provide covering fire and protect the point man) until the platoon leader can maneuver his men in response to the situation. When my platoon was on the move, the point man went first, then the slack man, then a machine gunner and ammo bearer, then another rifleman. These first five men are well-trained and have usually worked together over a period of time, learning and trusting each other (and their ability to survive the first moments of contact). They are a team, work well together, and respond instinctively when contact is made. Often the result of any given contact is predicated on how quickly the point man recognizes a dangerous situation and how well the "front five" respond when contact is made. I should have known better than to screw with what had been (up to that point)—successful.

It was the latter part of January, and I decided to demonstrate that I could walk point. My radio telephone operator (Chuck Cudlike) was none too keen on the idea and expressed it. Nonetheless, I persuaded him to be the slack man—still carrying his radio. We had broken camp early where we had set up alongside a trail—hoping to catch an unwary enemy using the trail at night. Having not done so, I was comfortable that we could move out—I would walk point for an hour or so, then give it back to the regular guy. We moved out, with me in the lead, my radio telephone operator, a machine gunner, his ammo bearer, and another rifleman. We had walked about ten meters, down a slight hill on the trail where it curved to the right. I could not see beyond the curve so I stopped and indicated to Cudlike that I would move slightly forward to a position where I could see beyond the curve and then call him forward. He got down on one knee to cover me and then I started moving slowly forward down the trail. I had not taken two steps when a Viet Cong soldier jumped from a spider hole on the left of the trail—not more than twenty meters from me. He jumped up firing and the tree next to me started shredding as he fired rounds towards me. I hit the ground as Cudlike started firing over me to cover. Out of nowhere came three other enemy soldiers, firing at us. I was literally pinned down, unable to move without fear of being hit as the distance between me and the enemy was too close. To add insult to injury, I was unable to get to the radio direct the rest of my men, and too far out front for them to hear me. Stupid shit thing to do. Fortunately, my lead machine gunner (David Tanton) assessed the situation in fewer than five seconds, maneuvered himself into a position to provide suppressive fire, and started firing down the trail. As soon as he did that, I chunked a couple of hand grenades down the trail, waited for the explosions, and then jumped up and ran back up the trail towards the platoon. My radio telephone operator was right behind me as we passed the machine gunner and dove in behind him. By that time, the lead element in my platoon had already begun a well-rehearsed maneuver towards the contact, fanning out and laying down suppressive and counterfire. Within two minutes, we were moving forward, down the trail in a counterattack. By this time, one enemy soldier had been eliminated, the others long gone. The platoon swept and secured the nearby area, forming up in positions around me while I was on the radio reporting the contact info to the company commander. The whole incident from start to finish probably took ten minutes. Sergeant First Class Sparks and his radio man came up and I told him what had happened. He was quiet as he listened to me. When I was done, he just shook his head, looked at me and said, "Lieutenant, you can't be doing stupid shit." I replied, "Roger that." We moved out shortly thereafter, me and my radio telephone operator near the front of the platoon, the "real" point man leading the way. I realized quickly how much my bravado had unnecessarily jeopardized the safety of my men. I never walked point again.

By the end of January, I had been in the field with my platoon for almost a month. We were told that the company was being extracted from the field, back to Camp Evans for a two-day rest. We made our way to a pick-up zone, and then airlifted by helicopters back to the base camp. I was still wearing the same field fatigues that I had put on the day I went out to join the platoon. (For the record, the extra pair of jungle fatigues carried by soldiers almost never got used unless the ones they were wearing became unserviceable.) It was a welcome respite from daily operations. Back in camp, the soldiers got to take a cold shower, get a clean change of clothes, and have a chance for a hot meal and a couple of nights' sleep (without guard duty) before being sent out again.

I took advantage of the respite. For the first time since I had joined my platoon in the field, I slept in the officers' hooch, on a cot, and ate a hot meal in a mess hall. After almost a month of eating nothing but C-rations, the hot meals were great, but a price was paid. Digestive systems used to a steady diet of small portions of canned food do not accept readily the comparatively rich diet in unlimited quantities offered in the base camps. There was a price to be paid for overindulgence—and I paid it. After spending most of the first day sitting in a "four-hole" outhouse, I learned (like most of the seasoned field veterans) to eat moderately when back at the base camp. I got to spend a bit of time with all the other platoon leaders. Some were more engaged and efficient than others. Eventually, the decision was made to dissolve fourth platoon and divide and distribute the men to first and second platoons. That decision brought my field strength up to about thirty-five men, sizeable for an infantry platoon in the 101st at the time.

Our typical, platoon-sized search-and-destroy mission commenced at dawn that morning and continued daily for the next month. We were still operating about five to ten miles east of the Laotian border, averaging enemy contact every other day or two. Sometimes these contacts were very brief—the single trail watcher, occasional sniper. Other encounters resulted in extended firefights—sometimes lasting two to three hours. My platoon was given an area of operations that was about six kilometers long north to south and five kilometers long east to west—thirty square kilometers—a lot of territory for an infantry platoon. The mission was to randomly patrol the area, seeking out enemy and/or their locations, engage when discovered, locate and destroy caches of food, supplies, arms, and ammo that had been stored by the North Vietnamese Army/Viet Cong. In that we were successful. After patrolling all day—dawn to dusk—the platoon would find a suitable location and set up for the night. The first platoon was working in a similar area adjacent to mine and depending on where we were at the end of the day, we would rendezvous and join up for the night; safety in numbers and it gave the platoon leaders and sergeants somewhat of a respite—maybe an hour more sleep than we usually got.

The sheer size of our area of operations dictated how we operated. We could not possibly patrol the whole area daily. I would pick random routes, in the jungle, along and off paths and trails, in and out of small villages, anywhere we suspected there might be enemy activity. Our area (with its systems of trails and overhead triple-canopy jungle) was reputed to be a major corridor for bringing in supplies from the North—and we could find evidence of that most anywhere. Local Viet Cong were most certainly in the area, and it was suspected that regular North Vietnamese Army units moved in and out with impunity. Outwardly, most of the villagers in the area were friendly—but you never knew. The South Vietnamese government did not have very much influence in the area. Most of the villagers were Montagnards, mostly older men, women, and a few children. Military-age men were few and far between—and it was wise to be cautious if you spotted them.

Conducting platoon-sized operations in these areas was efficient but inherently dangerous. That notwithstanding, support for any small unit in contact was a radio call away—and could be expected almost immediately. That support could be in the form of additional troops helo-lifted in to reinforce a unit in contact, extraordinary and accurate mortar and artillery fire (each rifle company had its own forward observer—FO—to call for fire), helicopter gunships, and under certain circumstances, support from Air Force fighter aircraft that literally flew 24 hours a day just looking for a call to drop or fire their ordnance. The Army's policy of using small units to cover and patrol relatively large geographical areas was effective in the northern part of South Vietnam.

Around the latter part of February '69, my platoon was patrolling the far western edge of our area of operations. As we headed out one morning, we were really on our toes. From our position that previous night, you could smell smoke from nearby wood fires. The local villagers used mostly coal for cooking, so generally, wood smoke meant enemy feeling comfortable and secure enough to prepare hot meals and obviously not aware the U.S. soldiers may be in the general area. We were moving up a trail into the mountains, under triple-canopy jungle where we had not patrolled before. The trail was joined by two other small trails and was now three to four times wider than a foot trail, hard-packed and showing recent use. We all started to get the little tingle you felt when contact with the enemy was imminent. The three lead men went forward more slowly now as the path started uphill. I stopped, checking my map and marking three or four locations to call for supporting fire quickly, and calling the company commander to tell him the situation and register the mortar grid coordinates. At that moment, just ahead of me up the trail, this loud voice cried out in English (with a significant amount of profanity)—sounding very much like someone either in significant pain, or maybe someone fighting hand-to-hand. Not hearing any gunfire, I and my radio telephone operator ran forward to see what was going on. We had not gone fifteen meters on the trail when we came upon one of my men, standing in the middle of the trail, his pants half down, holding his penis from which a very large leech was hanging. This soldier, like most ground infantry soldiers, had a habit of relieving himself just before suspected contact or a firefight—as did most everyone who had ever been in a firefight. Far better to go beforehand than to soil oneself—a lesson many had learned through experience. This poor guy was really forlorn, wailing and making more noise than could be imagined. Though funny later, it obviously was not at the time. There was no consoling him. I brought the rest of my platoon forward, setting up a perimeter for safety. All of us checked for leeches daily/hourly as needed—a necessary activity when in the field—just one of the many bodily checks one did as routine. We all carried the standard Army-issued liquid insect repellant—and what we carried was extremely effective. One or two drops on a leech was usually sufficient to make it release and just drop off. This trooper was having none of that—even when the medic suggested it. I ultimately had to call for a helicopter to take him back to base camp to have a doctor remove the leech.

Any element of surprise was now blown. As it turns out—it was a good thing. All the noise this soldier made spooked whoever was in the jungle ahead of us and they had quickly disappeared westward into the hills. After setting up a protective perimeter, I sent out a scout team to see what was ahead. They radioed back that we had literally stumbled upon a significant, heavily fortified bunker complex (about the size of half a football field), dug deep into the hills. There were cooking pots literally still boiling from several fires. I called the company commander, reported it, and he sent first platoon to join us, then he brought up the rest of the company for support. We spent the next two days investigating the tunnel complex and inventorying the military equipment. We had apparently discovered a North Vietnamese Army rest and recuperation location, located not five kilometers from the Laotian border. It was sizeable operation complete with generators, fuel, weapons and ammo cache, a small medical clinic, operations center, mess hall, small movie theater, and even a "comfort house" where apparently women "entertained" the North Vietnamese Army soldiers.

At the end of the two days, we had recovered and catalogued over five hundred small arms, associated ammo, rocket-propelled grenades, mines, medical supplies, and tons of rice. The maps from the operations center revealed the North Vietnamese Army had robust operations and plans in the area, and a working (and accurate) knowledge of the American military forces working and patrolling the area—which was somewhat disconcerting. We hauled what we could hand-carry to a small landing zone about a kilometer from the bunker complex and prepared to destroy the rest of the supplies and complex. The helos carrying the "treasure" back to Camp Evans returned with the explosive materials we planned to use to blow up the complex, preventing any further use by the North Vietnamese Army. The entire operation took four days. First Lieutenant Larry Jones (first platoon) was a combat engineer and had a working knowledge of the explosives being hauled in to destroy the complex. Just as soon as we cleared one bunker or room, Larry was setting up the explosives, shaped charges, and wires. By the end of the second day, we had taken all the useful materials out and were ready to blow up the complex.

The next morning, Viking took the company down into the lowlands about five kilometers away from the complex, leaving me with about half my platoon for security. First Lieutenant Jones was going to do the honors and actually detonate all the explosives—since he had set them up. About twenty minutes after Viking had taken the company out of the area, we were ready to blow the complex. Jones, me, and our radio telephone operators selected a convenient location about two hundred meters downhill, behind a sizeable boulder to shield ourselves, backs up against the big rock. Jones signaled he was ready—and with a flourish, squeezed the detonator. The first shaped charge detonated, then another, and then—without any warning—a massive explosion occurred, much larger than anything we expected. It seemed the whole side of the mountain shook, then exploded. Whole trees began flying overhead, cascading, and tumbling down the side of the mountain. Huge clods of dirt, rocks, and tons of debris came sliding by and around us in a mini-avalanche—the boulder we were hiding behind literally lifted off the ground before thudding back down. Apparently, the shaped charges had detonated an undiscovered cave in which the North Vietnamese Army stored high explosives—creating enough energy to blow away half the hillside—a surprising but totally unexpected outcome. It took us twenty minutes to uncover ourselves and climb up and out of the debris the explosion created—neither of our radio telephone operators were happy. Realizing we were okay, we gathered ourselves and men and headed down to where the rest of B Company was waiting—laughing and hootin' and hollerin' all the way. All said and done, we had destroyed a significant North Vietnamese Army complex, but in the process left no doubt we were in the area—and there to stay. We continued to patrol the area for another week—but never found another bunker complex nor any signs of the North Vietnamese Army. There were many, many jokes made about the soldier with the leech who had quite possibly saved my platoon from running into a significantly larger enemy force. The best one, however, was that second platoon had been saved by a "dickhead." Still makes me laugh.

About a week after destroying the North Vietnamese tunnel complex, B Company was called out of the field, back to Camp Evans where it was planned to take two days for stand-down—rest, hot meals, showers, clean clothes, etc. We were airlifted back to Evans around noon, and by 3:00 PM, we had all showered, cleaned our weapons, and repacked our gear for the next mission. The company rear detachment had planned a cookout. The food for the cookout consisted of steaks and baked potatoes, cooked on a 50-gallon steel drum with a chain-link fence as the grill surface. Simple but effective. Warm beer (free and provided by either Falstaff or Carling) or soda was available in abundance. Sergeant First Class Sparks and Hardcore supervised the cookout. It was a welcome respite from the field, enjoyed by all. War stories abounded, and we all had had good laugh at the constant stream of field-related jokes (and ever-growing and embellished story) about my platoon being saved by the "the leech on a dickhead."

We finished the cookout, and by dark were all in our respective sleeping areas, in my case—the officer's hooch. About 2:00 AM, the local Viet Cong started lobbing mortar shells sporadically into the base camp. In reality, these mortar attacks were not in and of themselves too damaging—they were meant to harass. Protection from these attacks could be had by getting to one of the many underground bunkers in the base camp—many of us simply got off our cots, laid up against the hooch's sandbagged walls, and hoped for the best. After about an hour of this mortar shelling, the inevitable effects of the steak and potato had its effect on Larry Jones, and he decided to make a run to one of the outhouses nearby. In the dim light, he got up and stood in the screened doorway looking towards the outhouse when a mortar round struck, obliterating the three port-a-potties where he was headed. Nonplussed, Larry took about five steps outside, dropped his pants, and did his business. When done, he dove back inside the hooch, laying up against the sandbag wall—lamenting ironically about how bad it would be to get killed taking a dump. The mortar attack stopped soon thereafter, replaced by the heavy rain, lightning, and thunder of the typical, early morning monsoon storms so prevalent that time of the year. By first light, any evidence of Larry's bathroom adventure had been washed away, substituted by six-inch-deep mud. The shattered remains of the port-a-potties were the only evidence left of the early morning mortar attack.

Most of the day was spent just resting. The platoon leaders went to the company orderly room to receive the mission orders for the following day. We were to be airlifted in a combat assault slightly north of the area from where we had been previously operating. The area of operations was similar in geography to our previous one, only there were more inhabitants and villages. Again, our mission was to seek out and destroy any enemy forces, eliminate their stores of food and weapons, and protect the locals from enemy operating in the area.

After a restless night, we assembled the next morning on the helipad in a steady rain and lifted off just after first light. We landed on a "cold" landing zone, and in less than ten minutes, my platoon was moving out, back into the (by now) familiar foothills for another month of combat operations. We started another three to four weeks of search-and-destroy operations, in and out of the villages during the day, climbing back into the foothills at night. This time, my platoon's operating area was about six kilometers wide east to west, about ten kilometers long north to south, about fifteen kilometers further north than our previous area with the western boundary being the border between Vietnam and Laos. Operations along the border were tricky, and one had to know the precise location at any given moment. I became pretty adept at map reading—an absolute necessity for both safety and combat support if needed.

The next three weeks were spent patrolling the platoon's assigned area of operations. We were in and out of small villages, taking refuge at night in the hills. We continued the practice of relocating after dark. North Vietnamese Army and Viet Cong were active in this new area. Almost daily we would have some contact with enemy forces—sometimes with two to three trail watchers, sometimes chasing groups of seven to ten enemy soldiers we would catch moving from place to place. Fear of ambushes kept us wary—fortunately we never encountered one.

Getting resupplied in the field was a challenge. We had to come down the mountain, find a suitable landing area for a chopper, and secure a landing zone. Once resupplied, we had to pack/repack, put refuse on the chopper, clear the landing zone, and move back up into the mountains. This whole process took at least half a day in addition to exposing our location to the enemy. We were now getting the new Army field rations called LRRPs (long range recon patrol)—essentially freeze-dried pouches of food that could be reconstituted with hot water. They were actually pretty decent—some of the meals better than others. My soldiers each had their favorites and some serious trading occurred on resupply days. My favorites were chicken and rice, chicken à la King, and ground beef and rice. I learned early on that anything with beans in it (chili for example) didn't fully reconstitute, leaving the beans crunchy. I also didn't care for the spaghetti and meatballs. Each meal came with assorted condiments and treasures—candy, chocolate, a pack of four cigarettes, and powdered coffee and cocoa—all great trading material—the cigarettes especially useful when trying to obtain information from the local villagers.

Getting fresh water daily in the mountains meant simply reading a map, finding one of the abundant flowing streams, and filling our canteens. We had learned to steer clear of standing water, including that in rice paddies. We all carried a small bottle of iodine tabs—putting one in each filled canteen for sanitization and purification. Whenever the water was used for reconstituting dried food, the taste was masked—but you could taste the iodine when drinking it. We always tried to climb to the highest point when looking for water, scouting along the way to make sure the stream was not contaminated (a favorite trick by the North Vietnamese Army/Viet Cong). On days when we were at an elevation too high to find running water, I would send a quartering party (six to seven men) down the mountainside far enough to find water, each man carrying four to five collapsible, two-quart canteens to fill for distribution among the platoon members. One day, we found this beautiful cascading waterfall high up in the mountains. We called first platoon to assist in securing the surrounding area, built a fire, then spent the day bathing, swimming, and enjoying the waterfall and natural pool as if it were a recreational park in the States. We departed at dusk, deeper into the mountains, fully bathed and relaxed.

Patrolling in the mountains posed an interesting environmental juxtaposition in terms of weather. Daytime temperatures in the triple-canopy jungle could reach well into the high nineties, nighttime temperatures would fall into the low forties. With that large of a swing in temps—clothes soaked in perspiration and rain—it was easy to get cold at night. Many times, my radio telephone operator and I would just sit on the ground, back-to-back, covered with a poncho liner and let our body heat dry us. Still—we would shake and shiver most of the night.

My platoon spent the next three weeks or so operating in this remote area near the Laotian border. Clearly the enemy was emboldened in the area, using it for both transit and sanctuary. We began to have contact almost daily—sometimes two to three enemy trying to avoid us, sometimes groups of ten or more willing to stand and fight it out. Invariably, with our firepower, combat support, and the ability to rapidly reinforce units in contact, we held the upper hand, defeating the North

Vietnamese Army/Viet Cong we encountered. Sometimes they cut and ran, seeking sanctuary across the border into Laos. We chased them on the ground, calling for gunship and artillery support that followed them all the way to the border—and sometimes, I am sure, a "stray" artillery round or two impacted across the border into Laos. Sometimes enemy soldiers died as a result of contact with my platoon. Seeing dead enemy combatants was something that took some getting used to for me (for all of us). Eventually I didn't even think about it. We were fortunate in that my platoon sustained no casualties—neither wounded nor killed. The longer this went on, the more confidence I gained in leading my men. In a very short time, their confidence in me showed—especially in the manner they responded when given orders during contact. There was no hesitation when I gave orders while in contact. I knew I could count on them—and they on me—to do the right thing. I attempted to be at the front of my platoon, all the time—trusting that in doing so my men would see that I was willing to put myself as much at risk as they were, and not ask them to do things I wouldn't. The Army Infantry School at Fort Benning [now called Fort Moore] motto "Follow Me" was no longer just words.

There were no weekdays or weekends, no Mondays or Sundays—just the steady pace of daily patrolling operations, interrupted by contact, resupply, a moment's respite—then repeat. Resupplying my platoon during field operations was a hit or miss thing. Getting food to us was paramount—however, many things had to come together for the resupply to occur. We had to be in an area where we could find a suitable and secure landing zone for a chopper. A dedicated chopper (as well as escort gunships) had to be ordered. The supplies we needed (food, ammo, med supplies, clothing, etc.) had to be requested, packed and loaded. Timing of the resupply mission was critical and of course, the weather had to cooperate. By this time, most of the field units were able to receive the MREs (Meals Ready to Eat) as opposed to C-rations. MREs were considerably more convenient, weighed less, and more meals could be packed in a rucksack per resupply than C-rations. Reasonably, one MRE could last me two full days, with a couple of snacks in between. Sometimes, we would receive LRRP meals—the freeze-dried packets of food, reconstituted with hot water. Both MREs and LRRP rations were preferable to the C-rations. The men replaced jungle fatigues only as necessary (ripped and/or unserviceable), but clean socks were a prized commodity. Most of us did not wear underwear (except for a T-shirt). Jockey or boxer shorts rubbed or chafed—and if worn, added another layer of cloth that had to dry out if you were wet, which was most of the time (whether from crossing streams, rain, or perspiration). Although it was nice to hear from family, most of us chose to not receive mail in the field to keep from carrying personal identifying information. I did not carry any personal or family information, not even a photograph. All I carried was my dog tags—I left my ID card in my footlocker in base camp. Obviously, there was no use for money in the field. One of the problems associated with resupply was that in doing so, the platoon's location was identified, so after resupply, we would have to move a considerable distance away from the resupply point, often using up a whole day in foot travel to get back into our area of operations for security.

Every soldier learned to carry those things in his rucksack that best suited his mission and personal needs. Unnecessary items were quickly eliminated. You tried to carry only enough food/meals to last until the next resupply (plus one extra day's worth). I had already given up carrying an extra dry set of fatigues—they took up much-needed room in the ruck. I carried two extra pairs of socks. A prized commodity was medicated body/foot powder (came in a plastic container about the size of a cigarette pack), and I usually had an extra or two. I had given up trying to wear contact lenses (too much trouble to keep clean and much less risk of an eye infection), so I carried two extra pairs of glasses. The rucksack frames were aluminum, lightweight, and designed to carry a heavy load. The ruck bags were large, equivalent to a civilian backpack in size, and could carry a lot. Two of the ruck bags could be mounted on the frame, one on top of the other. I adapted my loads to suit what I thought was appropriate. I carried food and personal items in the top bag, the bottom bag contained extra ammo, hand grenades, smoke grenades, an extra radio handset, a radio antenna plus two extra batteries, a claymore mine, two bricks of C-4 explosive (detonators in top bag), a coil of det cord, extra bandages/supplies for medical use, and two or three additional LRRP meals. With both rucksack bags packed, together they weighed probably sixty or seventy pounds plus. Most of the men carried a similar load. You got used to carrying that amount of weight. The rolled-up poncho and liner went on top with the steel-pot helmet. Most of us wore cloth boonie hats until we made contact—wearing a steel pot all day was cumbersome. If the platoon made contact, soldiers dropped the rucksacks immediately, keeping the LBE harness on (containing necessary fighting gear), donned steel pots, and started maneuvering. Two men would stay in the area where the rucksacks were dropped to guard them—also providing a rally point should it be necessary. One day, the platoon was ascending a steep mountainside, literally hand over hand to get to the ridge top using trees for handholds. One of my men complained that he just "couldn't go another step up" with his ruck. I went back down about twenty-five meters to check on him. He was sitting down, ruck off leaning up against a small tree. I told him I would carry his ruck if he would carry mine (to which he quickly agreed). I grabbed his ruck, heading back up the mountain. Ten minutes later, my platoon sergeant called me on the radio—telling me that the worn-out soldier couldn't even lift my ruck, let alone carry it. We had to wait for over an hour for Sergeant First Class Sparks to dismantle my rucksacks and parcel the bags out to two different men to complete the climb. When the complaining soldier got to the top, he quietly grabbed his ruck and reassumed his position in the platoon. Apparently, word got around. No one complained about the weight of their ruck again—and no one volunteered to carry mine.

My platoon continued its mission in this area of operations for another three to four weeks, one day blending into another. Each succeeding day found us encountering more enemy. Instead of sporadic contact, we were now engaged in some sort of contact with North Vietnamese Army/Viet Cong forces almost daily. Contact now lasted longer, the enemy more concentrated in our AO [area of operations], operating freely. Engagements were violent, rapidly developing into situations requiring immediate support from sister platoons, and in some cases another company in our battalion. It was clear that the enemy forces in our area were robust and did not intend to give up this area without a prolonged fight. Most of these encounters cost lives, especially those of the North Vietnamese Army and Viet Cong. B Company did not have any killed during this period but did have several soldiers wounded. I was fortunate not to have any second platoon members killed or wounded. Surprisingly during this time (I found out only later after I was back at Fort Benning) I was awarded the Bronze Star with "V" for some action I undertook during some/one of the contacts. I was too green to even know how a valorous award was earned/given—but later found out that one/some of the men in my platoon, having observed me during one of our encounters, recommended me for the Bronze Star with "V." Looking back—it's somewhat gratifying to know that though I had only been in command of the platoon for a couple of months, the men had confidence in my leadership and recognized such in my performance in combat situation(s). The award eventually caught up with me when I returned to Fort Benning.

An interesting event occurred during this period that shows the infrequent, unpredictable, but fortunate serendipity of combat. My platoon had made contact late in the afternoon and was pursuing five or so Viet Cong attempting to escape. We were operating on the edge of thick the jungle area and encountered a significant-sized enemy force. It was getting dark, and the company commander (Viking) decided to extract us to a safe area for the night and pursue the Viet Cong force the following day. We managed to move to an area about one kilometer from the edge of the jungle for the extraction, finding a suitable landing zone. The extraction went as planned with all but myself, my radio telephone operator, and one rifleman left as full darkness came. The Viet Cong had figured out what was happening and had surrounded the landing zone, shooting at the helicopters. We had Cobra gunship support, but clearly it was unsafe to attempt any further extraction. Our protocol for this was for any remaining soldiers to move to a protected location and hunker down for the night. I radioed Viking and he approved. I and my two remaining soldiers began moving east, knowing there was a sizeable, heavily wooded area about three kilometers away where I planned to hunker down for the night. About two minutes later, one of the Cobra pilots radioed me and said that if I could get to a small clearing about two hundred meters away they could provide cover for a pickup. I immediately headed for the clearing. As soon as we got to the clearing, the Cobras arrived, circling low overhead. I was expecting a UH-1 but the Cobra pilot called saying that we would be picked up by two of his aircraft and flown out on the skids. Sure enough, in less than a minute, two of his Cobras swooped in and touched down with their landing lights on. We could see them clearly, running to them as the pilots waved at us to get on the skids. I got on one, my radio telephone operator on the other side—hanging on for dear life. The remaining soldier got on the other Cobra's skids and away we went, low over the trees while the other two Cobras began firing into the clearing we had just left. They flew us at low level about five kilometers to where B Company had set up a night perimeter and dropped us off. Viking met us at the landing zone. Satisfied that all my men were accounted for, he directed me to where the rest of my platoon was. I joined back up with them and settled in for the night. The entire extraction operation had taken a little less than an hour. Instead of three soldiers having to hunker down in the jungle overnight, innovation, quick-thinking on the fly, and stellar execution of an expedient plan enabled us to get back to the unit safely. I was certainly glad. I never did find out who the pilots were (by name). However, I learned never to underestimate the ingenuity of the American soldier to devise unique solutions that weren't necessarily in the "soldier's manual."

Reading a map and knowing exactly where my platoon was was of paramount importance—as it should have been for every unit leader. Our area of operations was clearly defined, and I had the freedom to operate within it. Unfortunately, a platoon leader from one of our sister units (3rd Battalion, 187th Infantry) inadvertently wandered into my area and had set up an ambush along one of the many trails throughout the area. My platoon was reconnoitering the trail when the sister platoon sprung the ambush—fortunately way too early to hurt my point man. The ensuing exchange of fire between the two friendly elements wounded three soldiers, one of whom was in my platoon. We recognized immediately that the fire was coming from M16s and not the AK-47s used by the North Vietnamese Army/Viet Cong. There is a distinct difference in the sound, including the "crack" of the bullets flying past. It took about ten seconds to realize the mistake, but by then the injuries had occurred. I immediately assessed the situation and called for a medevac. We got the three soldiers out quickly and thankfully no one died. By the time Viking arrived we had everything sorted out. I had already had my "discussion" with the errant platoon leader—it was none too pleasant. The company commander of the other unit arrived, and he and Viking held a brief meeting, gathered the platoon leaders together, then conducted a full after-action review. It was clear that the sister unit platoon leader was lost and had erroneously led his platoon into my platoon's area. I'm not sure what (if anything) ever happened to him. I was thankful that none of my men had been killed—but the incident certainly reaffirmed the absolute necessity of having good map-reading skills and knowing exactly where you were at any given point.

The platoon had been operating in this new area for a little over three weeks. I was informed we would be returning to Camp Evans for a two-day respite. We were picked up by helos and returned to the camp around the beginning of April '69 for a couple of days' rest at Evans. After completing a two-day respite, the platoon's new assignment would be another three- to four-week mission in a completely new tactical environment—a sandy lowland area about ten kilometers wide and about thirty kilometers long that included MSR-1, the main highway running along the South Vietnam northern coast from Hue all the way to the North–South Vietnam border. This section of Highway 1 was the subject of a 1961 book called *Street Without Joy*, written by Bernard Fall, which I had read as a senior in high school. I was passingly familiar with the area and its historical significance during the First Indochina War and found it both odd and interesting to be operating in an area I had read about. The new area of operations was heavily populated by Viet Cong who generally hid during the day, coming out at night to harass American forces and village populations, and attack anything that moved along the highway at night. Our job was to interdict these local Viet Cong and destroy them—and we did just that.

We literally were now operating 24 hours a day. Men caught a little sleep in fifteen- to twenty-minute catnaps, when we rested momentarily. It seemed we were in contact constantly—day blending into night. Nights were much busier than day. The highway traffic was heavy, all day and all night—mostly American military convoys moving supplies to units up and down the highway to military firebases and camps located in the coastal areas. These truck convoys were usually heavily protected and escorted by American military police units, tanks, and/or armored personnel carriers. Huey gunships and Cobras flew all night (literally) and could be called upon almost instantly. The Viet Cong made it a priority to ambush these convoys, and we made it our priority to ambush the Viet Cong. Both were successful, American forces more so than the Viet Cong—and they paid a heavy price in mortality.

Two specific events occurred involving my platoon during this period that demonstrate the devasting effect(s) of these operations:

I had been given the mission of setting up my platoon for an overnight watch on a three-kilometer-long section of Highway 1 to provide backup support for convoys traveling on the roadway that night. We settled into our positions after dark in a section of elevated sand dunes about one kilometer west of the road. The area along our section of road could be clearly seen in the moonlight and, typical of this area, there was heavy underbrush along the road—a favorite location of enemy soldiers from which they could attack convoys. The area from our location in the dunes and the roadway was cultivated with large rice paddies all the way to the road. We had been watching for about four hours, convoys (six to seven vehicles or so) moving along the road. These mini-convoys were a mixture of deuce-and-a-half trucks and armored personnel carriers, a couple of tanks here and there—running back and forth about every twenty minutes or so with no problems. Suddenly, on the very northern boundary of my overwatch area, the Viet Cong ambushed one of the convoys, hitting one of the armored personnel carriers with a rocket-propelled grenade. The armored personnel carrier, severely damaged, veered east off the road, traveling about two hundred meters into the adjacent rice paddy where it got stuck in literally waist-deep muck. The rest of the convoy drove on (as was the protocol), leaving the damaged armored personnel carrier and crew to defend itself until help could arrive. I immediately started moving my platoon from its overwatch location to get to the armored personnel carrier and provide defensive protection. The driver of the armored personnel carrier as well as the topside turret gunner were wounded, and they had lost all the radios in the vehicle—could talk to no one. Armored personnel carriers were configured to meet the mission needs—this had a crew of five, was lightly armored, and was carrying a lot of cargo. The uninjured crew had already set up to defend and one of the crew was manning the .50-calibre machine gun on top of the armored personnel carrier. I moved my platoon into position along the roadway, getting ready to move out to the armored personnel carrier when the turret gunner started shooting at us! With no radio communications in the armored personnel carrier, I could not contact the crew. I made several attempts to let the crew know we were friendly—to no avail. Now we're stuck and we're going to have to wait until daylight to go out and secure the armored personnel carrier. The Viet Cong who had attacked the armored personnel carrier had now been reinforced and were attempting to get to it, not realizing that I had moved my platoon into position between them and the armored personnel carrier. We were being attacked now by the Viet Cong element and could not move as anytime we raised up, the turret gunner would fire at us. To make matters worse, a light observation helicopter arrived overhead and started firing at us. I was unable to contact the pilot on the emergency frequency. My machine gunner (David Tanton), realizing the situation, fired up at the chopper (not intending to hit it), knowing the tracer rounds (our M60 tracer rounds are red—the Viet Cong tracer rounds are green) would identify us as friendly. The pilot recognized the tracers and immediately stopped shooting at us—finally contacting us on an alternate radio frequency. About ten minutes later, four Cobra gunships arrived to provide my platoon support and cover for the armored personnel carrier. In another ten minutes, four M60 tanks came flying down the road to provide both support to my platoon and cover for the armored personnel carrier until dawn. Our mini-battle continued as the Viet Cong tried to flank our position. I was also on the radio calling artillery fire to stop the Viet Cong from breaching our flank. At one point, about fifteen Viet Cong gathered on the northern edge of our position and started to attack. One of the tanks quickly maneuvered into position to cover and fired a round into the Viet Cong attack force—completely decimating it. It became clear it was not feasible to approach the damaged armored personnel carrier and crew until first light—so we hunkered down. We spent another two hours laying in foot-deep rice paddy water and water buffalo crap; muck and mud until dawn when we figured it would be safe to attempt to get to the armored personnel carrier. At first light, I sent a scout team out to the armored personnel carrier to secure it. The driver had been killed when the rocket-propelled grenade struck the armored personnel carrier, which had caused it to veer off into the rice paddy. Two of the crew were badly wounded, including the soldier who had manned the .50-calibre machine gun overnight. We immediately called for a medevac which arrived in less than ten minutes. The tanks secured the roadway and called for a tank retriever to pull the damaged armored personnel carrier out of the rice paddy and tow it back to a base camp. The rest of B Company joined us, providing added manpower and security. About thirty minutes later, the 3rd Brigade commander (Colonel Joe Conmy—call sign Iron Raven) and the battalion commander (Lieutenant Colonel Charles J. Bauer—call sign Bushmaster) flew in to assess and review the actions that had taken place overnight. We had obviously encountered a much larger enemy force than had been anticipated, and the commanders were making plans on how best to continue the mission in the general area. Meanwhile, the rest of my platoon swept the area from which the Viet Cong had attacked us. They found at least twenty dead enemy soldiers. There were also clear indications that many others had been wounded, dragged away, or otherwise left the area. I had seen dead enemy before but had not experienced this level of carnage. The death and destruction inflicted by the combination of artillery, gunships, and especially the tanks was devastating and gruesome. Colonel Conmy, Lieutenant Colonel Bauer, and Viking went around to all my men, talking with them, congratulating them on a "successful mission." I remember Colonel Conmy telling me that Viking had told him I was the "most aggressive" platoon leader he had ever commanded—not sure whether that was good or bad. In any case, I thought we might get a brief respite, but instead, we were given the mission of pursuing the enemy northward. By 10:00 AM, the entire company was on the move, headed north along Highway 1, patrolling and pursuing the enemy.

Two days later, the company had moved into an area about five kilometers from the South–North Vietnamese border, about five kilometers from the coast. The area was basically flat, sandy, and covered with rice paddies. The area was much more populated—small villages interconnected with paths along the paddy dikes. Though the French had brought Catholicism to the area, it was still predominately Buddhist, which showed distinctly in the architecture of the many buildings and pagodas in the area. At night we would set up in or around one of the Buddhist temples, giving us some protection from the elements as well as providing limited, hardened protection from enemy attack. We had been operating in this general area for about two days, not having very much luck in finding the enemy. We were informed that around midnight, B-52 bombers were going to be dropping bombs along the border about ten kilometers north of us. Sure enough, just after midnight, the northern horizon lit up like a carnival midway. You couldn't hear the B-52s overhead, but you could sure hear and feel the effect of their bombs. The ground literally shook (like an earthquake). It was impressive, and I had no idea how anything could survive that type of pounding. Two nights later, we were informed that the battleship USS *New Jersey* would be conducting fire missions along the border in support of American Marine force operations. The B-52s were impressive—the *New Jersey* was awesome. Impact from just one of the rounds caused the earth to "move under your feet"—reminiscent of a later 1971 Carole King song. Imagine a shell the weight of a Volkswagen Beetle being hurled over twenty miles. And, if we thought the B-52s were stunning, the *New Jersey* was overwhelming. The ground rumbled and shook from the impact of her rounds. The fireworks and light show were indeed spectacular—and I had no idea why North Vietnamese Army or Viet Cong would want to go up against, let alone try to survive such overwhelming firepower. In any case, after the B-52 and *New Jersey* missions, we had very little contact with any enemy afterwards. Subsequently, by the end of the month, the command made the decision to pull the company out of operations for well-deserved respite.

The company was picked up incrementally by helicopter and flown back to Camp Evans. We spent a couple of days standing down. We showered (a lot), got fresh jungle fatigues, boots, and spent a lot of time cleaning our field gear and weapons. By now I knew better than to gorge myself on mess hall chow, limiting myself to grits in the morning and a few steamed veggies in the evening. And, even though the beer was on the house, I did not indulge. My digestive system was too used to field rations and I knew better than to gorge myself—I had already experienced the consequences.

By now, it was the beginning of May ('69). I had been the platoon leader for second platoon for a full four months. I was beginning to feel competent. We had experienced some significant events as a unit, and I felt that the men were confident in my leadership and my demonstrated skills. I was no longer a newbie—but I knew I still had a lot to learn and a long way to go. Some soldiers kept a mental calendar and could tell you to the day their scheduled date of departure (DEROS) from Vietnam. I didn't. I certainly did not want to keep a mental calendar in my head counting off the days I had left on my tour.

While we were standing down at Camp Evans, rumors circulated that the 3rd Brigade had something "big" planned for operations in and around the A Shau Valley, near where the 1/506th had been operating—very near the Laotian border. Most of the brigade's combat units were on various fire support bases in and around Camp Evans, getting rest, recharging for the upcoming mission. B Company was told that it was going to be flown as a unit to a place called China Beach for a week's R&R. China Beach was an American recreational facility located near the coastal town of Da Nang. It was a sanctuary of sorts for the American military, pretty much left alone by the North Vietnamese Army and Viet Cong. Soldiers usually got to go there once during a year's tour—and it was a welcome respite from the grind of daily field operations—especially for the grunts.

The next morning, my platoon loaded onto a Chinook helicopter and we flew to China Beach—scheduled for a five- to seven-day R&R at the beach facility. Upon arrival, the platoon members were assigned to three Quonset Huts (ten to a hut)—the platoon sergeant and I were given rooms in a very nice, air-conditioned hut divided into individual rooms by plywood. Nothing fancy but it was clean, and the showers/bathroom had hot water—quite a change from Camp Evans and the field environment. By mid-morning, most of the guys in my platoon were laying out on the beach, enjoying the sun, the surf, and the free beer dispensed from a thatched hut near the beach by the China Beach staff. Most of the staff were civilians (men and women), employed by the military to provide restful accommodations and entertainment for soldiers. There were also many "Donut Dollies"—American Red Cross gals there to entertain (in a wholesome manner) the soldiers at China Beach. There were plenty of activities—volleyball, horseshoes, a baseball diamond, tennis, swimming, surfing—most anything you'd expect to find at a decent, low-end summer resort. There was a PX, a barber, and a basic cafeteria-style restaurant (you could get anything from burgers to steak to shrimp and lobster). There was also a mess hall where you could eat for free. In essence—except for being in a war zone—China Beach had all the comforts of a stateside recreational facility, including movies and a bank of telephones where troops could call back home at no charge using MARS (the Military Affiliate Radio System).

I spent most of the day on a lounge chair under a palm tree just off the beach. I wrote a couple of letters to mail home but did not try to use the phones—there was always a line [of people] waiting to use them. Sergeant First Class Sparks and I just rested as best we could—knowing that we would be best served by doing that, not overindulging on either food or beverages. Sparks and I were in bed by 9:00 PM, looking forward to a few more days of just lounging and doing nothing.

I had just finished breakfast the next morning when Viking's radio telephone operator came to me and said that the company commander wanted to see me. Viking told me that he had some "bad news and some good news." The bad news is that I was being "relieved of command" of the second platoon. I had this sinking feeling in the pit of my stomach that I had done something terribly bad, sufficient to warrant relief from command. He then told me that the battalion commander had decided to make me the battalion's mortar platoon leader—an assignment with the responsibility of providing fire support for the entire battalion (all four line companies) and of course, with which I had absolutely no experience (except to have called for fire support). I was both dejected and elated at the same time. I did not want to give up leading the infantry platoon, but at the same time I knew that this new responsibility was indicative of the commanders' confidence in me. He then told me that I was to depart back to Camp Evans "right away" so that I could take over the mortar platoon and "get ready" for the upcoming mission into the A Shau Valley. Sparks gathered up the platoon, I told the men what was going on, packed up my ruck, and headed off to the helipad to catch a ride back out to Camp Evans.

At Evans, I went immediately over to the battalion's TOC (tactical operations center) to get a briefing on mortar platoon, its personnel, equipment, and upcoming mission. By 4:00 PM, I had met the mortar platoon sergeant and received a full briefing on the platoon's men and equipment. The platoon consisted of 34 men with eight operational 81 mm mortar tubes (two spare tubes) and all associated equipment. The platoon was organized into four sections, each section having four men, two mortar tubes, and all the associated fire direction paraphernalia necessary to provide mortar support to the battalion. The men were well trained, literally on alert 24/7 to provide instant support to any battalion unit (and others as well). That night, I got to see them in action for the first time—as they conducted interdiction fire to a sister battalion conducting patrols around Camp Evans. It was all new to me, but impressive, nonetheless. I spent the next few days getting familiar with both the platoon's men, equipment, and how they responded and conducted their fire missions.

By now, it was the end of the first week in May '69. I had now had about a week to become familiar with my new duties as the mortar platoon leader. On the morning of the of May 7, I was summoned to the battalion TOC to receive a briefing on the battalion's upcoming mission, designated as Operation *Apache Snow*—a mission to reinsert the battalion into the A Shau Valley in an attempt to interdict, disrupt, and eliminate the North Vietnamese Army/Viet Cong forces operating there, keeping them from using the valley as a staging area for attacks into the coastal areas and also using the valley's many trails as escape routes back into Laos. The operation was scheduled to commence on May 10, with an air assault into the valley with the 1/506th Infantry, 3/187th Infantry, and a South Vietnamese Army regiment. My mortar platoon would follow the 1/506th insertion to provide immediate fire support to the 1/506th.

Operation *Apache Snow* began at dawn, with the first element of the 3/187th being inserted by 9:00 AM, followed by the 1/506th. My mortar platoon was inserted to support 1/506th operations around mid-morning on May 11. The platoon provided supporting fire to 1/506th for the rest of the day. Due to injuries sustained that day, I was evacuated off the mountain shortly before dusk.

After examination by field medics and a brigade surgeon, I was given a cot in a tent in one of the temporary holding tents pending further evaluation. It was shortly before midnight, May 11, 1969. On May 12 about 2:00 AM, I was awakened by one of the medics and escorted to the brigade helipad. A real medevac helo was already there, waiting to transport four of us to the MASH (mobile Army surgical hospital) at the 101st Airborne Division headquarters location in Hue/Phu Bai. We arrived at the division headquarters hospital about 3:00 AM, where I was again given a brief exam, then put in a temporary holding tent with cots until I could be further examined by a division surgeon later that day. By now, whatever adrenaline had been generated by the day's activities was beginning to wear off—and I was dead tired. I was also starting to have more trouble walking (balancing) and I still could not hear a thing—except for the constant ringing in my ears. I laid down on one of the cots and drifted off.

In the coming days, I found I had severe damage to my ears, a fractured lower back, and I had separated my left shoulder. Besides the numerous "dings" from shrapnel, I also had several deep tissue bruises (probably from being tossed about during the explosion). In short—I was a mess. The doctor frankly indicated to me that my hearing problem was severe, and that he did not know whether or not I would ever regain it. Due to that, he determined that there was no facility (in-country) that could address the issue. I was taken out to the hospital's helipad, loaded onto an Army medevac chopper (with three other soldiers), and flown to Cam Rahn Bay. The four of us were immediately loaded onto a waiting C-130 medical evacuation plane, set up to transport wounded (both ambulatory and on stretchers). I was being transferred to the American Naval Hospital in Okinawa for further evaluation.

We arrived at Kadena Air Force Base, Okinawa, sometime in the very early morning, May 13. I was transported to the naval hospital complex near Kadena, processed in, and given a bed in a semi-private room. I turned 21 there in that hospital in Okinawa. My medical care included an ear operation. The repairs surgery went as well as the doctor expected—he told me that I should eventually regain my hearing—but there would be no returning to my unit in Vietnam. By the middle of June, I was discharged from the hospital and booked on a military charter for travel to the States. My orders indicated that I had to report to Martin Army Hospital at Benning as soon as possible. The ear doctor on staff there removed the tubes in my ears and repacked them with cotton and sent me on my way. I was given a 30-day convalescent leave and told to get my ears checked once a week—then report back for further evaluation. The ringing in my ears was still there, but I could at least hear (faintly) and mostly understand what was being said. It could have been worse.

The four months plus I spent in Bravo Company under the able leadership and guidance of Captain Harold J. Viking Ericksen were beneficial. Under his command, I rapidly progressed from a green lieutenant to a reasonably competent infantry platoon leader. I was confident that to the extent of my capability and knowledge, I could lead men in combat. Emulating Viking served me (and my men) well. Most importantly, I learned to lead from the front and never, never (though I knew it more than once) show fear in front of my men. Equally important was to be aggressive and not to be reticent when commanding—to take action and not be reactive and let the enemy dictate the battle. For actions on May 11, 1969, as the mortar platoon leader, I would be awarded the Silver Star. I am forever grateful to Viking for his guidance in leadership, setting the example—and for the men who valiantly fought by my side and thought me worthy of such recognition.

Those lessons, put into action daily, served me (and my men) well later one fateful day on a remote mountain in the A Shau Valley in Vietnam—the "Mountain of the Crouching Beast." It is the venerable Viking to whom we all owe a debt of gratitude. And to the men I was privileged to lead and who followed me without fail, I am humbly thankful—for it is to them I owe my life. They kept me safe.

After a second tour in Vietnam, Jim Tarleton received a branch transfer to the Army Signal Corps—serving in various assignments in Europe, Korea, the Middle East, and the States. He retired from the Army after 26-plus years of service as a lieutenant colonel. After retiring from the Army he transitioned to public education, becoming a high school social studies teacher, golf coach, and administrator. He retired from public education in 2011.

CHAPTER 7

John Sasse

In Vietnam January 1969–January 1970

> "I didn't want to kill people. I didn't grow up to kill people. It's just the politicians said, I got to go kill people."

The following was compiled by the author from John Sasse's contributions to the Battlin' Bastards private journal and his September 2023 oral history interview with George Bogdanich, conducted for this book and a documentary film project.

I was born in Chicago. My dad died when I was eight. And then the real world started, you know what I mean? Because in my neighborhood, if you didn't have a dad, everybody's got to fight with you. But I was a little tough son of a gun. I didn't like people with authority telling me what to do. So that's probably built into my character. And then I went on to high school, Hammond Technical Vocational High School, and I got married May 12, 1968. And then I went to the draft board—I was supporting my mom, my wife, and her mom [who] was dying of throat cancer. So I went to the draft board. I go, "I'm supporting my mom, I'm married, etcetera, etcetera." But I got drafted in '68, and I arrived in Vietnam on January 11, 1969.

I wasn't [sent over] in a unit, at that time. They had a rotation, it's called. It's not where they'd send a whole company over. So everybody was new all the time, you know what I mean? At the reception center, I spent one day there, and you get there, and then you do a lot of paperwork, and then they try to tell you how to brush your teeth. "They will be black! They will rot in your mouth!" And you learn all that. And then I think it was the next morning, they had roll call in the morning, and then they'd assign you, and—"John Sasse, 101st Airborne," like that. I'm not jump qualified, but … they became air mobile. So there's no parachutes over there. It's all helicopters—and the 101st had plenty of helicopters.

So I start at Camp Evans, and then I got into the first platoon, the first squad, all year long, all 365 days. Eventually I became a squad leader, machine gunner, which is, that's like the quarterback, in the center. You know what I mean? Bravo Company is often associated with Hamburger Hill. Well on May 9, we were on Firebase Blaze. I remember working out of Blaze. We followed a trail that went straight down. We slid on our rucksacks down until we fell into a river. We were cut up by the jungle. I got cut all up by elephant grass. We returned to Blaze and we were told to build bunkers and fill sandbags. The next morning my hand was three times larger, I had an infection throughout my body from the cuts. I was transported to the hospital (where I spent six days). So I returned from medical treatment, and joined what was left of Bravo Company at Hamburger Hill towards the end of that battle.

After Hamburger Hill I went on R&R, but then I was back in the thick of it. I earned my Bronze Star [on] August 24 at Firebase Berchtesgaden, for example. That night, the guys on guard duty started firing and throwing grenades and yelling "gooks." I thought they were just freaking out, until I heard the enemy myself. I started firing from a position where they couldn't penetrate. I grabbed the M60 machine gun and did what I had to do. My Bronze Star citation tells more of the story:

> AWARD OF THE BRONZE STAR MEDAL WITH "V" DEVICE, August 24, 1969
>
> Republic of Vietnam
> By the direction of the President of the United States under the provisions of Executive Order 11046, for heroism in ground combat against a hostile force in the republic of Vietnam on August 24 1969:
>
> Specialist Sasse distinguished himself while serving as a machine gunner in Company B, 1st Battalion (AIRMOBILE), 506th Infantry, during combat operations in the vicinity of the A Shau Valley, Republic of Vietnam. Company B was at Fire Support Base Berchtesgaden when an undetermined-size force of enemy sappers and infantrymen attacked the perimeter. Specialist Sasse was one of the first to detect the enemy sappers and alert his comrades. He immediately began leveling a heavy volume of machine-gun fire on the insurgents. In spite of the heavy volume of enemy automatic weapons and rocket-propelled grenade fire directed at his position, Specialist Sasse held his position and continued to fire a heavy volume of suppressive fire into the enemy ranks successfully repelling the attack at his bunker. He picked up his M60 machine gun and moved through the intense enemy fire to another bunker more heavily besieged than his own.
>
> Reaching the bunker, he noticed a wounded comrade subjected to further enemy fire. While his assistant gunner returned for more ammunition, he fed and fired the gun, providing a base of suppressive fire until the wounded man was removed to safety. It was mainly due to his courageous actions that his squad's sector of the perimeter was not penetrated. Specialist Sasse's personal bravery and devotion to duty were in keeping with the highest traditions of the military service and reflect great credit upon himself, his unit and the United States Army.

But I have a lot of stories like that. That's why I'm sick. That's why I'm not like … calm and all that. You don't do combat, and be normal anymore. Twenty-two American veterans kill themselves every day. Like—I didn't want to kill people. I didn't grow up to kill people. It's just the politicians said, I got to go kill people. And it doesn't leave you. It's like cancer. I mean, you wish you could wish it away.

CHAPTER 8

Jim Sherlock

In Vietnam January 1969–January 1970

"I guess we were doing some kind of reconnaissance, but I don't know. I was just there in the line."

The following is a lightly edited summary of the author's May 2024 oral history interview with Jim.

I was born in 1948 in Akron, Ohio. We moved from Akron down to North and South Carolina. My father was in the military and we lived in South Carolina until I was seven, and then moved again to San Diego County in California. I wasn't really into school too much, but I used to go fishing and hang out at the beach. And then as I got older, as a teenager, got into surfing. So surfing was kind of like my life. I looked forward to getting out of high school, not that I really had any plans for afterwards. And then I was drafted. I was surprised when I received it; shocked. And then I just went in. I remember coming home, and my brother's friend was living with us at the time, and he just came out of the house, screamed like, "Hey, you got drafted! You got drafted!" So it was kind of a shock.

When it came time to go, I remember jumping on a bus. My mom and stepdad drove me to Oceanside to catch the Greyhound bus for my eight-hour ride to Fort Ord. I don't recall drill sergeants coming out and screaming and yelling in our faces or anything. And I think it was kind of what I expected. Maybe not even as hard as I expected. And then advanced individual training, same thing, it was kind of what I expected, I guess. I mean, I was 19 at the time, so I hadn't really thought about it much. It's just something that happens to you. As far as understanding what the war was all about, I think had some idea because of all the protesting and all the stuff that was in the news at the time. So I think I had an idea of what was happening, although of course the reality when you get there is a little bit different than anything you picture.

Because I was being deployed January 20, we got to go home for Christmas, I believe. And then when we got back, we were not given the right to go back home again [right before the deployment, as you would normally get to do]. We had just been off for Christmas. So a whole bunch of us guys went away without leave (AWOL) for a weekend to go home, because we wanted to go and see our family and friends before we went. We were all given Article 15s, but Article 15s don't leave the base with you. So when I left Fort Ord to go to Vietnam, it was kind of a dropped situation.

When it came time to go to Vietnam, I flew out of Travis Air Force Base up by San Francisco. It was a long flight. There were a few stops. We stopped in Hawaii, stopped in the Philippines, and one other stop—I can't remember the third stop now. I remember we flew into Da Nang, and seeing a whole bunch of smoke in the air. It was actually from the latrines, they were burning waste. I remember getting off the plane, it being extremely hot and humid. And that was it. We went through some type of a week-long orientation, and everyone was given their different areas that they were going to be shipped out to. I was shipped to the 101st. Other guys went to different areas of the country. The whole airplane didn't stay together. They kind of dispersed us throughout the country, as needed.

They took me to Camp Evans. And when I got to Camp Evans, there were a few other guys were kind of just getting in-country also, so we kind of formed a bit of a relationship there. Probably within a week we got designated to platoons, and they flew me out and dropped me off in the field. We would set up and sit all day long in our little area and we'd go out and do little short patrols at night as a group, the whole company from what I remember. And then we'd go back and we'd set up our area again and then stay there all day. I don't think we really moved around too much during the day, from what I recall. I guess we were doing some kind of reconnaissance, but I don't know. I was just there in the line. I guess we were probably patrolling for Viet Cong, because we were in the village areas. So I'm thinking that's what we were doing, but I don't think they really told us. They just said "We're going out on patrol," or whatever, and you go.

I was extremely fortunate over there. When we were on Hamburger Hill, I got bronchitis, so I was back in the hospital. So when that all started happening, I wasn't there. And then, when I was out of the hospital, combat was so heavy they couldn't get me out. I was in a staging area where they were flying [out] food and stuff, just kind of stuck there until things calmed down. And then when they finally got me out there, I got wounded a few days later and was taken back out the field and ended up going to Japan. I got wounded after we went on patrol and got fired upon; there was a rocket-propelled grenade fired. It kind of exploded in front of me. So they flew me out. I was evaluated, and then released, and it was kind of weird because I got released and I [was] just supposed to make my own way back to Camp Evans. So I kind of limped around with the wounded leg until I found a chopper ride back to Camp Evans, and then went on a sick call the next day because I took my wrapping off, the medic at Camp Evans looked at it, and he decided to send me to Da Nang. And the doctor there sent me to Japan with a bunch of other guys.

So I ended up going to Japan for a couple months. My wound was actually pretty minor. It wasn't a bad wound at all. In fact, I kind of felt guilty on the medevac to Japan because there were a lot of badly wounded guys and I just had more or less a deep flesh wound on my leg. But I was in Japan for a few months. So as far as my combat action—I kind of was one of the lucky guys where, things just kind of worked out the way they did where I wasn't in all the heavy stuff for the most part.

Overall, I think our morale was pretty good. I guess just because we had good close relationships with each other, we were all friends, so I don't think any of us really got too down. I think the morale might've been bad after Hamburger Hill because we lost some guys there, but even then I don't really remember morale getting real low. I remember just getting towards the end of our tours, we were all kind of happy and in fact, I have a calendar somewhere with all my days that I checked off, I scratched out every day.

When I came home, I flew back to the Seattle area. And then from there, somehow I got a flight to California. There might have been some anti-war sentiment, but I just think that my attitude was, none of that bothered me. I don't know why. I don't think I've had a lot of the problems, or being bothered by a lot of stuff, that others can have. I guess it's just my mental outlook. I guess because I'm just a laid-back surfer dude!

I got a job working for Alpha Beta, which is a grocery store. I got sick of the schedule; I couldn't go out with my friends and go to parties like they did. So I got out of working retail and my mom got me a job with a heating company. I did that for probably five, six years and I ended up getting out of that and going into trucking. I went back to heating, air-conditioning; eventually bought the business from my boss. Now I'm enjoying retirement. While I haven't struggled with PTSD, I have dealt with health issues due to Agent Orange.

CHAPTER 9

Doyle Cable

In Vietnam January 1969–May 1970

> "You never forget any of the firefights. They're pretty prevalent. And in your mind 50 years later."

The following is a summary, edited by the author, of Doyle's September 2023 interview with George Bogdanich, conducted at a Battlin' Bastards reunion for use in both this book and a documentary film project.

I was an apprentice meatcutter, and I had a deferment when I was cutting meat. And you had to renew that deferment, I don't know, every six months, something like that. But I just wanted to get it over with and get in, and get it over with. So I went ahead and I let that deferment lapse and as soon as I let that deferment lapse, within a couple months' period, I got my draft notice. And that was 1968.

I went through basic and advanced training at Fort Polk, Louisiana, what they called Tiger Land, down there. There was advanced training there to prepare you for jungle warfare. It was real hot and sultry down there. It mimicked the weather over in Vietnam. And if you went to Tiger Land, you were just about a hundred percent sure you was going to go to 'Nam. And I did.

I was a young kid, only 20 years old. After my training at Fort Polk, I came home for a month on leave, and that was the middle of December until the middle of January, and then off to Washington. Flew out of there to 'Nam. My dad and I were talking while I was home on leave there before I flew to Washington, and he asked me—I was out in the garage and he asked me, he says, "Are you going to Vietnam?" And he didn't know at the time, of course. And I just said, "Yeah"; he kind of hung his head down. And my dad wasn't one to really tell you that he loved you or anything, but he did it by his actions. He kind of hung his head down. And we kind of parted ways there. We kind of parted ways right there. Didn't give me a hug or anything, but that was my dad. I was okay with that. I didn't really have any feelings that I didn't want to go. I wanted to go and get it over with. I was okay with going. I was afraid to go, but I didn't have any animosities toward anybody about going. My country wanted me to go, and that's what I was going to do.

So we stopped over at Japan, somewhere in Japan to refuel for just a short time, I don't know, maybe an hour. And then flew into Cam Rahn Bay. I spent about three months in the combat engineers—we didn't really see any combat. But that's what they called us, combat engineers. They had road graders and things of that sort, that we would go out into the villages with and help the villagers maybe build a bridge or tear a bridge down or grade a road, that sort of thing. And that was it. My military occupational specialty was 11 Bravo, which is infantry. But evidently they didn't need any infantry at that time. And so that's why they stuck me in the engineers. And I thought, *Wow, this is great.* I thought, *Man, I can do this for 12 months. This ain't bad at all!* Two square hot meals a day, and a dry warm hooch to sleep in. Life was good. Life was good. The first week in April came along, and I got orders for the 101st. And that's where things changed. That's where things changed. I always like to tell people when I'm having a conversation about my experience over there that I would've never known what war was like had I not gone to the 101st. Not to put down what anybody else does. It's just a fact. I saw both sides.

So I needed some new training; I did some rappelling out of the helicopter, and we kind of went out and did little maneuvering things there. And it was only a week long. I forget what all we did, but I know I did some rappelling out of the chopper. And after that week, I made my way up to Camp Evans, which was just outside of the A Shau Valley. And I spent two or three days there doing some paperwork and getting my gear together. And then after two or three days there they flew me right out there, to the jungle, and I think it was Firebase Blaze, and it was right from the get-go, unlike any type of thing I'd ever been through. I didn't know what to expect. Didn't know exactly how to act, what to do.

The company commander was Harold Ericksen, and we called him Viking. His call sign was Viking. What a guy. I mean, we all loved him. He was a great leader, a fierce guy. I don't think you'll hear a bad word about Viking. It wasn't too long until we went out into the jungle, the surrounding jungle. I wound up serving as the radio telephone operator. Evidently, a radio telephone operator was not a hot job that somebody likes to do because you got to carry an extra twenty-five pounds on your back, and you're already carrying sixty-five, seventy pounds, so you carry another twenty-five. It makes a big difference. So I wound up being radio telephone operator, going into the Hamburger Hill battle.

They called us into the battle on May 13. So we started up—the hill that we started on was not Hill 937, which was Hamburger Hill. It was further down the ridge line. I remember that we had to scale, climb a vertical hill of dirt, dirt, and vines and jungle stuff before we actually got to where it was not—where you could not climb, and it was more of a slope. But we climbed, it took a while to get up … twenty, twenty-five feet.… And it was straight up and down ninety degrees, and it was tough getting up there. And I didn't know what was happening. I was only three weeks into the 101st. And we finally got up there, and then we climbed up.

We were going up the slope to the trail that went to the top of the ridge line there. And the lead platoon, when they got to the top of the ridge line, they came into contact, they came into firefight, they came into contact. All this is an eye-opener for me. I've never done anything like that. They don't do that stuff down there in the combat engineers. You don't see anything like that.

Actually, Hamburger Hill wasn't my first firefight. My first firefight was about two weeks earlier. I was only with the 101st about a week or so and I was already in my first firefight. And that was a real eye-opener. And I didn't really know, once the shooting started, all I did was hit the ground. I didn't know what else to do, but to hit the ground, that's what I did. So it didn't last long. It lasted maybe fifteen minutes or so, and then things were quiet. So I waited a few minutes. I got up after things quieted down, I walked over to a group of guys that were kind of standing around, and we were looking down at two North Vietnamese that we had killed. And they looked to be, to me about fifteen, sixteen, seventeen years old, just kids. That was a shocker my first time, to see something like that. And one of the guys standing there, and I'll always remember this too, he tore off his 101st patch, and he pinned it to one of their necks, kind of like a calling card, that the 101st had been there. And that was a message, that—don't mess with the 101st. And so that was my first firefight, and that was about the first week. And then two weeks later, we ascended the hill on May 13, the top of the ridge line there, and caught the trail. The lead platoon came into contact. And so I'd been in my first firefight. I'd already seen death like that, which I'd never seen before. And so we just, from day to day to day, you fight all day long for, I don't know, forty, thirty, twenty yards of real estate. And then you dig in for the night. You dig a foxhole every night just in case, and get up in the morning, and you do the same thing all over again. You fight all day long. And that was quite an eye-opener.

So this went on. By May 16, we weren't the lead platoon. Roger Pedue, he got killed that day. He was walking point. He started out walking point, and he didn't have to, he was a sergeant, Sergeant Pedue and his radio telephone operator.... I learned later on that Pedue only had about thirty days left in-country. And he didn't even have to be out there. Usually a lot of times, if you've only got thirty days left, you can go back to the rear to the company and have a nice cushy job doing something and spend rest of your time at base camp doing something. Well, he chose to be out there with us. Pedue chose to be out there with us, and it cost him his life. He lost his life because of that. And the crazy thing about it, years later, I learned that he only lived twenty-five miles from me back home. I think about that a lot. He didn't even have to be there.

As we go into the 17th [of May], that night we dug in on this hill like we did every night, dug in. When we got up that morning, the 18th, we got hit sometime that morning. I'm not sure if it was late or whatever, but we got hit from behind. The enemy had got in behind us. And so when the firefight started that morning,

I was carrying the radio for the lieutenant. They threw me into that spot because nobody else wanted it. And so during that firefight, I don't know how long it was, but it got real crazy. I got separated somehow from the lieutenant, and it was just—something that I remember, I remember the mortars coming in and explosions going off around us, the AK-40s, the gunfire, the rocket-propelled grenade rounds. It was just like total chaos, a lot of yelling, a lot of screaming in a firefight like that. And so I got separated from the lieutenant, and as somebody must've yelled about leaving, getting out of there, as I was making my way down the hill, I looked out to my right, and my lieutenant was in the foxhole. He was slumped over dead, so I didn't stop. I didn't really don't remember anybody else being around me. Once I got down to where the rest of the company was, that's when I saw the medevac coming in to pick up the wounded. And there was a bunch of wounded, ten or twelve, something like that. And it came in there, and the wounded were jumping on, getting on it any way they could. Guys were helping them on the chopper.

I'm watching this, like watching a movie, I'm watching this, the wounded getting on there and people helping, soldiers helping the wounded get on. One guy, there wasn't room for him—and so as the chopper was lifting off, he wrapped his arm around the skid of the chopper, and it took off over the tree line of the jungle. And I'm watching him hang onto the chopper skid as it was going off the tree line of jungle. And I followed—my eyeballs followed him. I didn't see him fall, but I followed him until he was out of my eyesight. And I didn't know immediately that he fell. And then I learned later on that he did fall and was never—his body was never recovered.

We did eventually get to the top of the hill, but not that day, or not the next day or the next day. None of us knew what to do. Not even the platoon leaders. One of the sergeants was kind of in charge, whoever it was. I'm not sure who it was at this point, but no, I mean, they didn't fly another lieutenant out because—so one of the sergeants took over, and so nightfall is coming on, and this blond kid, he was a spec four, I was a private first class, he came up to me, walked up to me and says, "Cable, you're going out on listening post tonight." Well, it didn't sit well with me. I didn't want to do that because a listening post is where you go out about ten, fifteen yards and set up for the night, and actually usually two guys go out. Well, this night we were pretty depleted, so only one guy went out in each direction. I was one of the guys that was supposed to go out. And so I had a little argument with this blond-haired kid. I said, "I don't want to go out." Whatever was said, it was a heated argument because the direction I had to go was right where they ran us down the hill. I knew they were knocking on the door. I knew that. And we couldn't go the direction we were going because we were pinned out. We were getting sniper fire from in front of us and in the back of us. So we were pinned down. And so nightfall [was] coming on, and I had a little argument with this blond-haired kid, and I don't want to go. To me, it was like a suicide mission. I'm going to be the first one to catch the bullet, if not from the North Vietnamese then from one of our guys, because we were all trigger happy. Everybody was pretty trigger happy at that moment. But even though I didn't want to go, I knew I had to. I just wanted to put up an argument. And he knew we were all trigger happy, and I didn't want to go right back up in the direction that I just ran down. But I went out, I got my gear together. I went out about fifteen yards and set up for the night. The thing about it is usually you set out claymores and trip wires. Well, I didn't have any claymores and trip wires to set out. We were out of them. I just went out there, myself and my M16, and didn't get a lot of sleep that night.

I mean, in a situation like that, I knew I wasn't going to make it. I knew I was not going to make it that night till the next morning. I knew that, and probably everybody else thought the same thing. But I'll tell you what, I reached out to God that night. I made my peace with God that night because I knew I wasn't going to make it. I knew this was it. I didn't want to die in the jungles of Vietnam, but I knew that's what was going to happen. And I reached out to God that night, and I just made my peace with God, and I was okay with that. After that, I didn't expect to see daylight, and I don't think anybody else did either. I really don't. I know we were all praying that night. It was that type of situation.

So morning came. I was thankful for that. Morning came. I didn't have any food or water. We were out of food and water at that point. We would try to go forward, but we couldn't because we were catching sniper fire. And we didn't try to go backwards—we had to go forward, but we couldn't because of sniper fire. So later that afternoon, we did get a chopper. They came in, it hovered about, I don't know, twenty-five, thirty feet in the air and pushed out these canisters full of water. They pushed out quite a few of them. And I remember filling my canteen up. I carried six canteens, a gallon and a half of water. That's how much I carried, along with the radio and everything else. Water is a precious commodity over there, no doubt about it. And so we all filled up our canteens. I remember taking a sip because I was so thirsty, we all were. I took a sip of this water. We usually have what they call the purification tablets. Iodine we were supposed to drop in there, shake it up, wait ten, fifteen minutes, and then you can drink it. Well, I didn't wait until ten, fifteen minutes. I was thirsty. So I took a sip of this water and you could taste the gun powder in it, that was in the canister. You could taste that gun powder, but nobody minded because it was water. We had water. And thankfully it gave you the strength to get out of there.

The next couple days, we circled around and came back on the trail that we were going on. They had bombed out and put napalm on Hamburger Hill. So the battle was pretty much over at that point, the heavy fighting, on the 20th and 21st. We probably came into a little bit of fighting, but not like we had. And so every once in a while, I remember running across an area where there were just dead North Vietnamese, laying all over the place. I remember I stopped once when there was a bunch of North Vietnamese laying all over, and I looked at this one, I looked at him right in the face. I looked at him in the eyes. Well, he didn't have his eyes. He didn't have any eyes. They were either burned out or sunk back in his head. I'm not really sure. But he didn't have any eyes. It was just holes there. So that kind of hit me kind of hard. So we made our way back down.

I arrived just in time for Hamburger Hill, but then plenty other firefights followed. And one that I can remember pretty vividly is—I didn't carry the radio a hundred percent of the time, but probably about ninety percent of the time I carried the radio. So this other firefight, it was June. June 4th. I was carrying the radio. In fact, that was the firefight where Steve Conroy and his radio telephone operator, Jim Sherlock, got wounded, in that firefight. And I was carrying the—Sherlock was carrying the radio for Lieutenant Conroy, and I was carrying the radio for my platoon sergeant. So the firefight is going on, and I got the horn to my ear. You always got to keep—the radio telephone operators, got to keep the horn to their ear. The phone, I call it the horn. We call it the horn. Keep the horn to your ear. So you've got to let either whoever you're carrying it for, your platoon sergeant or your platoon leader, you got to let them know what's going on. So you keep the horn to your ear, and the firefight is going on. I'm listening to Viking. He is calling in air support from a battleship. So they're coming in and the firefight is going on. Myself and my platoon sergeant, we were hugging the ground, what I like to call, hugging the ground. You get the lowest you can because the rocket-propelled grenade rounds are coming, and rifle fire. And so Viking, he gets on the horn and I'm looking right at him to my right, about eight to ten feet to my right. And it's thick jungle, so it, it's not like I can see real clear, but I can see him about ten feet to my right. And he gets on the horn there and he says, "Second platoon, get your butts up here." And he probably used a little bit stronger language, but I'll use "butt." "Get your butts up here." So I'm looking right at him when he says this, and I said, "Sir," I say, "we're up here. We're right to your left." So he looks at me and I'm already looking at him, and we give the nod and then the firefight continues. So that was another firefight, one of many. You never forget any of the firefights. They're pretty prevalent. And on your mind fifty years later.

Another one—it wasn't a firefight, but we were just out in the jungle humping wherever we were going. And it's kind of a funny thing, but we stopped to take a break. So I take my ruck off, I'm carrying the radio, and so I keep the horn to my ear, even if I'm not carrying my rucksack, because you never know if somebody needs to get in touch with you. So I'm listening to the radio and Viking comes on the radio and he says, "Alright!" He says, "Who took a shit and didn't cover it up?" And he says, "From now on, tell your guys to cover it up!" So I kind of chuckled to myself. And so the little group of guys that was kind of around me right there, I told them, "Hey, Viking says from now on, if you take the crap, cover it up!" It was kind of a funny thing.

Another time I went out on a patrol, me and another guy, and he must have come from the rear area because I certainly didn't have any weed on me. So he must have brought some in. So we're out there on patrol twenty yards out, fifteen or twenty yards out with the radio. You call in your sitreps every hour in the nighttime. And he had some weed. So we kind of toked a little bit. And Warren Sutton was Viking's radio telephone operator then. And they call every hour on the hour, what they call sitreps, situation reports. So you got to do a squeal when he calls out to you. Well, I missed the couple of sitreps calling back to the command post to Warren. And so the next morning he questioned me. He got ahold of me and questioned me. "Why didn't I respond to his sitrep?" He said, "You fell asleep, didn't you?" I denied it. But I didn't want to tell him, "Yeah, I was out there smoking weed!" I never did that again. I realized what jeopardy I could have put everybody in; what a foolish thing to do. I never did that again.

Another firefight that really sticks out in my mind is Hill 996. That was July 11, 1969, and 996 is where Gordon Roberts came out of that battle with the Medal of Honor. We went to Hill 996 to help out Delta Company. Delta Company was pinned down, and so we were sent there to help them out. And I wasn't carrying the radio then for whatever reason. I don't know. But I remember as I was going up that hill, I was keeping in contact, eye contact with this other soldier about eight or ten feet away from me to my right. And we were moving up the hill real slow. It was a slow pace, real slow pace. And the further we got up the hill, the little more intense the fire became. So we got close to the top of the hill right there, and everything went silent. *What's going on?* I was thinking, or I imagine we were both thinking that. So I took the opportunity to run the rest of the way to the top of the hill, and I did, and I jumped in this foxhole, and as I looked around, I realized we had dug in for the night there about two weeks earlier in that same spot. So I'm in there looking around, and actually that was a pretty stupid thing to do, as I looked back on it, jump in that foxhole because it could have been booby trapped. I could have lost a couple of legs. And I think about that. What a stupid thing that was to do. So I just looked around for a few minutes and I got out and I went over, I pulled up one dead of our guys up the hill, and that was a pretty eerie feeling. I'd never done that before. Pull a dead guy up and he was already stiff. I remember that. Pulled him up the hill to be bagged up and evacuated for later on in the day.

But I went over and I sat down with a soldier that had got shot in the arm, and a medic was standing there. So I sat down next to the soldier, and everything was over. The shooting was over by then, pretty much. So it wasn't like there was any shooting going on, it was over. So the medic, myself, this guy that got shot in the arm [were] sitting there talking, and we were trying to cheer this guy up because he was kind of moaning. He was in a lot of pain. And we were saying, "Hey man, you got the million-dollar wound, you're going to be going back to the world! This is it! You're out of here in a few days." And he was moaning. He says, "Doc, doc, can you give me a shot of your morphine? My arm is killing me!" So the doc said, "Yeah, yeah." So he gets the syringe out, he gives him a shot of morphine in the arm, and about thirty, forty-five seconds go by. And this guy says, "Hey, doc, can you give me another shot of that morphine? My arm is still killing me." And the doc says, "No, I can't give you another shot of that, if I gave you a shot this soon, it'll kill you." So we all kind of chuckled.

Another thing I want to note is, when we combat assaulted into a landing zone, it could be real hot. One time, we were making a combat assault and I had the radio, had the horn right to my ear, because it's real noisy and windy in there. We were about the third bird in when the radio man for the first chopper yelled into the radio "Hot LZ! Hot LZ!" [LZ meaning landing zone.] The closer we got I could hear the crack of the AK-47. I in turn yell to my guys, "LZ hot! LZ hot!" Thank God when we landed it must have been only a couple North Vietnamese taking potshots at us. Nowhere to run, nowhere to hide.

I served two years. Two years was plenty. I told them, I don't want to spend one more second over here. I'm not going to re-up with 11 Bravo MOS. I don't want to spend one more second over here. Because from day to—you just live day to day. You're not guaranteed. And I know nobody's guaranteed from day to day, but over there you're really not guaranteed from day to day. I mean, Sergeant Pedue was in my mind, that he didn't need to be out there. He could have been in the rear area and been alive, could come back home alive. But no, I didn't want to re-up for anything."

I think personally I just went because I was drafted, I wanted to go and do what my country wanted me to do. I didn't know much about anything else. I wanted to get in there and do my duty—what I thought was my duty—and … I just did what I was told. Really, I was 20 years old. I did what I was told and I was proud. I was proud to go over there, whether it was to fight or whatever it was, and it turned out to be fighting. I didn't like it. Once I got into the fighting part of it, that was a big eye-opener. Seeing death around the corner every day. You don't know whether you're going to get up the next day. Is it going to be, am I going to die this day or what? You don't know. I was just doing what I was told and I was okay with that. I just wanted to serve my country.

When Doyle returned home, he moved in with his parents, went back to his old job as a meatcutter, and, as he puts it, "tried to drink up all the beer in Northwest Indiana." He married in October 1976 and he and his bride are still together 48 years later.

Secretary of Defense Robert McNamara pointing to a map of Vietnam at a press conference, April 26, 1965. The first American combat troops had arrived in South Vietnam earlier that year, building upon the thousands of "advisors" already stationed there. (Courtesy Library of Congress)

Secretary of Defense Robert McNamara (right), President Lyndon Baines Johnson, and Secretary of State Dean Rusk seated at a table after McNamara's return from South Vietnam, July 21, 1965. Decades after the war ended, McNamara would write a book, *In Retrospect*, expressing regrets over the way the war unfolded. (Courtesy Library of Congress)

Clergy supporting the Vietnam War march with signs near the White House, at a demonstration sponsored by the American Council of Christian Churches, February 2, 1967. (Courtesy Library of Congress)

An anti-Vietnam war protest and demonstration in front of the White House, January 19, 1968. (Courtesy Library of Congress)

President Richard Nixon, circa 1970. Nixon would ultimately pull the last American troops from Vietnam in 1973. Over fifty-eight thousand Americans had been killed there. South Vietnam would fall in April 1975. (Courtesy Library of Congress)

Battlin' Bastard Gordon Roberts received the Medal of Honor for his actions in the A Shau Valley in July 1969. (Courtesy the Congressional Medal of Honor Society)

Jim Sherlock and a friend "enjoying a bowl" on an Eagle Beach weekend break from the field, 1969. Jim notes that it was "great to be on the beach (being a San Diego County kid) and enjoy the smell of the ocean and feel of the sand." (Courtesy Jim Sherlock)

Jim Sherlock and a friend at the hospital in Japan after being wounded, 1969. (Courtesy Jim Sherlock)

Jim Sherlock cleaning his M60, possibly at Firebase Berchtesgaden, circa 1969. (Courtesy Jim Sherlock)

Camp Evans, circa 1970. Left to right: Don Rollings, Tony Liguori, Roger Fitch, unidentified, and Wylie Glover. (Courtesy Don Rollings)

Bravo Company Headquarters, Camp Evans, circa 1970. Left to right: Joe Szuch and Tom Tibbetts. (Courtesy Danny McNair)

Firebase Kathryn, circa 1970. Left to right: Doug Turner, Danny McNair, and Staff Sergeant Gist. (Courtesy Doug Turner)

An interpreter coming out of an overnight bunker during monsoon season. Jerry Hoffman recalled that the interpreter, whose name he could not remember, was a "really good guy; a good friend." Jerry later heard that the interpreter was imprisoned for 20 years after Saigon fell. Upon his release, he is said to have opened a bar called The 101st. (Courtesy Jerry Hoffman)

At Firebase Berchtesgaden in the summer of 1969. (Courtesy Jerry Hoffman)

Jerry Hoffman's platoon, having just gotten off a helicopter in a landing zone in the A Shau Valley in the summer of 1969. Note the density of the vegetation. Jerry recalled that, even during the middle of the day, you could hardly see as you trudged through the jungle. (Courtesy Jerry Hoffman)

Jerry Hoffman and his platoon medic Danny "Doc" Caeb out in the field, circa 1969. (Courtesy Jerry Hoffman)

A typical bunker, circa 1969. (Courtesy Jerry Hoffman)

An unidentified soldier on the radio, circa 1969. (Courtesy Jerry Hoffman)

Platoon Sergeant Cecil Vancil in front of the command bunker on an unidentified firebase. Note the sandbags—the command bunker was always the best protected. (Courtesy Jerry Hoffman)

A view of the rice paddies. (Courtesy Jerry Hoffman)

Unidentified men waiting for helicopters, circa 1969. (Courtesy Jerry Hoffman)

Mike Serrano with a bandage on his arm, circa 1969. Jerry Hoffman noted, "Lot of times we would get jungle rot, so they'd try to put antibiotics on it, and patch it up." (Courtesy Jerry Hoffman)

A lieutenant coming out of the command bunker with a *Playboy* magazine, circa 1969. (Courtesy Jerry Hoffman)

Jerry Hoffman and Mike Steam manning a perimeter bunker at Camp Evans, circa 1969. (Courtesy Jerry Hoffman)

Jerry Hoffman and Mike Serano getting orders on the radio, circa 1969. (Courtesy Jerry Hoffman)

Roger Harrison and an unidentified interpreter, on a small firebase, circa 1969. Note the radios. (Courtesy Jerry Hoffman)

Though the Battlin' Bastards were usually in the mountains, there were a few places where tanks could be used. Circa 1969. (Courtesy Jerry Hoffman)

Max West, at the front of the line here, was the "flower child" of his company, according to Jerry Hoffman, with peace signs on his helmet. He would lose a leg in a booby trap. Circa 1969. (Courtesy Jerry Hoffman)

A view of Eagle Beach, circa 1969. Jerry Hoffman noted, "We'd go in the field for forty to sixty days and if everything went good, they'd fly us to Eagle Beach and we'd get one day to clean up and have hot food and they'd have a band play for us. The salt water helped clean up your jungle rot." (Courtesy Jerry Hoffman)

A view of Eagle Beach, circa 1969. When some of the Battlin' Bastards made a return trip to Vietnam in 2017, they stopped here and planted a cross in honor of the brothers they had lost, pointing it towards the United States. (Courtesy Jerry Hoffman)

Jerry Hoffman recalls of helicopters, "They were our taxis everywhere." Circa 1969. (Courtesy Jerry Hoffman)

Warren Sutton in Vietnam. Circa 1969. (Courtesy Warren Sutton)

Rich Smets, [first name unknown] Hosler, John Dalton, Doug Turner, and "Doc" Lohm. FSB Kathryn, July 1970. (Courtesy Doug Turner)

William Shue, 1970. (Courtesy William Shue)

Hank Bow. Circa 1969. (Courtesy Hank Bow)

Don Rollings, 1971. (Courtesy Don Rollings)

Danny Mitchell, 1970. (Courtesy Danny Mitchell)

The Battlin' Bastards who served with him all speak reverentially of Captain Harold J. Ericksen, known by his call sign, "Viking." Viking would be on R&R leave at the beginning of the battle for Hamburger Hill, but he would eventually return to his command and, as Jim Tarleton writes, would continue "to lead his troops splendidly. His uniform was festooned with many awards testifying not only to his leadership but also his personal bravery and courage—and his men willingly and loyally followed him. There are many soldiers from B Company who survived and returned home because of Viking's courage and leadership." Viking spent 25 years in the Army, retiring as a colonel. He died on July 26, 2019.

Viking posed with his men in Vietnam. Undated. (Courtesy the family of Harold J. Ericksen)

Viking addressing his men in Vietnam. Undated. (Courtesy the family of Harold J. Ericksen)

The handwritten caption on this undated photo sent to Viking's wife reads, "Giving some of your candy to some children." (Courtesy the family of Harold J. Ericksen)

Near the Hue Citadel and military museum during a 2017 return trip to Vietnam. Left to right: Mike Smith, Jerry Hoffman, Pete Falco, Terry Ostendorf, and Steve Conroy. (Courtesy Steve Conroy)

The Battlin' Bastards' 2024 reunion in Mississippi. Back row: Rick Farris, Daniel Denton, Warren Sutton, Jerry Hoffman, Terry Ostendorf, Don Rollings, Jim Monroe, Chuck Choney, Terry Taylor. Second row: Doug Turner, Bob Harasick, John Brown, Danny McNair, Danny Mitchell, John Sasse, Mike Bookser, Steve Conroy, Pete Lohm. Front row: Roger Harrison, Lou Bowen, Wannie Cook. (Courtesy Marlene Van Matre)

CHAPTER 10

Jerry Hoffman

In Vietnam March 1969–March 1970

"To this day I still feel that we let the Vietnamese people down to a certain extent."

The following is a lightly edited summary of the author's May 2024 oral history interview with Jerry.

I was born in 1949 in Fairbury, Illinois. It's a small farming community in Central Illinois. I grew up with my mom, dad, brother, and sister. My dad was a tool and die maker and in 1964 he started his own tool and die shop. My mom worked as a cook in the school, and some other jobs in grocery stores. It was a good place to grow up; fairly safe. We were able to run pretty much on the streets and ride our bikes wherever we wanted to; go out to farms and help (or pester the older people, depending on how you look at it). My dad was in World War II; he was a belly gunner in a B17. He was stationed in England but flew missions over Germany and France. He didn't talk about his experiences a lot, but he had a scrapbook that we would sometimes sneak out of the closet and look at when we were growing up. He was not a person that talked an awful lot.

Growing up, I pretty much liked school. I was on like the National Honor Society and captain of the football team and president of the Letterman's Club, so I would say I was fairly active in high school. I went to college for a year at Illinois State, Bloomington. My grades were good. I was on the Dean's List, but I decided to volunteer for the military because I wasn't really sure what I wanted to do, and I thought—me and another friend went in together on a buddy plan. We went to basic and advanced individual training together, flew to Vietnam together, and at Cam Rahn Bay we got separated. He went to the Americal, and I went to the 101st, and he was killed in June of that year.

When I volunteered to go, it was, I guess, partly because of my dad, and knowing that he had served. Although I didn't tell my parents before I signed the papers, and they were not real happy with me. Not because they disagreed with the war, just because, you know, they knew it was dangerous. But I kind of grew up with the idea that, kind of like John Kennedy said, "Ask not what your country can do for you, but what you can do for your country?" And I—unlike the typical college person of that time, I kind of went to the other side of it and thought it was our responsibility to do something. And to this day I'm not a hundred percent sure I agree with some of the things that we did, as far as leaving Vietnam. Because I felt like the people were good people. I like the Vietnamese people, and especially the kids in Vietnam. The children were very friendly towards Americans.

I thought I knew a lot about the situation in Vietnam before I went, but I'm not sure that I really understood the politics. Both the corruption of the South Vietnamese government as well as understanding how fickle the American decision-making could be. One time they're in favor, and the next time they're not in favor, of a certain course of action. But to this day I still feel that we let the Vietnamese people down to a certain extent. I've met some people from Vietnam that were the boat people [who fled after the country was united under the communists]. Many of those people said that when the North Vietnamese took over there was an extreme amount of cruelty. One lady that I met, she had a brother and an uncle, I think it was, that were Catholic priests, and they were executed after the North Vietnamese took over. I'm not sure that the average person here in the United States knew the extent of the division between the Catholics in Vietnam and the Buddhists in Vietnam. So yeah, there was a lot I don't think I understood.

Anyway, I went to basic at Fort Campbell, Kentucky, and then advanced individual training at Fort Lewis, Washington. I was a fairly physical guy. I was in the judo club at and like I said, I was a captain of the football team.... So physically, I was probably much better prepared than the average person. However, I don't think I was really prepared for the structure of the military at the time. The Army is—there's a right way, and a wrong way, and then there's the Army way, and the only thing that matters is the Army way. I don't think we were particularly well-prepared for jungle fighting, at least the people who came out of Fort Lewis. I have heard people that went to Fort Polk, Louisiana, were much more prepared, or much better prepared for the jungle environment at least, than we were. We went from the wintertime in the northern part of Washington, with snow and five-degree weather, to one-hundred-degree heat in the jungle. And some of the tactics that they—they could have done a better job of explaining the tactics, of how we should do things. Because the unit I was in in Vietnam—we spent the majority of our time in the jungle. We would go out for fifty, sixty days and come in for a day, and then go back out for another fifty to sixty days, and that can be very hard on your body in the jungle.

My first impression when I arrived in Vietnam was just—the HEAT! I remember as soon as I stepped out of the plane where it was air-conditioned, and the intensity of the sun and the heat and the humidity. We had just come from the winter! So it was kind of a double whammy. So that was my first impression, was how hot it was; wondering how this was going to work. Then we got sent to Saigon, for an orientation, and they kind of talk[ed] to us about some of the things that we were going to see and encounter, and we pulled guard duty. Then we went to Camp Evans. And then it was just one or two days at Camp Evans and the next helicopter out, I went out without really all of the gear that most people had, because they were short on some things. But I had all my ammo and stuff.

The first real encounter for me was April 4, when Walter Chase and Mike Flood were killed and our Kit Carson [Vietnamese] scout was killed. We went out on a—we were at Firebase Veghel, the company was. We went out on a patrol with just our platoon. Actually, it may have just been—because there wasn't a lieutenant with us—so it may have just been our squad. And we ran into, or made contact with, the North Vietnamese. Initially, we had one guy wounded, and the Kit Carson scout was killed. Then we drew back, kind of regrouped, and then we kind of moved back down the hill on the trail. They had brought in some napalm, and hit the area. One of the guys gave me his M60 machine gun, which I'd only had maybe one day of training on at advanced individual training. And he took my M16, and the sergeant told me to go down this trail. I went down there, and the gun was jammed, which might be why he gave it to me, I don't remember. But my assistant machine gunner got shot, and I dragged him off the trail. In the meantime, the recon platoon came to join us, to help us out, and they took some casualties. And I went down to help some of them get to the landing zone to get medevac'd out. And while I was helping that person up the hill, kind of all hell broke loose, and that's when Walter and Flood were killed.

I went back down the hill, and they were bringing other wounded up, and I helped get them up to the helicopter. Then the rest of the platoon pulled back up, what was left of them, and we medevac'd out the guys who were wounded. But Doc Flood and Walter Chase, the decision was made to leave them down there because they were already dead, and not to go back down that night. The next day Delta Company came to help us and they lost about five guys killed, trying to get to us. So we went back to Veghel the following day, and I remember feeling like, *what the heck have I gotten into?!* Because you can't see in the jungle, very well, so it's kind of hard to fight when you can't see.

So we try to regroup. Viking talks to us, gave us a, almost a football-type speech of, "We're gonna go get them," and all. But it kind of—I was kind of thinking, *are we really doing this the right way?* It's kind of hard to judge. And because—it was my first combat, and I wasn't sure what was going on yet. I barely knew all the guys in my squad, let alone the platoon or the company. I've been in the field about a week to ten days. But, fortunately for us, they had left—the North Vietnamese had left the area. So we recovered the bodies and then after that we pretty much got into the A Shau Valley, and we're in contact almost every day. A lot of, not major firefights until we had the firefight at Hamburger Hill, or the battle.

So that was a real tough time for our company. We went from 126, I think, down to 23 that weren't wounded. I was wounded in that battle, but it was more of a, the kind of wounding guys like to get, because it got me out of the field. So I think we went there on the—we started towards there on May 10. I think it was on the 12th or 13th that we actually made contact. We broke on to the top of the ridge line, and our job was to break onto a ridge line that ran down to Laos from Hamburger Hill. And there was communication wire running down the hill, from Hamburger Hill to Laos, where they had more troops. So we ended up having quite a few guys wounded, quite a few killed. One guy that was killed, fell off a helicopter. One day some of the guys were—we're getting hit on both sides. We lost the lieutenant in the second platoon; he was killed that day. One of the guys I had walked point with quite a bit was killed. I was hit on the 17th, but my wound wasn't bad enough that I was in danger of dying. It was enough that I couldn't walk real well. I always wondered why I was so lucky to not get shot or wounded worse than I was, because there was lots of times when I should have been.

Despite all this, I have a lot of respect for the North Vietnamese soldiers that we faced. They were very well trained, very determined in the face of horrible odds for them. Because we had air superiority. We had firepower superiority. For every GI that was killed there were probably ten North Vietnamese that were killed. I don't remember the exact statistics, but their statistics were horrible compared to ours. We got resupplied with food once a week; they were pretty much down there by themselves, living off the jungle. I watched one time we had some South Vietnamese troops with us, and the South Vietnamese troops, as we were getting ready to go, get to the high ground for the night, to be able to set up a perimeter, they were picking up snails and pieces of vegetation. And I asked one of them, "Why?" And as best I could understand, that's pretty much the way they lived. When they were out in the jungle, they lived off the land as opposed to having their C-rations brought in. I watched how he prepared his food, and he just kind of put it in a little container and kind of mixed the snails in, and ate everything. They really were tough soldiers, I mean they—they would, you know, if they were given an order to attack a firebase, they were walking into an awful lot of firepower, and they just did what they were told. I don't have as much respect for their leaders, because they sent them into meat-grinder situations on a regular basis. And I don't quite understand why they were that committed. I went back to Vietnam in 2017 or 2018. And the Vietnamese people are very capitalistic. The country that we went to is thriving. They're building skyscrapers. They're doing all kinds of stuff, because of their foreign trade with the United States. After we left—the Chinese were helping them, and the Russians were helping them. But after we left the Chinese and Vietnam got into a fight. I later learned they'd been fighting for centuries. And I didn't quite understand why they were so against the United States, that they would send that many of their people to die when, if they basically just shook hands, we probably would have helped them tremendously, economically, twenty to thirty years sooner than they saw the increased economic activity that's going on today.

Anyway—back to the war. At one point I became the radio operator. For us, communication was probably more important than it was for the Vietnamese, because they really didn't have medevacs to call in. If they got wounded, they had to basically walk back or just die where they were at. That's part of the reason for the attrition rate—they really didn't have anybody to call. For us, most times, except for a couple of times, we were able to get a medevac back in within a half hour of when a guy was wounded and get him out. And I have nothing but praise for our medevac pilots. They were super.

Another factor in our favor was the ability to call in air strikes. The ability to call in artillery. To me, one of the reasons I wanted to be a radio telephone operator was I wanted to know what was going on. When you were just one of the infantrymen, a lot of times, you don't exactly know what's happening. Sometimes you barely know where you're at, other than you're in Vietnam. Now, radio telephone operators were a target, because the enemy wanted to knock out communications. But still, I wanted to know what was going on. And the AN/PRC-25 performed really well, it was dependable, it was rugged. The downside of all that was, it was heavy. I think it weighed twenty-five pounds by itself, and then you carried a spare battery, which was another three or four pounds. It was not light like a cell phone. And the range was not the best. If you got down in the valley, you might have communication problems.

Part of the reason enlisted men were so desperate for information was that there was a definite feeling at the time that some of the officers didn't know what they were doing. For our company, Viking was on his second tour in Vietnam, and he was a born leader. I thought he was probably the best captain in Vietnam, I mean, the guy was phenomenal. But some of the lieutenants, I think they had the short course, and hadn't really—didn't really understand everything yet. After I came back I got to thinking about it, and really it wasn't fair, our critique of them. It was more a critique of the Army and their training, rather than the individual lieutenant or captain. They were put through, in many cases, maybe thirty days to six months longer training than us, but they had never been under fire. They had never seen—they had never really called in an air strike. They maybe had done it in practice, but not when it really meant something, so I have more respect for them now than I did at the time. But we did have some lieutenants that were really, really good, and we had some lieutenants that weren't quite so good. I think sometimes the expectations that we had, were that our leaders were going to be like they are in the movies, and that just isn't realistic. In many ways. I began to feel kind of sorry for them, because I know a lot of them carried guilt with them for years after, and still do to this day. For instance, when we were on Hamburger Hill, we got a captain dropped in to our company practically on the day we broke onto the top of the ridge line headed towards Hamburger Hill. Viking was taken out of the field by orders of his commander, and he didn't want to go. But he was ordered to leave.

And the new guy was dropped into a situation where he didn't know his officers. He didn't know his sergeants. He didn't know who he could trust, who he couldn't trust; who was a good leader, who wasn't. It's a terrible disadvantage heading into a major battle, and the result was less than ideal for our company. But at the same time I've begun to feel pretty sorry for him, in what he was faced with, and I don't think he had ever been in combat himself, either. So, it really wasn't a fair situation for him. But at the time, I think we were expecting more out of people than what the service or their experiences had really taught them. Because the guys, the older guys in our company would look at us, and the term was a cherry, or a new guy. But we didn't give the officers the same leeway, though they were really brand new to the experience, too.

When I came back from Vietnam, it was a really bad time in the country [the United States] because there was not a lot of respect for the soldiers. Later on I wrote a letter to Viking, telling him that the one thing he did was to instill a sense of pride and respect in our minds for the job we were doing, when most of the country didn't have that same respect for what we had done or the sacrifices that so many guys made. He called me up and thanked me for the letter, and actually was crying on the phone about how much it meant to him to hear that. But he did a lot in terms of making me proud of the job we were doing. I was thankful that we didn't work around villages, so I didn't see personally see any of the types of atrocities towards civilians that were being reported on and responsible for a lot of anti-war, anti-soldier sentiment. I really didn't understand how anybody could do that, or get themselves into that kind of a mind frame, that they would think that killing kids would be acceptable, or something that they should engage in. I didn't understand why they did it. I understood the pressure that we were under, and the feeling after you see your own friends getting killed. I think the one thing that bothered me most about the stories was not that they were telling stories of Americans committing atrocities—which I think did happen for some of the troops that were around villages—but that they didn't mention or seem to make much of the atrocities the North Vietnamese committed against the South Vietnamese. For every My Lai-type incident that I heard about, I probably heard about ten or fifteen stories of where the North Vietnamese had done similar things to the Montagnards or South Vietnamese people, and not much was said about it. And then, later on, after we left, and the North Vietnamese took over, the South Vietnamese suffered tremendously. I mean, it takes some pretty brutal things for people to just jump on a raft and head out into the ocean without knowing if that raft or that boat is going to be seaworthy. You have to be pretty desperate.

Overall, I was very disappointed in the way we conducted the war, in that it seemed like we had pretty much made up our minds by the time I got to Vietnam that we were leaving. And for that reason it seemed like it was futile that we were there. We'd already made a decision to lose. I think that's been one of our biggest issues since World War II, in every war that we've been in. We've not been willing—first of all, before you go to war, you should understand what war is, and that war is not a clean endeavor and innocent people are always victims. And I don't know if it was the guilt of dropping the atomic bomb on civilians in Hiroshima and Nagasaki, which was a terrible loss of life, but since that time—and I see it today with some of the situations in Israel, and the Hamas situation—we're just not willing to do what war takes. So people should be a lot more careful about going into war. But once you go into war, you've only got two choices, and that's to win or lose. And somehow people seem to think we can win a war without bad things happening, and I'm just not sure that that really can happen.

Upon his return to the United States, Jerry went back to school, started a family, and ran several successful businesses.

CHAPTER 11

Hank Bow

In Vietnam August 1969–August 1970

"We ... were very short [of] men at all ranks in Bravo Company."

Battlin' Bastard Danny McNair took the initiative to interview several veterans who, quite understandably, were more comfortable speaking with a fellow veteran than an author who is not. What follows is Hank's story as told to Danny for the express purpose of this book, lightly edited by the author.

I am from Jamestown, Tennessee, which is on the western edge of the Cumberland Plateau not far from the Kentucky state line. Jamestown is the home of the famous World War I hero, Sergeant Alvin York. I graduated from Alvin York High School in Jamestown in 1967 and began working at a friend's grocery store for a little over one year when I was drafted into the Army in February of 1969. I was inducted into the Army with another friend, Daniel Smith. We rode the bus to Fort Jackson, South Carolina, for basic training. I completed all my basic training and advanced infantry training with a friend named Dewey Byerly who would eventually end up with me in Bravo Company, 1/506th, of the 101st Airborne in Vietnam.

I received my orders to leave for assignment to Vietnam in the later part of August 1969, along with some of my friends who had trained with me. My friend, Daniel Smith, drove us to Indianapolis, Indiana, and from there we flew to Oakland, California, to be processed out for Vietnam. When we arrived in Bien Hoa, Vietnam, I remember the hot, humid weather and the distinct smell. The first night we actually slept in old bunkers and the base received incoming fire, but it was not close to our position. We were only there a few days when orders came across for Dewey Byerly, Pete Ancona, and myself to be sent to the 101st Airborne. My friend Daniel Smith received his orders for the 199th Infantry. We then flew up to Phu Bai where Camp Eagle (home of the 3rd Brigade) was located. We were processed on up to Camp Evans where Bravo Company, 1/506th, was located and attended SERTS [Screaming Eagle Replacement Training School] before actually checking in at Bravo Company. SERTS is where we were taught everything about infantry air assaults from Huey helicopters. This included preparing all of us replacements for what to expect in the field and some practice firing weapons. Training also included all aspects of air assaults from helicopters. This would include rappelling, combat assaults from helicopters, how to prepare the order of squads and weapons before boarding up the helicopters, unloading of the troops, setting up security, and then moving out from the landing zone towards our objective. We would actually practice a CA outside the wire at Camp Evans during SERTS. There would be many real combat assaults over the next year and other travel by helicopters as part of the infantry in Vietnam, so this training was crucial. We were then sent to Bravo Company to prepare for duty in the field. We picked up our M16 rifles, rucksacks, ponchos, poncho liners, canteens, helmets, masks, entrenching tools, first aid kits, insect repellent, body armor, C-rations, and extra clothing. We would later pick up M16 ammunition, grenades, M72 LAW, claymore mines, C-4 explosives, and any other items depending on the type of weapon we would be assigned. There were always other veterans in the rear that would help us by telling us to bring more canteens, showing us how to pack the rucksacks, and other useful information. I was picked up on the helicopter pad and taken out to an area around firebases near Berchtesgaden. Bravo Company had been hit very hard in August on Berchtesgaden, losing several killed and wounded. Some of the men I arrived with in Vietnam, such as Dewey Byerly and Pete Ancona, would end up in first platoon together as replacements. Many others would soon follow in the next two months, who would also be in my squad. We had some very good non-commissioned officers and officers who helped prepare me as a rifleman. Lieutenant Silverthorn was our platoon leader. Max West was a veteran who had walked point and began to work with me as a point man, which was one of my first jobs. Dewey Byerly, Pete Ancona, Sam Brown, Bob Caloud, Aaron Livingston, Rod Taylor, Donnie Tritt, Danny Mitchell, Terry Atkinson, Bob Haberle, Doc Peter Lohm, and Leon Heaton would all become part of my platoon over the next couple of months and we would be together for most of our time in Vietnam. I picked up the name "Hound Dog," from someone in my platoon. I was from an area in Tennessee where we did a lot of hunting and I did have my hunting dogs, so that is probably how I got the name.

My first big operation in the field would be at an old Special Forces camp in Mai Loc, north of us nearer the DMZ at the end of September 1969. The 101st was to relieve the Marines located in that area. We were told that a B-52 strike would be conducted before we were sent to Mai Loc, to prepare for our arriving. We were flown up on fixed-wing aircraft that landed at the air strip at Mai Loc and then CA'd into the area around FSB Victory which is where Bravo would be located. When we CA'd near FSB Victory we unloaded from the choppers and jumped into a large bomb crater that was created by the B-52 strike. We were forced to put on our gas masks as we were hit by gas that had been dropped into the craters by our support aircraft to keep the enemy from using them. Bravo was divided up into six-man teams working out of FSB Victory. We did not have any contact, but began to gain experience in the field.

Sometime around the first of November 1969 we were CA'd to FSB Rakkasan and again worked on six-man teams. This was monsoon season and it was very wet, cold, and muddy. Falco would become our new platoon leader. He was a great officer who loved and cared for his men. He was a very good leader and probably the reason many of us were able to return home after Vietnam. Staff Sergeant Mike Turner would become our platoon sergeant and was also a great leader. Captain Lee Sullivan would become our new company commander about the same time. In December and January, we would be moved between the old French fort that was around the Rocket Ridge area. We also operated on six-man teams from FSB Jack, which was very close to Camp Evans. The company spent Christmas on FSB Jack. My friend Sam Brown and myself were picked up at Jack and flown to the Bob Hope Show at Camp Eagle, which was a great surprise.

This time period allowed more time in the field all around these flatlands and Rocket Ridge on the six-man teams. Some of the teams I was on were assigned to blow new landing zones. Our team would be flown by Hueys to the area to blow the landing zone, taking C-4 plastic explosives on the chopper with us. We would kick off the case of C-4 and climb down ladders to blow the new landing zone. I was also on six-man teams that sought to ambush the enemy, and some where our team was to remain in place and silent for observing any enemy activity. One night we were on the silent-and-observe team when a wild animal came up on my position. I kicked at the animal which caused it to leave. I was thanked by my team members for not firing my weapon to expose our position. We think it may have been a wild boar, which other teams had also encountered in that area.

The weather continued to be wet and cold with many leeches to contend with in the lowlands. In February, we would move farther into the mountains west of Camp Evans where we would find many more enemy signs and booby traps, and get in some firefights. The first part of February the lead part of first platoon hit a booby trap, wounding some of the men. Still, we had to press on. A few days later Lieutenant Falco would lead us on a mission, looking for reported North Vietnamese not far from us. We began advancing up a hill, firing our weapons at two Viet Cong and one North Vietnamese. One of the North Vietnamese was killed near a small stream. We also received supporting fire from a Pink Team, which was an armed light observation helicopter. They hit two more of the enemy, with another North Vietnamese killed and one wounded. When the firefight was over, I picked up a boonie hat that was dropped by one of the North Vietnamese and brought it home with me after Vietnam.

In the days following this contact we began to find more signs of larger enemy forces in the area such as trails, bunkers, supplies, ammunition, and hooches. This made us all aware that contact with the enemy was going to increase. This would be the routine over the next several months with the frequency increasing all the way up into July 1970. I had been the AG (assistant gunner for the M60) for a guy named

Donnie Tritt. I can't remember the exact timing, but Donnie had to be sent to the rear for medical treatment for a severe case of boils. I became the M60 gunner at that time. The M60 weighed 23 pounds and was a most important part of our fire power. I had learned a lot [from my time as an assistant gunner so] we carried an extra barrel plus 100 rounds in the gun at all times. It was a big responsibility and the M60 had to be kept very clean. I knew that if the weapon and the ammunition were not kept clean that it was prone to jamming. I used a shaving brush to keep it clean, especially around the area responsible for the firing mechanisms. I draped a towel over it while humping to keep it as clean as possible from rain, dust, dirt, and other debris. There was definitely a lot more dirt and dust when we were on firebases. The M60 was easy to break down and clean especially after heavy firing or when it rained. When we set up in the night defensive position the extra rounds carried by the rest of the platoon would be dropped off in the 100-round belts to me and my AG. The belts were hooked together to provide a great amount of firepower. My AG was a guy named Reynolds.

We were in the same area in March and the North Vietnamese presence became even more evident, with bunker complexes found, ammunition, supplies, and enemy contact resulting in enemy casualties and prisoners. We had Chieu Hoi (Vietnamese scouts) with us, who provided intelligence and could also interpret with any North Vietnamese we captured, and read captured information such as North Vietnamese maps. On March 3, 1970, we were in an old North Vietnamese Army bunker complex when we heard moaning very close to us. We found a wounded North Vietnamese hidden in a spider hole. He was in very bad condition, but the medics were able to give him aid so he could be sent to the rear for interrogation. He was able to tell the intelligence personnel with us at the time that that bunker complex was previously occupied by a lot of North Vietnamese. We continued to find large amounts of ammunition, and supplies.

We were sent into Camp Evans for a stand-down in March. The night of March 19, FSB Granite was attacked by sappers. We knew there was a large number of casualties and that Bravo Company was the reactionary company at Camp Evans that night. Our previous acting third platoon leader, First Sergeant Frank Foronda, had just been transferred to Charlie Company, 1/506th, in March when Lieutenant Chuck Choney arrived and became the platoon leader of third platoon for Bravo Company. We were CA'd to FSB Granite the next morning [March 20] to reinforce Charlie Company. The casualties were very high with many Charlie Company killed and wounded. First Sergeant Foronda made it through the battle and was awarded the Silver Star for his bravery, and preventing FSB Granite from being completely overrun. We were placed on the perimeter of Granite and conducted patrols all around the firebase. We found some of the dead North Vietnamese outside the wire as well as weapons, trails, and hooches. We also set up ambushes and tracked some of the North Vietnamese, but did not find any alive. We continued to patrol around FSB Granite into April. We did go into Camp Evans for a stand-down, and to Eagle Beach, the first part of April; but then went right back to the area around Granite. We were also around the Rao Trang River and FSB Maureen.

On April 25, we were to CA onto FSB Maureen. Our first platoon was to be the last to CA into the landing zone. The first two platoons received fire and we (first platoon) were diverted to another landing zone close by the rest of the company. The second platoon would move into the middle of an ambush and were hit and pinned down for hours that afternoon. There was a lot of artillery being fired in our support and we held our position up the hill from second platoon. It was dark when the fighting stopped, with many casualties from second platoon. We lost Eudell Kotrous from first platoon, who was killed when he went with Sergeant First Class Isaacs to assist second platoon. Isaacs was the acting platoon leader for first platoon because Lieutenant Falco and Staff Sergeant Mike Turner were assigned somewhere else during that time. It was raining and none of the casualties could be evacuated out until the next morning. Doc Lohm, our first platoon medic, was also wounded (by our own artillery), and was helicoptered out too. Sergeant First Class Isaacs would later be awarded the Distinguished Service Cross for his action that day coming to the aid of Second Platoon.

The company moved away from the area of attack and continued to find enemy positions and equipment. There would be some contact during the next few days and some of our first platoon were wounded. We were very low on supplies and began to walk off of Maureen down a finger until we got to an old landing zone. We stopped there at that old landing zone to resupply. I was at the bottom side of that landing zone where first platoon was set up in the perimeter for the resupply. Second platoon was placed on the upper side of the landing zone facing the uphill finger we had just walked down, and third platoon was also on the perimeter above us. When we were attacked the second platoon was hit very hard. Cobra gunships were called in and were firing all around us in support, coming very close to our positions. First platoon was not being engaged by the North Vietnamese because they were attacking the top of the perimeter where second platoon was located. The second and third platoon had been hit very hard and we would find out later some of the casualties were from our Cobra air support friendly fire. It had been a long day of resupply and then the evacuating out of the large number of wounded and killed. Lieutenant Falco was rotated out of the field that same day, and it was a major loss for the men of first platoon. I remember Captain Sullivan was the only officer left at the end of that battle. We were very short [of] men at all ranks in Bravo Company.

We still had a very good leader in Staff Sergeant Mike Turner, who would become our acting platoon leader. Staff Sergeant Sandy Porter was also a very good leader in first platoon. Captain Sullivan led what remained of Bravo Company out of that area as quickly as possible. We all thought that we would be attacked again that night. I think we all dug in the deepest defensive positions ever in anticipation of being attacked that night of May 1, 1970. We did not get attacked that night and would be sent back up on Maureen and then down around the Rao Trang River. We were then flown to FSB Rakkasan for a few days. Rakkasan was attacked by rocket-propelled grenades right after we arrived and there were some wounded from Bravo. We were also on FSB Kathryn for a few days before walking off back into the area around Kathryn. The first night after walking off we were in our night defensive position when we could hear the sound of North Vietnamese mortar tubes. The North Vietnamese were firing back into Kathryn. Artillery and air support was called in to take out the mortars but not before Kathryn received a great number of casualties. We continued the same routine of security around the firebase, finding more signs of the enemy with artillery being called in at times for North Vietnamese that were spotted or to destroy enemy positions.

We were sent into Camp Evans the first part of June for a stand-down and also received a new company commander. Captain Bob Harasick would assume command of Bravo Company from Captain Lee Sullivan, whose six months in the field as an officer had been completed. After the three days stand down, we were CA'd back to the same area around the Rao Trang River and Maureen. On one occasion we were CA'd into an area near FSB Ripcord where the 2/506th was in a major battle on and around Ripcord. I remember it was a very weird feeling about that area, I guess because we knew what battles had taken place there. We were only there a few days and CA'd back to Maureen area. We did not have much contact with the enemy until June 25. We had advanced up Maureen and were near an old landing zone taking a break when second platoon engaged some North Vietnamese. A rucksack was found with valuable intelligence information inside that was after picked up by helicopter and taken back to the rear area. We eventually set up a night defensive position with first platoon in the same night defensive position as headquarters platoon. The second platoon set up a short distance away from our night defensive position.

I remember we were on high alert because there were intelligence reports of a great number of North Vietnamese in the area and [it was] likely we could be attacked. Early the morning of June 26 the second platoon was attacked. I could see the large flashes from the explosions and gunfire from second platoon and the North Vietnamese Army. It was obvious it was a major attack. There was also support fire exploding all around as well as illumination rounds. I could hear the screaming and knew it was very bad. We were then ordered to move out in support of second platoon, so we cautiously began moving in their direction, crawling part of the way. When we got close the battle had subsided and we entered the perimeter. There were dead North Vietnamese and second platoon wounded and killed. Some of the men from second platoon that I knew were unrecognizable due to the nature of how they were killed with satchel charges or grenades. We took over positions around the perimeter for security. When it was light enough, we began to help move our dead, or put the North Vietnamese dead into a pile in a defensive position. I remember one North Vietnamese whose head was completely blown off, maybe by a claymore mine, as second platoon was defending their positions. After the wounded and killed were medevac'd, we moved out of the immediate area of the battle and remained in the area of Maureen for a few days. We then began moving down a ridgeline toward the base of the mountain Maureen was located on. This continued on into July.

There were increasing signs of the enemy like graves, bunkers, enemy supplies, and ammunition. We had tracking dogs assigned to our platoon and they began to alert. We knew they were all around us and that it was only a matter of time [until] we would be attacked. On July 3, 1970, Danny Mitchell and I celebrated our birthdays. On July 4, we were hit from behind by rocket-propelled grenades that wounded Collins, Heaton, Henderson, and Brown; all friends of mine. We set up a night defensive position on July 5, and the weather was very poor with a lot of rain. The next morning, July 6, we received a call for support for the rest of the company in another night defensive position who were under attack. It was early that morning and there was no time to eat breakfast. We just grabbed our gear and moved towards the direction of the night defensive position where headquarters platoon, second platoon, and third platoon were all located. Our acting platoon sergeant, Turner, had been sent in a few days before for medical issues. We had a very good staff sergeant in Porter, who led the first platoon out that morning. We were nearing the night defensive position where the attack had occurred and we heard an M16 firing. Porter had been mistaken for a North Vietnamese soldier and was killed instantly by a Bravo trooper on the perimeter of the night defensive position. Sandy Porter was one of the best and a tremendous loss for first platoon and the entirety of Bravo Company.

We proceeded into night defensive positions on the perimeter that had been vacated by the large number of wounded. The medevac arrived and the evacuation of the wounded began. The first lift up in the penetrator was dropped from a good height, further injuring the two men going up. We all thought the helicopter was receiving fire. Finally, the evacuation resumed and evacuated all the wounded. We moved out later that day thinking another attack would be coming very soon and were fortunate we were not hit again over the next few days. We were finally flown out to FSB Bastogne for a few days to receive replacements. I was assigned to truck security that traveled the nearby road, and also was on some six-man ambush teams. The next six weeks is a blur of constantly moving from one firebase to another with a visit to Eagle Beach in between. I was finally approaching my departure date in August and was assigned to a sniper team at Camp Evans the first part of August. I do remember Sammy Daniels was on that three-man team, but can't remember the third member. The men I came to Vietnam with left with me to go home, along with a few other men. Dewey Byerley and Pete Ancona went back with me. We all arrived back at Fort Lewis in Washington State to receive orders for our next assignment.

I arrived home in Jamestown and then was stationed at Fort Riley, Kansas, for six months. I returned home to Jamestown and enrolled in a continuing education curriculum to prepare for a career in the construction industry. I was hired by a major construction company that was involved in the growth in the Knoxville, Tennessee area. I became a construction superintendent responsible for many projects over the years. I was fortunate to work in an industry I enjoyed and [was] able to finish my career and retire there.

CHAPTER 12

Chuck Choney

In Vietnam January 1970–December 1970

> "They were just talking about cars and girls. Next thing you know … we've turned them into killers, turned them into hardened soldiers."

The following is a lightly edited summary of the author's September 2024 oral history interview with Chuck.

I was born and raised in Lawton, Oklahoma. I grew up in a home with both my parents and my two brothers and sister. My dad was a baker. He worked in a bakery all his life, and my mother was a nurse. And then in the later part of her career, she got into administration. As a child, I enjoyed school. I went to public school from grades 1 to 12, and played sports year-round.

My first two years of college, I went to a junior college in my hometown of Lawton. It was called Cameron College. It was a land grant college, therefore all male students had to take ROTC (Reserve Officers' Training Corps). And the latter part of my sophomore year, I started getting interested in a military career. And since it was a junior college, I was going to have to transfer to a four-year school, and I elected to go to Oklahoma State University, which also had an ROTC program. So I applied for and was accepted into the senior ROTC program. Upon graduation, I was commissioned [as] a second lieutenant in the Army. I graduated in January of '69. I knew that if I didn't go into the ROTC, I probably would've been drafted—as were a lot of my friends I went to high school with. They were all drafted. And then I thought, well, if I'm going to be drafted, I might as well stay in this program and come in as an officer rather than as an enlisted man.

All I knew about Vietnam was that it was a war, and it was government policy. And in my household—my mother worked in civil service, as did most of my family—we were all staunch supporters of our government. I didn't have any qualms. I knew I was going to go to Vietnam, so I accepted it early on. When the time came, I flew over. It was a 22-hour charter flight, so the whole flight was nothing but Army guys and a few Air Force people on board, and of course we all knew where we were going, and everyone was pretty calm about it. A lot of laughing, and fun—but the closer we got, I kind of noticed how serious everyone started to get.

When we get off the plane the first thing noticed was the heat and the awful smell. I mean, it was very, very oppressive. Everyone on the plane was loaded onto buses and shipped to the replacement center. There was this big auditorium they took us to. They told us orders for assignment will be coming down. There were a few people in our group who had orders to a specific unit and the captain giving the brief said, "All you people who have specific orders, just throw 'em away because they don't mean nothing. It's the needs of the Army. Wherever the replacements are needed, that's where you'll be going." So they took our whole group, and sent us to all different units all over Vietnam. Because of the way they ran the replacement system, when I got to my unit, I didn't know anybody. And they didn't know me, they didn't know anything about my capabilities. And I didn't know anything about their capabilities. So that was a big disadvantage, but you learn in a hurry.

I was pleased to get assigned to the 101st. By the time I got to Vietnam, there were certain units that I had studied and would have wanted to go to, and the 101st was one [of them]. Of course, we didn't have a choice. We couldn't go up there and say, "Hey, can I have a choice?" Right? But when they posted our orders, and I found my name on the bulletin board, and I saw where I was going, to the 101st, I was very pleased. They issued us all kinds of equipment, and then we went to the airfield and all the people going to northern part of Vietnam loaded up into this plane and they flew us up to Phu Bai. My first impression of the base camp was how big it was. Second impression was how busy the base was when we got there at 2:00 AM. After various trainings and orientations, I got on a helicopter with all my equipment and they flew me out to Bravo Company, and then my company commander Lee Sullivan then introduced me to the platoon I was going to lead.

Some of the guys were Hamburger Hill veterans. They had been out there for a long time, and they'd seen a lot of action. In fact, I had about six guys in my platoon that fought on Hamburger Hill. So actually I got those guys off to the side and introduced myself. I said, "I want you to help me learn." Plus I had a great platoon sergeant, Frank Foronda. But he told me, "I'm going to be here for two more weeks, than I'm transferring to Charlie Company." He said, "You got two weeks to learn." And I told him, "I appreciate that." I said, "I will learn from you." And he was my mentor. Two weeks was up, and he left, and I really hated to see him leave. By then, though, I'd gotten acquainted with a lot of the veterans, who did help. And then I also found out there was quite a few guys that only got there a couple days before I did. So I wasn't the only new kid on the block.

Our job was long patrolling, up in the mountains. We worked in the lowlands. We were up in the mountains of northern I Corps, and it was just patrolling. The 101st's mission at that time was to have a presence up there in those mountains. Because they found that during Tet that's where a lot of the North Vietnamese troops staged when they hit the lowlands and attacked. So we were up there, I think, to have a presence to keep the North Vietnamese out of there. And then we were also on the edge of the A Shau Valley. That's where a lot of North Vietnamese troops were. Patrolling was our main course of action.

I was there for one day when we had our first contact with the enemy. So from then on, it was periodic contact. We'd run into them, or they'd run into us, and there'd be a firefight. But God willing, we didn't suffer any casualties other than that first day. One of my men got shot and I don't remember his name, because I'd just got there. It just happened so fast. It's my first day; we'd just gotten settled in for the night. They woke me up at two in the morning because it was my turn for a radio watch. I had that for thirty minutes and I passed it on to someone else, and I went back to sleep and then got up. As soon as the sun came up, we'd start gathering our stuff. Then we'd start heading down this trail. We went about maybe a hundred meters, and I'm kind of back in the column and I hear gunfire. Of course, everybody went down and a sergeant said that we needed to go up front and see what's going on. So we basically crawled up there, to the front, and the guy who got hit was the point man, and I said, "What happened?" He said he went up this little rise and there was a North Vietnamese soldier just standing there, and they opened up on each other, but the North Vietnamese soldier beat him to the draw, hit him in the leg, and of course he was medevac'd and he never came back. We looked for a blood trail to see if he hit that soldier, but he didn't. And I asked, "Is this the way stuff like this happens?" And they said, "Sure is. We stumble on them or they stumble on us."

The medevac system saved a lot of lives versus the previous wars. More soldiers actually died from shock or infections before. When we were able to get them out of the field, get them to the rear, to our medical aid stations, then to evacuation hospitals to get the treatment they needed, they could survive. All of the people that were in our company that were wounded, all survived, except for one. He passed from massive injuries. But all the others who were medevac'd, all survived. That's because they were able to get out the field as fast as they could to get to proper treatment they needed.

When I got to my platoon, we didn't come out of the field for about ninety days. We'd come back for a stand down and go back out and just stay out there just for forty-five to fifty, sixty, up to ninety days at a time. But we had good equipment and we had a good resupply system, and we were resupplied every four days with food and any other equipment we needed. And I always thought that the supply system and the equipment we had was adequate. The AN/PRC-25, later changed to the PRC-77, those were good radios. They were good pieces of equipment.

I don't want to get into any personalities, but there were some people over there that shouldn't have been in leadership positions, and they didn't do a good job. And as a result of that, it got some men killed and wounded. It was just carelessness, poor leadership, is what it boils down to. But a lot of the soldiers there, the officers and non-commissioned officers, they did well. They handled themselves like soldiers should and as a result of it, kept the casualties down.

The one incident I would like to talk about, it still bothers me to this day, and this is when Captain Sullivan was our commanding officer. He had my platoon go over to help another, because they got into some heavy contact and they were pinned down. They had two guys that were killed. They couldn't get them back because the fire was too heavy. So they had my platoon go over there to augment. So the battalion commander comes on the radio and orders the company commander to recover the men that had been killed. The commanding officer advised the battalion commanding officer he couldn't because it would cost more lives. Well, the battalion commander insisted, and he got two more of his men killed. So he pulled back. Finally the brigade commander got on the radio, told the battalion commander, "Do not send any more troops down there. It's ridiculous!" He said, "I want more artillery put in there before you send anybody in." So after the barrage is over, they brought back those guys who were killed. They had them wrapped up in poncho liners, and they were all crying—because that's their friends that were killed down there. So the scene of those guys bringing those dead bodies back remains with me to this day. Later on that battalion commander was relieved from his command and rightfully so.

Our company had some fine Non-Commissioned Officers (NCOs). We called them shake 'n' bakes, or we called them instant NCOs. These guys were draftees and selected right out of training to go to NCO school and upon completion were made E-5s. If you wanted to get an E-5 regular, it would take you three to five years to make E-5. These guys were making it in 90 days. They were coming over and had no leadership skills. They barely had enough skills to be infantry, much less a leader. But they learned in a hurry. Luckily, they also had a program where spec fours could be made temporary sergeants, and that's who most of my squad leaders were, because they had the experience and they'd been out there; they knew they had leadership skills.

Our patrolling went on until May 1. We came out of the mountains and came to a flat area. We set up a company-size perimeter. This is the first time that the whole company came together with all three platoons. We always acted separately from each other. While we were in this perimeter the battalion commander came in with his operations officer and were conferring with the company commander, Lee Sullivan. And the battalion chaplain came in to talk to the troops, and it was just kind of an administrative type of day. After I got my sector of the perimeter set up I sat down to read my mail. All of a sudden machine-gun fire started raking the area. Everyone was scrambling for cover. I didn't know what was going on. I got on the radio to find out what's going on. Captain Sullivan said, "We're receiving fire from above the second platoon area." He said, "Send one of your squads around to the left to flank them and bring fire on them."

I took one of my squads to flank the attackers. We brought fire on them and they broke off contact. At this same time a Cobra gunship began a rocket run. Unfortunately, his rockets fell a little short and they exploded in the trees right above us. All the shrapnel came raining down on us. It got about four of us from the squad that I was maneuvering with. We were all hit with shrapnel. It was a short firefight and I think we killed several of them. The second platoon had four of their guys killed. I was then medevac'd with the other wounded. I spent almost two months in the hospital in Japan recovering and rehabilitating my right hand.

Since I had injuries to my hand, a little bit of shrapnel in my left shoulder, and on my back, I thought I would be headed back to the States. Usually, if you got as far as Japan, you would be going back to the States. That's what I thought when I first got there especially when they asked me, "Where's the nearest Army hospital from your home of record?" For me, it was right there in my hometown, Lawton, Oklahoma. That's where Fort Sill is located. So they wrote that down and I thought that's where I would be going. But was I for a surprise when I was sent back to Vietnam.

When I got back, we had a new battalion commander, Lieutenant Colonel Porter. I went in and introduced myself and he said, "Oh, yes, I recall seeing your name." And while I was sitting at his desk, in front of his desk, he had this big, large manning board behind him in his office. It was for the officers and NCOs in the battalion. I just looked at him and I thought, there's a lot of open slots for officers, for lieutenants. So he looked at me and said, "What would you like to do?" And knowing in the back of my mind that the normal process is six months in the field, then back to the rear as an assistant staff officer. I said, "Well, sir, I see you got a lot of open slots." I said, "I'd like to go back to the field. If I could go back to Bravo Company and if I could get my old platoon back, the third platoon." He says, "You got it." He was actually smiling because I actually solved the problem he had of officer replacements. He needed to get some experience out there in the field. So there I went. Next thing you know, I'm on a helicopter going back to the third platoon.

A lot of the old hands were still there. They came up welcomed me back and slapped me on the back. Captain Robert Harasick was the new commanding officer, having replaced Lee Sullivan. We continued the same mission of patrolling. I stayed with the platoon until I was hit again on July 6. On this day, we awoke before daylight to begin our daily routine and security procedures by going on alert, looking and listening, and being aware of anything out of the ordinary. Next, we prepared our breakfast and began to pack our rucks for the eventual moveout. The last thing would be to bring in our claymore mines.

At this time, we heard a loud pop which wasn't as loud as a gunshot but more sounded like a firecracker. Everyone went down and grabbed their weapons and began to scan the tree line. I shouted out if anyone knew what that sound was.

At the same instance that I realized the sound was a blasting cap detonating a large, loud explosion went off to my immediate front. At this time, I was standing and Captain Harasick was kneeling to my left. The explosion knocked me on my butt and rattled my cage. I regained my feet and senses and noticed Captain Harasick had a large amount of blood flowing down his face from a severe laceration on his head. I immediately noticed no one was firing their weapons so I began to shout for them to start firing. Captain Harasick began to coordinate with the forward observer (FO) to bring in artillery fire. It was at this time that I realized that my upper lip was lacerated and my front tooth was knocked out. All wounded were extracted by jungle penetrator. This proved problematic in that two soldiers were dropped due to high winds and suffered more serious injuries.

This day turned out to be my last day with Bravo Company. The policy of the 101st was if you're hit twice, you don't go back to the field. I went up to battalion staff at Camp Evans and then to 3rd Brigade S-3 to be a Liaison officer with the 1st ARVN Division's 1st Brigade at Camp Nancy.

When I got home, I went back to the 82nd Airborne Division and stayed there for two years. I then transferred to the 7th Special Forces Group. I stayed there until December of '74 when I came on orders to the infantry officers advanced course at Fort Benning. That's a nine-month course. After that I received orders for Germany and that's where I finished up my career and decided to leave the Army. I then spent the next 26 years as a special agent with the FBI.

I saw a lot of futility in Vietnam, that we were not able to do more. I felt like we should have just packed up and gone home sooner if they were not going to let us do what we needed to do to win. And eventually that's what they did. I regret what we did to these young soldiers. A lot of them got drafted, trained, then right over to Vietnam. One day they were talking about cars and girls. Next thing you know ... we've turned them into killers and hardened soldiers. We had to do that for them to survive. But I counter that by saying that when they came back from Vietnam, they resumed their lives. They went back, got their education, got married, raised children, now grandchildren, and they are retired now. They all did well with their lives—in education, law enforcement, business, the fire brigade, farming, and construction. These guys did well for themselves, and that's what I'm very pleased about.

Today, I am enjoying my retirement, travelling, spending time with my family, and reading. One thing I really enjoy is getting together with the Currahee guys anytime we can get together.

CHAPTER 13

R. L. Farris

In Vietnam August 1969–August 1970

"Welcome to Vietnam."

For his participation in the book, Mr. Farris chose to share an essay about his arrival to Vietnam. He went from dorm to battlefield in the blink of an eye.

I stirred awake from a light slumber and looked at my Bulova watch. The cabin lights were dim, but I could make out that the hands were both straight up in the air. I rubbed my tired eyes. September 1, 1969, was only a few seconds old and yet, I already knew I would remember this day for the rest of my life.

I looked around the cabin of the Boeing 707 and saw most guys were not sleeping. They were probably as excited as I was. It wasn't really excitement as much as it was anticipation; the anticipation of finally arriving at a place that I had heard about every day of my life for the last five years. It was a place that was provocative and hated by many. This was my chance to see it for myself. I was only a couple of hours away.

During the next two hours my thoughts wandered elsewhere as they do during the boredom of a long airplane flight. You think about the past. You think about the future. The present seems stagnant even though you're hurtling above the earth in excess of five hundred miles per hour. My thoughts turned to my parents. The day that just ended was their 23rd wedding anniversary. Next, I thought about my two young cousins, Terry and Bob. Then, I even recollected the two crazy guys that lived next door to me in the dorm last year. They were probably preparing to go back to school within a week or two. I wondered what time it was back in Indiana. My mind was too muddled to do the math at that moment. I pondered what the next year would be like. Suddenly, the cabin lights snapped on and the pilot informed us we would be landing in about twenty minutes. The Bulova told me it was 2:10 AM or 0210 hours military time. I still had to convert from civilian time in my head.

A few minutes later the 707's wheels touched down and we braked at the end of the runway. The large jet turned and stopped. The front cabin door was opened. After a couple of minutes, a soldier wearing E-5 sergeant stripes entered the airplane cabin. He grabbed the PA system microphone and spoke, "My name is Sergeant Henley.

We are at the end of the runway in Bien Hoa. We are going to taxi to the main terminal. If, while we taxi, the Viet Cong decides to send a rocket our way, the airplane will stop and we evacuate. There are sandbag bunkers along either side of the runway. Get into one of those and wait it out. Any questions?"

Silence. No one raised a hand. If someone had made that statement to me six months earlier, when I was a civilian, I would probably have crapped my pants. Now, after five months of basic training and infantry school, it was just part of the experience. The airplane rolled to a stop on the tarmac. Apparently, the Viet Cong didn't care about us that night. They had plans for us later in other places. So far, so good.

We stood and quietly shuffled forward toward the exit. A standard airport stair was rolled into position at the forward door and guys were slowly moving out. I checked my Bulova; it was 2:30 AM. The soldiers ahead of me were slowly navigating down the steps and being led into the darkness by Sergeant Henley. I exited the door and stood at the top of the stairs. That moment the air-conditioned cocoon of the airplane cabin evaporated and a stifling heat and humidity slammed into my face. It even smelled musty, like air trapped in the basement of an old house that hadn't been opened in eighty years. My only thought at that moment was, *If it's like this at two thirty in the morning, what the hell is it going to feel like at two thirty this afternoon?* Later that day I found out.

The group walked single file toward what looked to be a terminal building. As we walked along the tarmac in the dark, I was able to make out bundles of freight on skids and wooden boxes randomly placed in cargo nets along our path. My eyes darted behind each bale of material, half expecting to see a small man in shorts and a cone-shaped straw hat stand up and point a rifle at me. *That's silly,* I thought. *We are in the middle of a protected airbase.* However, in the darkness I couldn't completely shake the feeling. In the distance, I saw a wooden structure with a roof and no sides. It was like a picnic shelter you'd see in the park. There were five or six dimly glowing light bulbs, each hanging on a single cord from the shelter ceiling. Packed under that roof was what looked to be about a hundred and fifty men.

As we approached to within twenty-five yards of the shelter, our faces became illuminated by the glow of the dim lights. To a man, all of the shelter inhabitants broke into wild cheering. I thought it odd the Army would turn out a bunch of guys in the middle of the night to welcome us peons. The closer we got; the cheering became louder. Sergeant Henley explained that the guys under the roof were waiting to board the airplane we came in and go home. It became the Freedom Bird for them. We were the replacements. I wondered if I would be lucky enough to be standing under that shelter on August 31, 1970. Only time would tell.

We entered the dimly lit terminal building. We were directed to assemble in ranks in front of a wooden platform. We separated into a block fifteen men wide, ten deep, and became quiet. An E-6 sergeant climbed four wooden steps to the podium and turned to face us. He then uttered those three little words. No, not "I love you." They were, "Welcome to Vietnam." I glanced down. The Bulova said it was 0300 hours. I had arrived.

At that moment, the Bulova's hands became time counters on a stopwatch starting at zero/zero. They began counting down my year in Vietnam. The circulating horror stories at home and opposing viewpoints about the war were all rolling around in the back of my mind. My personal beliefs about Vietnam would start being tempered by my own real-time experiences and, sometimes, painful observations. Indeed, welcome to the real Vietnam.

CHAPTER 14

William Shue

In Vietnam September 1969–August 1970

"Metal has come out over the years from the wounds, and I still have a piece in my finger."

Battlin' Bastard Danny McNair took the initiative to interview several veterans who, quite understandably, were more comfortable speaking with a fellow veteran than an author who is not. What follows is William's story as told to Danny for the express purpose of this book, lightly edited by the author.

I was living in Norwood, North Carolina, and working as a brick mason and carpenter before I was inducted into the Army in 1969. I attended basic training at Fort Bragg, North Carolina, and advanced infantry training at Fort McClellan, Alabama. I was married at the time and my wife went with me to the airport when I left for Vietnam. My flight was from Charlotte, North Carolina, to Oakland, California, for final processing to Vietnam. I landed in Cam Rahn Bay, Vietnam, and was assigned to the 101st Airborne. There were some delays, but I finally attended Screaming Eagle Replacement Training. This was the training to prepare us to operate as combat troops from helicopters. It included rappelling, combat assaults from helicopters, patrolling, and anything else required to become acclimated to operating as a combat soldier in the 101st.

I was issued an M16, equipment, and supplies, and then flown out to Bravo Company in the field. My initial time in the field was spent becoming familiar with the men in my platoon and learning how to operate as a member of a squad. I was more comfortable staying up at night and sleeping during the day to remain alert to possible attack. The first few months in the field we were assigned to six-man teams and also security for engineers working on the Rakkasan Road, which was being built from FSB Rakkasan to Camp Evans. Most of my time was on a six-man team that had a very large area of operation from the north near the DMZ back south to most of the firebases in our area, and as far west as the A Shau Valley near the countries bordering South Vietnam. We were responsible for blowing landing zones. We would pick up our assignments to blow a landing zone for many reasons. The landing zone could be to take out wounded and sick, bring in supplies, or for a combat assault.

On February 1, our six-man team was blowing a landing zone when we heard a helicopter hit by an explosion, and then saw the smoke after it was downed. That particular day we linked up with the rest of the third platoon. The main body of the third platoon was then directed down a hill and we followed in behind them. There was contact ahead of us and we heard by radio about those killed and wounded. Our six-man team had been divided up that day, and Louis Moretti, who was on my team, was wounded. A Cobra was called in and began heavy firing directly behind us over our heads in support. I believe we may have had another wounded by the Cobra, but I am not certain, because the support fire was so close. A medevac picked up the dead and the wounded and we were directed back up the hill to the landing zone we had been blowing. Wannie Cook was walking directly in front of me when there was an explosion from a booby trap and I was blown backwards. I immediately jumped up and went to him. He had both legs blown off, and was black from the explosion. The explosion had evidently cauterized his legs because there was not much blood. He was still in control of his thoughts and his first question was, "I didn't lose any of my family jewels, did I?" I answered and assured him that he still had them. Guy Pleickhardt was with me and we immediately took off our belts and put one on each of his legs as tourniquets. I think it was Doc Riggs who then came up and gave Cook a shot of morphine. I had doubts he would make it due to the severity of his wounds. We proceeded to the landing zone where I began probing the landing zone, checking for more booby traps. Guy and I then stayed with Cook until we put him on the medevac.

I then had some time to go sit down and gather my thoughts about what had happened. When I tried to sit down, I felt numbness in my right leg. Doc came over and asked if I had been hurt. I told him I didn't know and then noticed blood from shrapnel wounds on my hands. Doc checked my legs which were also bleeding from the shrapnel. Captain Sullivan flew out to our position after that and told us that he was sending another platoon to help third platoon. I did not go back to the rear for my wounds at that time, but went back later with my platoon to Camp Evans. I was sent to Phu Bai for X-rays and to be checked out. I was on crutches for a few days. Metal has come out over the years from the wounds, and I still have a piece in my finger.

In March, we continued to remain in the field with more combat assaults and sightings of the North Vietnamese. I remember the day we lost Cecil Dobson, who suffocated in a cave. It was a very sad day for our third platoon. We were sent to Camp Evans that month for a stand-down. I remember the attack on FSB Granite and the large number of casualties they had. Third platoon was sent out to reinforce. I can't remember exactly when I was sent to the rear permanently. I did not have much time left in-country and was promoted to supply sergeant, working on the helicopter pad. While I was supply sergeant, I scrounged everything I could to send back to the field for the men. I knew how important it was to get out dry clothing, hot food, or anything else I could find.

I received a 10-day drop for my DEROS [return home date] and went home the end of August 1970. I returned to my hometown of Norwood and began the same work building homes. The brick mason and carpentry work continued to progress until I finally went to school and obtained my contract license. I have continued this work for about fifty-three years, building very large homes on the lake. I have brought my son into the business, to carry it on and we work together to this day.

CHAPTER 15

Lou Bowen

In Vietnam October 1969–May 1970

"I became closer to those men than anyone I had known … anywhere else."

This is Lou's story as told to Danny McNair for the express purpose of this book, lightly edited by the author.

I was living in Wickett, Texas, which is in western Texas, when I was drafted into the Army in 1969. I worked in the oil fields at that time. I received my basic training at Fort Bliss in Texas and advanced individual training at Fort Ord in California. I married my fiancée before I reported to Oakland, California, for my deployment to Vietnam. I reported to Oakland in my full-dress uniform, which was collected when I arrived and mailed to my wife—she received my dress hat in the mail sometime later.

I arrived in Vietnam the last part of October 1969 and was quickly processed to the 101st Airborne at Camp Evans. I picked up my equipment, which included my M16, rucksack, canteens, canteen cup, poncho, poncho liner, helmet with liner, entrenching tool, insect repellent, body armor, some basic medical supplies, spare socks and clothing, and a protective mask. I would also pick up an ammo box for my personal items such as toilet tissue, writing materials, and personal hygiene items. We would receive M16 ammunition with bandoliers for carrying the ammo magazines, fragmentation grenades, smoke grenades, claymore mines with detonators, wire and caps, C-4 explosives, an M72 LAW [antitank weapon] and 100 rounds of M60 ammunition. Ammunition was issued at different locations depending on the circumstances. There were times we were not permitted to carry ammunition on the helicopters. I also carried a knife with me, that I brought with me from home. We were issued a case of C-rations which was to last for four to six days depending on resupply. We also received a P-38 can opener for opening the C-ration cans, and I carried a spoon in my top pocket for convenience.

I was flown out to the field with another replacement by helicopter, which was an experience I will not forget. The chopper was loaded with sheets of steel matting, which was used for making helicopter landing pads. The steel was not secured to the helicopter floor, and we had to load up right on top of it for the trip out to our company. The steel was sliding all over the helicopter and we were moving with it, holding on the best we could. Each time the helicopter banked the steel moved and so did we. This was not a good beginning as we did not think we would even make it out to join Bravo in the field.

We finally landed at FSB Rakkasan and were assigned to second platoon on six-man teams. We spent the next few months working on ambush teams and also blowing landing zones. We were picked up by helicopter when we were to blow landing zones, carrying C-4, detonation cord, detonators, and sometimes dynamite. The C-4 cases and dynamite were kicked off and depending on the circumstances we would jump from the choppers (depending on how far off the ground the helicopter was hovering).

The weather was cool and wet much of the time. FSB Jack was close to Camp Evans and we spent Christmas 1970 at Jack. We were also up around Rocket Ridge, where rockets were sometimes fired by the North Vietnamese at Camp Evans. There was not any action during that time I can remember. I began to learn how to operate with the rest of my squad, and remember being with Harry Ebaugh and Sergeant Bruce Keplar (who were on the six-man teams with me). We began to move deeper into the higher mountains away from Rocket Ridge. The company began to come into more contact with the enemy. First and third platoons would make contact with the enemy with some major casualties during this time. We did locate graves, enemy supplies, and bunkers with second platoon. The longer we remained in that area the greater the number of enemy graves and supplies we found. Second platoon would also come into some minor contact with the North Vietnamese. I do not remember many of the specific details of these actions. There was some artillery support from nearby firebases, Cobra gunship support, and strikes by B-52s, but I do not remember the specific times or locations.

We had been in the field for a long time and were finally sent to Camp Evans for stand-down in March. The day we were sent to Camp Evans for the stand-down, FSB Granite was attacked by sappers and had a great number of casualties. I was picked up by a quickly assembled reactionary force and sent to FSB Granite that same night. I guess I was in the right place when they came by looking for men to send out to reinforce Granite. The rest of second platoon did not arrive until the next day, on March 20, 1970.

When the helicopter brought me in that night, I was directed to a position out on a point in the perimeter for security. When I got to the assigned position, we had to drag two dead North Vietnamese out of the position. There were killed and wounded all over the firebase. We did not have any contact that night. Second platoon arrived the next morning and we were sent out on patrol around FSB Granite looking for North Vietnamese. We found campsites and bunkers with supplies such as rice, equipment, and satchel charges. We found a cave that had been used to discard old uniforms and put on new ones. It was also used as a barber shop before the attack on Granite. We did not make any contact while around Granite after it had been attacked on March 19.

By this time, I was beginning to assume walking the slack position behind a guy named Boyd Magee from Louisiana. His nickname was "Lightning" because he moved very quickly. Boyd continued walking in that point position while I was there. We had been patrolling all around the same general area of the Rao Trang River near FSB Maureen. My squad leader was Donnie Brewer, who was from Mississippi. Nathanial Griffin was our M60 machine gunner. We were in that same general area until April 25, 1970, when we were combat assaulted to the old Firebase Maureen.

The first helicopters that day came in on a hot landing zone. Sometime after we landed, my squad moved off the old firebase down the mountain to the bottom and began back up a small rise when we spotted a North Vietnamese soldier and a bunker complex. There was contact and we were ordered back up the hill in the direction we came from. Artillery fire support was called in on the bunkers with 155s. The rounds were mostly hitting the top of the trees and exploding before reaching the ground. When the artillery ceased firing, we were ordered back down the same way with Boyd at point, me at slack, Griffin carrying the M60, and his assistant gunner behind me.

When we reached the bottom a machine gun opened up on us, hitting Magee immediately. A call for a medic went out and Robertson moved forward to attend to Magee. I was firing from behind a small tree over Magee and Robertson at the direction of the enemy fire. A sniper started firing from a tree and hit Robertson two times. I could see the sniper in a tree who was well concealed. I began firing at him, but could not hit him. Robertson could not save Magee and got up to move back. He was shot two more times in the legs. I was also hit by the same sniper in the groin.

We were pinned down, but Griffin tried to help me and was shot in the back by a machine gun. (I would find out later that Robertson was shot four times and Griffin nine times that day.) I put my thumb into the wound in my groin to stop the bleeding, but did not know until later that the shot had sliced across my penis and blew a hole out my buttocks as it exited. It was most likely a ricochet from the sniper round. The sniper was finally killed, but we continued to be pinned down for a long time because every time someone moved, they were hit.

I knew it was getting very late in the day. Finally getting close to dark, the last bunker was taken out by Sergeant First Class Jesse Isaac (who received the Distinguished Service Cross for his brave actions that day). I was picked up and carried back up the hill. I had no feeling from my groin down the right leg. I was given morphine and was told about the other wounds. I asked if I still had "everything intact." I was assured everything was ok. I was fortunate that the bullet had missed any bones or major blood vessels, but it did hit a major nerve. I knew we could not be medevac'd out that night. The bottom of my right foot felt like a bee sting and I requested my foot be massaged. Someone took off my boot and did massage my foot.

Sometime the next morning I was moved to a landing zone to be helicoptered out. The chopper came in and lowered a basket. Mike Bookser, who had also been wounded, was put in the basket first, and me next, with both of us lying in opposite directions facing each other's feet. Mike put his arms around me holding both of us in the basket. The basket was lifted and going up through the canopy when I think it brushed a tree and the litter went from horizontal to vertical. Bookser was then face up and I was face down with the basket trailing out behind the chopper.

We were both taken to the Quang Tri Surgical Hospital, not far from Camp Evans. When we arrived, I was to be taken to surgery and was told the knife my wife gave me could not be taken any further because I was going into surgery. I gave the knife to Bookser and it had a bullet in the handle. I had been wearing it also on my right side and it probably saved me further wounds that day. I was taken into the operating room and my boots were cut off. I was not happy with that because my dog tags were in the laces and my boots were also a special size that were hard to find. I never saw those dog tags again. I was given a shot of morphine and they were about to cover me with a sheet when I told them no, I wanted to watch what they were doing. My head was propped up so I could observe. They took care of the front side and then flipped me over and knocked me out completely. The procedure had been to clean up the wounds and leave them open for debriding. The wounds were covered by several layers of gauze. Each day all of the layers of gauze, with the exception of the ones next to the wounds, were removed and replaced with new gauze. I was flown to Japan after about one week.

When I arrived in Japan, I did not see a doctor for about three days. Dressings continued to be changed daily with the exception of the ones next to the wounds. A high-ranking doctor, who I think was a colonel, and a head nurse, who was a captain, came in to see me. The doctor began removing the outer layer of dressings from the first wound. The doctor then ripped the dressing off that was next to the wound. I immediately reacted and came around with a fist that knocked the doctor to the floor. I did not expect him to pull the dressing off, nor did he expect me to react either.

The head nurse began to chew me out, threatening disciplinary action against me. The doctor then took charge and told the head nurse to back off because he should have informed me before yanking off the last dressing next to the wound. The doctor was also not pleased that the dressings next to the wounds had not been changed daily. The next dressing was done by first soaking the one next to the wound. The wound in the groin was closed with seven stitches made of stainless-steel wire and twisted together at the end. The wound in the buttocks required seven stitches as well as the penis, which was also seven stitches, all stainless steel. I remained in Japan for two to three weeks before I was put on a gurney to be flown back to the States with other wounded. Nurses were on the flight to care for us [as we flew] back to the United States.

We landed in Anchorage, Alaska, first, and the nurses were replaced by a new crew. There was one nurse in particular who was rather buxom, who was giving back massages. When she gave me a back massage the stiches in one of my wounds broke out due to the swelling from the excitement! We were flown to a hospital in St. Louis, Missouri. I was placed in a bed and given more morphine that was being used to take care of my pain. I was in St. Louis one night before we were flown to the William Beaumont Hospital at Fort Bliss in Texas. I had written my wife from Quang Tri and the Red Cross had also contacted my family, but there was not a definite schedule of when I would be back home. They were finally informed that I would be sent to Fort Bliss and when I arrived my wife, my sister, my mother, and my brother-in-law were all there to meet me.

This was already a long journey. I was wounded April 25, 1970, and this was now the first part of June 1970, but my journey was far from over. I was wheeled in on a gurney and placed in an older hospital building. The building had 24 beds in its main part. Screened porches on either end of the building had six more beds each. I was placed on one of the porches. The building housed some of the most severely wounded Americans from Vietnam. My porch included a Special Forces medic named Sam, who I will mention again later. Sam had lost a foot and part of his leg. There were other amputees, with one in particular who had lost three limbs. There were other types of cases, such as one that had been bitten by one of the poisonous spiders in Vietnam. The bite had caused all of the flesh in one arm to die, leaving a large hole all the way to the bone.

Two days after arriving I was placed on crutches, but informed I could not go home on leave until the stitches were removed. I was with my wife and family at the hospital, using my crutches for the first time, when I fell down some stairs. My brother-in-law caught my head, saving me from some possible serious injury. That crisis averted, it was soon time to remove my stitches. A male nurse removed the stitches from my buttocks by cutting the stainless steel and pulling them out fairly easy. The nurse attempted to remove the stitches from my groin, but they were buried in the crease of the skin, making them impossible to remove. I talked to the doctor because I just wanted to go home. He agreed that if I was feeling ok, I could go home for a few days' leave.

It was a six- or seven-hour drive home to Pyote, Texas, and all of the family came to visit. I woke up about 3:00 AM that morning, and there was a large spot of blood on the bed. We drove back to the hospital on Sunday and met with the doctor on Monday morning. The doctor was able to remove the stitches in the groin, but told me something was going on inside the wound area, which might be blood clots or internal bleeding. The front and back had already healed outside on both sides, but the outside edge was extremely swollen.

The next thing I knew he used three fingers and quickly pushed them into the groin wound, ripping the wound back open. He told me when I fell on my crutches, I had broken the wound back open on the inside and it could not heal without being reopened for debriding. He said the way he opened it back open was the easiest way to handle it. He then instructed me on what to do next to heal the wounds from the inside out. He gave me a jar of Betadine with ten yards of gauze soaked inside. I was to begin by pushing the gauze down into the wound from the groin side all the way to the bottom that was the buttocks area. I used a long swab to pack the gauze on the bottom slightly and more firmly as I moved back up toward the top of the wound each day. The next day I would grab the end of the gauze and pull out all ten yards and repeat the procedure. This procedure would prevent infections and help with the long healing process.

I would remain at William Beaumont Hospital until June 1971, but would receive leave until I was finally sent home permanently. I became good friends with that doctor and the other patients in my building. There were never enough doctors and nurses to take care of everyone at all times. We had nurses assigned to the building and a doctor would make rounds each week with a candy striper. There was more than one candy striper who passed out watching me pull out the ten yards of gauze from my wound over that year.

I could not have made it without the other patients in that building. Sam, who was the Special Forces medic with only one foot, took care of many of us. He would hop around on one foot attending to what was needed at any particular time—even if all you needed was someone you could talk to about Vietnam who understood. We had all been severely wounded physically, but, in that hospital, also had a very unique and positive experience as we helped each other heal emotionally. I became closer to those men than anyone I had known in Vietnam or anywhere else. We helped each other make it through a very long ordeal that may not have happened without supporting one another.

We understood each other because we had all been through the severe wounding experiences in Vietnam. We were now going through the physical, mental, and emotional experiences of recovery together that no one else could ever understand. We were able to adapt and make the adjustments in our lives from those bad circumstances that allowed us to heal and overcome. When I was able to go home on weekends, I occasionally took men home with me as guests. I remained in touch with some of the men over the years.

I was finally released from the military and returned home. I was not able to pursue working for another year. I was fitted with a spring-loaded brace from my shoe to my ankle to assist in walking for the next 18 years. I initially went back to my job in the oil fields. I later attended a school to learn welding/HVAC [heating, ventilation, and air-conditioning] and was able to have a successful career working in many states and Canada for the next 40 years.

CHAPTER 16

Ed McCrystal

In Vietnam October 1969–October 1970

The following is a summary, lightly edited by the author, of Ed's September 2023 interview with George Bogdanich, conducted at a Battlin' Bastards reunion for use in both this book and a documentary film project.

Back in 1968, I was working for an HVAC contractor. Then I got drafted and went into the Army. I did my basic at Fort Gordon and my advanced individual training at Fort Jackson. And then I qualified for officer candidate school. So I went into the OCS program and then graduated back in early '69 and went to jump school, then got assigned to the 82nd Airborne. I spent about six months there. Then, in October, I got orders to go to jungle school down in Panama. Gave us five days, six days to get to California. So I went back home for the three days and then flew back out to California, and then got shipped over to Vietnam. And then I got assigned to the 101st at Camp Evans.

I was a second lieutenant, but a brand-new cherry when I got there. I was in second platoon, but we worked mostly in smaller teams. Either we were out in 12-man landing zone clearing teams, where—you would go out, they would drop you off and tell you "When I can land, I'll pick you up." So you had to build a landing zone, so he could land. Or you might be in three-man sniper teams, which was a joke for the most part because—I mean, it was, like, they'd pick three men out of the platoon and say, "Here's a radio," and drop you off in a location. No one knew—or, very few people knew, how to read maps and work the radio. I was the only one who had the radio telephone operator and a sniper with me. Everyone else just had a regular M16. For the most part, Gary Horner was my radio telephone operator. So yeah, most of the time we worked in small groups. Even if we had a platoon that was only twenty or thirty people, that was it.

I had a company commander called Miller. He was gone, then Lee Sullivan came in. My tour was initially pretty quiet. We walked in the jungle and never saw much. Then came FSB Maureen. We came in—my platoon and my helicopter, we were the first one landing. There we were—that was on April 25, 1970. So we landed there with no problems, started to walk off. I think the third platoon got waved off because it was a hot landing zone at that time then. But we were there. So we started walking off the top of Maureen, and it's strange that you normally don't get artillery talking to you. Me, as lieutenant, normally, I'm talking to the captain. So I had him on my phone, my radio, giving him directions in there. So we started out with artillery, about a thousand yards out, a thousand meters out. And as we walked, we brought the artillery in close to us, and then we were probably a hundred meters in, one hundred and fifty meters in when we were attacked by people in the bunker.

And I had just called in the artillery. And then when the shooting started, I called for more. So when it came out, it was almost on top of us at that time. Everyone shook. It was a scary thing, but we spent a good portion of the day in contact with them. It was weird. When we were walking—you have a point man, a slack guy, one or two others. And then me and my radio telephone operator, I had just passed—I just stepped into a tree line and my radio telephone operator was killed, and the people in front of me were killed. It was a shock. So I spent, unfortunately, most of the time stuck between the tree because the way it was lined up is, the people in the bunker can shoot directly into those lines, and the only thing saving me was the tree in front of me. So we spent a long time there, tried to get the rest of the platoon to move up, but they couldn't. Then Isaacson came down from the other side of the tree, a trail, and came down and was able to eliminate those people there. So that freed us up. Now my memory of the thing is two, three hours. I lost a lot of time. Everyone says it was most of the day. We lost about four or five people on that day, and a few more wounded. It was an eye-opener for us.

Then we went back the next day to survey the situation. Didn't find anything. And at that time too, we were low on ammo and food, and so we had walked off—this is April 26 [1970]. We walked a little farther down, into May. And May 1, we had to resupply, and again, we were hit again, and that's when we lost some more people. Again, I lost a radio telephone operator. During my tour, I lost three radio telephone operators. At one point, I was behind a big boulder, and there's an enemy behind the other side of the boulder, and we were, I guess throwing things around and trying to call in the artillery from the birds. And he kept on saying, he can't see anything. He can't see anything. Someone threw a frag and the black smoke. He said, "Oh, I can see that!" I said, "Okay, that's where you shoot." And so he did that. That was another day we lost a handful of people. A lot of people were wounded, too, because [of] the way it was structured—and not only my platoon lost people and had wounded, but the third platoon had some casualties. Their lieutenant was hit, Chuck Coney, and I was hit. So we all medevac'd out. And Captain Sullivan had no officers left in the company there. Sullivan was a good guy. You didn't really spend much time with him, though. Even if you're in a company situation, you may go in for a quick meeting, but you have to always go back to your platoon to make sure that they're all squared away. But he was a good officer, kept us safe for most of the time, and we miss him.

So we'd gone from six or seven months of walking, stopping, walking, stopping, walking, stopping—with no one shooting at you—to people shooting at you, people dying. No one really knew about maps.... I usually knew where we were, but even sometimes even I didn't know where we were. We would be on a hill like, "Okay, I know where I am now." They'd pick us up and drop us off, two, three clicks away, but never tell us where we are. And so you have to call in artillery to find it. Find out where you were. When we got into it at FSB Maureen, I think it was just—there was a whole big North Vietnamese Army group down below the other side of it, and leadership just had us trying to get in there.

At one point I was in the hospital for 10 days, then came back. I had shrapnel, in my leg and my arm. Then I came back and rejoined the company sometime later on, when the company was hit *again* near Maureen. I came back, took over the company—became company commander for a short period of time, as a lieutenant. But now it's first lieutenant. I was only acting for two weeks, three weeks. Our numbers were really down. Normally we'd have three platoons, but we didn't have—the company may have been forty men at that point. So we were divided by two.... And then soon enough, my time was up.

I've struggled with both post-traumatic stress disorder and the impacts of Agent Orange. But for the most part, it was—I don't want to say enjoyable, but it was—nothing happened. Because it was late in the war. It was just a year out of my life, except for me, it's really just two days, April 25 and May 1. Everything else just happened, just passed by. And when I came home, I got back my old job and then just kept on moving ahead, and now I'm basically retired and enjoying life.

CHAPTER 17

Leon Heaton

In Vietnam October 1969–October 1970

> "You go back to Vietnam almost every night. But you don't stay as long—you know what I mean?"

The following is a lightly edited summary of the author's January 2024 oral history interview with Leon.

I was born August 22, 1949, in Charleston, Missouri. I grew up with my mom, dad, two sisters, and a brother. My dad worked for a trucking company, and my mom was a homemaker.

My dad served in World War II. He brought my mother home with him. She was from Scotland. They met in England, and they got married over there, and she came over on the *Queen Mary*. But he never talked about his service.

I didn't really like school, growing up, but I wasn't like the other guys that would, you know, get left back because they didn't pass. I was a pretty good student. I'd say I got As and Bs. I played baseball, football.... but college was never really on my radar. I didn't care about school that much. When I got back, I did use the GI Bill, and I went to college. But right after high school, I got married; a year later we had a son. And that didn't last too long. We got divorced and I got drafted. I didn't even know where Vietnam was at. If I hadn't gotten separated from my wife, I would have never got drafted. But, it is what it is. I couldn't live with her, but once I get the Vietnam, I wish[ed] that I'd put up with her butt.

Once you got drafted, you didn't have very long. I was working as a machinist. I got home one day and mom said, "There's a paper on the table for you." And I opened it up and it said, "Greetings, you are hereby ordered...." First I went to the federal building downtown, in Cleveland. And then they sent me to Fort Campbell, Kentucky, for training. Basic was pretty rough, but not as rough as advanced individual training. For that, they sent me to Fort Polk, Louisiana. It was called Tiger Land, and as you take the bus in, it says, "Welcome to the birthplace of the fighting man for Vietnam," so we knew where we were going. And it was hot there, as it was in Vietnam, which was a good thing. I had my training there June, July, and August.

We did firing ranges, and I fired expert on M14 rifle. They said anybody who could fire an expert would get a three-day pass. Well, I never did see that three-day pass. Still waiting on it! While in training, I could call my mother once a week. After training, we had 30 days' leave. I wish they had sent me straight over there.

When the time came, I boarded my flight to Vietnam. We stopped, I think, twice to refuel, but we couldn't get off the plane. We, you know, had to stay on the plane the whole time. You kind of lose sense of time, until everybody looked out and said, "Well, we must be close," because they had two jet fighters on each side of us. And we went into Long Binh outside of Saigon. We stepped off the plane and they boarded us on a bus to take us to our training facility, and I just couldn't believe how people lived. You know, Americans were complaining about, this and that but, in Vietnam—they ain't got nothing. The Vietnamese ain't got nothing. I mean, they sleep on the ground. They got grass hooches. Their bathroom was the rice paddies. That's why most Vietnam vets don't eat rice.

But anyway—I reported to the 101st for in-processing, right outside of Saigon. You learned how to walk, like you were in the jungle; and they taught you how to ambush and recon. We did it with BB guns at first. I do feel I had very good training; I had excellent sergeants. I had excellent officers. I was as prepared as I could be for the circumstances we were thrust into, most definitely. I did observe other squads with leaders that maybe were not so good, but I had good leaders who knew what they were doing, and they always told you what was going on, and where we were going, and how long we were going to be there—although how long we were going to be there was never right. One time, we were out on a six-man patrol. We're supposed to be out there for a week, we ended up 30 days. We got socked in, which means the helicopters couldn't fly. So we actually walked out of the mountains to the lowlands.

Altogether, I went on 37 combat assaults, jumping out of helicopters. Sometimes we were on search-and-destroy missions. Sometimes we were recon. Usually, if you went with six men, it was recon, because you didn't want to.... You don't want to engage with the enemy with only six guys. Of course, we did have good air support, and we had the choppers or the Cobra. You always had good air support. In general, we were always well equipped, well supplied. At first, you didn't know—well you know what, I *still* don't know why we were there. Still don't. I have my *thoughts* about why we were there. It wasn't about the Vietnamese people, and it wasn't about communists. But for us in the field, we're just fighting to stay alive and protect our brothers. I mean, when you're out there with the company, and platoon, you get to know your brothers real well, and I still keep in contact with a bunch of them. We have a reunion every year.

Our lifeline in the field was the "prick 25," AN/PRC-25 radio. We had a radio man, radio carrier, and as long as you had your good batteries—we carried extra batteries.... And, by the way, the radio man is the only one that didn't have to carry gun ammo. And we would all have our poncho, not our poncho, but our jackets around us so you couldn't tell who was carrying the radio. Because the Vietnamese, that's the first one—the radio man is the first one they wanted to take out. On patrols, you had the point man, the slack man, and then your—whether it be a sergeant or lieutenant or captain, whatever he was—and then the radio man behind him. But like I said, everybody had their jacket around their rucksack so the Vietnamese didn't know who had the radio.

Your first 30 days in-country, you're scared because you don't know what's going on. And then 10 months in between there, you don't care, you just—you don't care. You have no feelings. Especially after you're in that first firefight, that changes you. The whole year I was there we lost 30 to 34 guys, and 67 were wounded, I think? That's out of 125 guys. But we all had it in our head, you know, "It don't mean nothing." And we would drive on. We'd make sure the wounded or the dead were properly taken care of, and then we would—like I said, "It don't mean nothing," and you drive on. You got—you got used to it, I guess. Nobody cried. Nobody shed a tear. Nobody. The whole time I was over there, I never saw it. I don't know if they did ... if they went off and did it away from us, but nobody in my company cried.

Though I joined Bravo Company after Hamburger Hill, I heard about it. And the ones that went through it, you kind of followed in their footsteps, and you watched them. And then you became seasoned yourself. And when it came almost time for you to go home, you just started counting down your days. Seven days before I was supposed to come home, I was still out in the jungle, and I was terrified until I got on that plane. And you got on that plane. You got airborne. Oh, man, what a good feeling, until you got home.

I had been wounded on July 4. I just got back from R&R in Hawaii. I got back on July 3, and we got mortared on July 4, first thing in the morning. And first squad was picked to go down and take the mortar pit out, and so we did. And then we were ordered go down and find them on the trail, but it, like I said, it was when I got wounded. It was 4:24 PM. So we knew we shouldn't have gone down there. That's why I said—the officers always talked to us. They told us what was going on. Everybody said, "You know it's kind of late to go down the hill. Gonna be dark here soon." But we said, "We've been ordered to go down, so we go. Well, let's go." And then once we got down there, we had almost walked right into a U-shaped ambush.

When they got a man in the front and a guy in the back that closes the door on you wherever you're at, you ain't getting out. I was the last man on the trail, and I spotted the enemy coming in. I fired his butt up, and I didn't see his buddy, but his buddy shot a rocket-propelled grenade. And the only thing that saved me was a tree. It hit the tree instead of me. But it blew me probably thirty yards down the hill. I was the fourth man—four of us got wounded that day. Three of us were medevac'd on a helicopter, that took us back to our base camp, Camp Evans. After that I don't remember too much. I know I didn't go back to my unit. I had a concussion, scrap metal all over, pieces of wood and all. I was lucky that ... if that rocket-propelled grenade hadn't hit that tree, I wouldn't be talking to you. Like I said, it wounded four of us. But they put me right back into the field. Only it wasn't with my unit. I don't know where they sent me. But our numbers had dwindled so much, they couldn't send me back to my unit.

When Leon got back to the States, he served five months at Fort Carson, Colorado, before leaving active-duty service. He then worked for Good Year for 28 years.

CHAPTER 18

Peter "Doc" Lohm

In Vietnam November 1969–October 1970

"All the officers had been wounded and we had very few men left."

Battlin' Bastard Danny McNair took the initiative to interview several veterans who, quite understandably, were more comfortable speaking with a fellow veteran than an author who is not. What follows is Doc's story as told to Danny for the express purpose of this book, lightly edited by the author.

I was living with my parents in upstate New York in West Monroe, just north of Syracuse, before I left for Vietnam. My brother-in-law drove me to the airport for the long flight ahead. The first leg was to Oakland, California, where many were being deployed from during the Vietnam War. We flew through Hawaii, but remained on the plane for the layover. I landed in Long Binh, Vietnam, in November 1969 and spent two weeks there waiting on assignment to my unit. We were standing in line waiting for our orders and the other soldiers were announcing where they were being sent. I looked at my orders and it said the 101st. I said out loud, "What is the 101st?" One guy told me, "You are going to the 101st Airborne." I flew on a C-130 to Phu Bai where the 101st was located and went through the training required by all the replacements arriving in Vietnam, preparing us how to operate. I was sent to Camp Evans, to the aid station where medics were sent, to get adjusted to being a medic. I remained in the aid station until about January and was then sent to Bravo Company for my permanent assignment in the field. I met Doc Riggs, who was the Bravo Company head medic. Doc Riggs would travel with [the] headquarters platoon in the field. There was an additional medic in each of the three platoons in the company (when we were fully staffed), making a total of four medics, counting Doc Riggs. I would be assigned to first platoon. To this day I am still referred to as "Doc Lohm" by all my friends from Bravo Company at our reunions. I would find out very soon there would be times, due to casualties, that we would not always have four medics in the field.

When the time came, I packed up my aid bag, getting ready to go to the field. The aid bag had an assortment of items that would be used frequently. I had a scalpel, field dressings, tape, cravats, antibiotics, pain medicines, morphine packet injectors, alcohol, malaria pills, salt tablets, and various other medical supplies. I was responsible for administering the malaria and salt tablets to all the men in the platoon on a routine basis. The medic bag would end up fairly large with all I carried. I also carried an M16 and all my other equipment, such as a poncho, poncho liner, water canteens, helmet, C-rations, ammo can for personal items, mask, body armor, and anything else required while in the field. I was flown out to the field to first platoon and the first person I met was Bob Haberle, who was the radio telephone operator for Lieutenant Pete Falco (our platoon leader). Haberle introduced me to Falco, Danny Mitchell, and other men in the platoon. There were many routine things I did to help the men due to the issues with the heat and humidity, insects, rainy wet conditions, and sometimes more minor wounds that could be field dressed. The more serious wounds required evacuation from the field at varying levels of care depending on the severity of the wounds. Heat exhaustion was a common issue and the reason I gave the men salt tablets; and of course malaria was also a concern and the reason for the malaria pills. The dirty and wet conditions also resulted in cellulitis that sometimes required me to use a scalpel to remove the infections. Boils were a major issue, which I also had myself. There were very large spiders in Vietnam as well as very large centipedes, both of which were venomous. There were also extremely venomous snakes, but I did not have to treat anyone for those issues.

I would experience my first casualties as a medic with first platoon on February 2, 1970. The day before, on February 1, 1970, third platoon was hit and a sergeant would be killed, with three men wounded. Sergeant Wannie Cook in third platoon was seriously wounded after he stepped on a booby trap, and would lose both legs. Given how hard third platoon was being hit, our platoon was sent to support. We were moving down a trail when the lead men from first platoon set off a booby trap. Gary Stahley, Max West, and Platoon Sergeant Freeman were all wounded. Lieutenant Falco and I moved the men to safety. Stahley and West had serious leg wounds; they would eventually each lose a leg. Due to the seriousness of the wounds, I began treating Stahley first. Lieutenant Falco would begin attending to Max West. I immediately applied a tourniquet to Stahley's leg and administered morphine. I moved to Max West and then Freeman, who had less serious wounds. We had them stabilized until they could get put on a medevac.

During this period of February and March we would continue to find greater numbers of the North Vietnamese through finding bunker complexes, weapons caches, hooches, enemy graves, and supplies that included their medical and food supplies. There were some firefights resulting in enemy killed, wounded, or taken prisoner. There are a couple of instances that I remember our medics were called to treat wounded North Vietnamese. On March 1, 1970, for example, I was called to the front after a firefight to treat a North Vietnamese soldier who had been wounded by our platoon. There was an American officer with the North Vietnamese, who I did not recognize, ordering me to save him. He was frantically telling me he had to be saved. I put my aid bag down and as soon as I saw the guy I knew there was no chance to save him. He had an exit wound though his head and had already died. I later found out that the officer telling me to save the North Vietnamese was from intelligence, who had been inserted with our company with a Chieu Hoi to gain intelligence. This North Vietnamese soldier could have supplied important intelligence if we were able to save his life.

There was another time a few days later that we had set up in an enemy bunker complex that contained all kinds of enemy supplies. While there I began to hear moaning very close to where I was located in the bunker complex. I reported this to those in charge, but I think it was discounted as not credible. Other men also began to hear the same sounds and eventually a wounded North Vietnamese was located inside a spider hole in the same area we were located. He was pulled out with a leg wound, but he was in a badly deteriorated condition after being there so long. Doc Riggs, who was our head medic, was called in to administer aid and the prisoner was put on a medevac out for interrogation. We continued in the area until being sent back to Camp Evans for a stand-down.

Later in March we were sent to FSB Granite, which had been hit by a sapper attack. There were many from the 101st killed and wounded. We were sent to secure the area in and around FSB Granite. The next major battle was April 25, 1970. Bravo Company made a combat assault onto FSB Maureen and first platoon had to land in another area close to the rest of the company due to heavy enemy fire at the planned landing zone. We were receiving artillery support from .155 Howitzers when a round landed behind me and shrapnel from the shell hit me in the right arm. Portions of the company were already right in the middle of heavy contact and not only could I not be evacuated, it was also thought important I stay because I was a medic.

Our second platoon had moved down below us and became involved in very heavy contact that afternoon, with many wounded and some killed. We did not have our platoon leader, Lieutenant Falco, that day, nor our platoon sergeant, Mike Turner, so Sergeant First Class Isaacs was our acting platoon leader (he was actually normally assigned to second platoon). The company commander, Captain Sullivan, radioed in for Isaacs to go to the aid of second platoon, who were pinned down by heavy fire. Isaacs left with two men, and went towards the area of second platoon.

I soon began hearing a call from Isaacs for a medic. I proceeded in the direction of his voice, crawling at times. I finally reached Isaacs, who was behind a dirt mound. He pointed to one of the men he took with him who had been wounded (Eudell Kotrous) and told me to begin an IV. When I got to Kotrous, I immediately saw a severe chest wound and knew I had other things to do before an IV. Kotrous's wound proved fatal. He died before I could go any farther. It was very late in the day, close to dark, and beginning to rain, with second platoon pinned down. We had dead and wounded, with no way to move.

While in the position with Isaacs I heard an incoming shell that hit the top of the trees right over us and then hit the ground right next to us, but did not explode. It was another 155 mm artillery shell and it was luckily a dud or both of us most likely would have been killed. Isaacs got up and told me to stay in my position and not move. He ran from our position into some tall grass, flanking around where the fire was coming from the North Vietnamese. He then disappeared from my view and I then heard explosions and gunfire. Isaacs had taken out the enemy fire. By this time, it was very late and the weather was not good. There was no way to get a medevac to all the wounded from second platoon. We would have to wait until the next day to begin evacuation of the wounded.

When I woke up the next day my hand and arm was really swelling up. Doc Riggs stepped in and declared my injuries too bad to remain in the field. I got a medevac to the hospital at Camp Eagle and was then sent to Cam Rahn Bay. I was operated on at Cam Rahn, to remove the shrapnel. Doc Robertson, who was a new medic with second platoon, was also medevac'd out the same day. He had been shot four times while administering aid to one of the second platoon wounded.

I returned to the field three weeks later, about the middle of May. Bravo Company was still in the area around FSB Maureen. The company was still in the field and also on a couple of firebases. I remember FSB Rakkasan was hit one night with a few wounded. I also remember FSB Kathryn being hit by a mortar attack right after we had left Kathryn to go back into the field. The rest of May was more of the same: patrolling with signs of the enemy everywhere. We would then go to Camp Evans for a stand down the first of June. Later that month, we would head back out to the same area of FSB Maureen. By June 25 we were up on Maureen, near an old landing zone, and the second platoon had some contact that day. We stayed in the same area and set up our night defensive position, along with the headquarters platoon, a short distance away from the second platoon night defensive position.

Sometime in the very early morning hours of June 26, the second platoon was hit in a very heavy attack. We could see the intense fire and explosions at the second platoon night defensive position. There was also a great deal of artillery fire in their support. We all realized it was a very bad situation and that there was nothing we could do immediately, but we were eventually ordered down to their position for support. The second platoon medic, Rodney Koerner, had been killed in the attack. There were our killed and wounded, as well as dead North Vietnamese, all in the area of the attack. Doc Riggs and I attended to the wounded and later that next morning the wounded and killed would be put on a medevac out. We were in the same general area for a short time before we began to move down the mountain ridge on into the first part of July.

I remember we received a couple of dog teams about that time and as we moved down the ridge line we found more bunker complexes, enemy graves, enemy ammunition, and other signs. On one occasion the dog handlers went out from the platoon for signs of the North Vietnamese. They returned and reported the dogs had alerted to enemy presence. I learned that once the dogs alert, their job is over at that point and so they returned with the information. We were all on high alert knowing it was just a matter of time before we would be hit again as we proceeded down the mountain the first few days of July.

We had a new platoon leader and I do not remember his name, but he was new and "green" for sure. One day he said to me, "Doc, we are proceeding on down into the Valley, are you ready?" I basically told him that I thought it was a bad idea. I remember on July 4 the enemy got in behind us and attacked the rear part of first platoon with rocket-propelled grenades, wounding four of our men. Collins, Heaton, Henderson, and Brown were all wounded in the attack. On July 5, we were well down the mountain when we set up a night defensive position. We were separated from second platoon, third platoon, and headquarters platoon, who had set up together in a night defensive position away from us.

Early the next morning the other platoons were attacked in their night defensive position. We were ordered to move out in support and so we grabbed our equipment and started in their direction. While approaching the site of the attack I heard gunfire and screams. I was called forward, as the first platoon medic, to the front of our formation. I grabbed my aid bag to start moving when I was told to disregard. I would later find out that the acting platoon sergeant had been killed by friendly fire while leading our platoon to support the rest of our company.

When we arrived at the night defensive position there were many wounded, including our head medic, Doc Riggs, and the third platoon medic, Haney. They were doing what they could do to render aid. I was attending where I was needed the most. Some were more seriously wounded than others. We began to load the wounded on medevacs. The first two most seriously wounded were put on the jungle penetrator. I was standing there watching the two men being taken up when they were dropped, injuring them both. They would be evacuated out later. Eventually all the wounded and one killed were taken out. I was the only medic left in the company. All the officers had been wounded and we had very few men left in second platoon, third platoon, and headquarters platoon. The remainder of the company finally moved out, away from that night defensive position where the attack occurred.

Later that afternoon after moving a good distance away, we set up another night defensive position. There was a strong feeling that we could be hit again that night, but for some reason the North Vietnamese did not attack us again. The remains of Bravo Company moved for a few more days until we were finally picked up and flown to FSB Bastogne. I served in the aid station for the next week or so at Bastogne and the remainder of the company was assigned to ambush teams or security for truck convoys until being moved to another firebase. The remainder of July we were at FSB Kathryn and also sent to Eagle Beach for a short rest before returning to Camp Evans.

The month of August, Bravo Company was moved between firebases as the company received replacements. The first part of September my replacement was assigned to first platoon as the medic, and I was then assigned to the battalion aid station at Camp Evans. The Camp Evans assignment did not last long as the head medic had some bad news for me. He regretted [having] to let me know I would have to go back to the field until second platoon received a replacement medic. I was getting very short then because I had also received a two-week drop from Vietnam. I spent another couple of weeks in the field until the replacement was assigned to second platoon. I went back to Camp Evans until I received my orders home.

I flew back to Fort Lewis, Washington, and then returned home to New York before being assigned to Fort Benning for the remainder of my six and a half months left in the Army. I moved back to civilian life in West Monroe with my wife and son, and worked on a dairy farm for four and a half years. I then made a decision to reenlist in the Army. I remained in the Army, working in the hospital, until I retired with 20 years of service. I then went to worked for General Electric. I have spent a great deal of time with the men of Bravo Company over the years that our Company Commander Lee Sullivan and my platoon leader from Vietnam, Pete Falco, reunited us all back together. I am proud to share this true story from my experiences in Vietnam and am proud of my service with Bravo Company, 1/506th, 101st Airborne.

CHAPTER 19

John Brown

In Vietnam December 1969–November 1970

> "I was hit in the helmet with a piece of shrapnel that stuck in my helmet and also hit my ear. I was very fortunate to have my helmet on or probably would have been killed."

This is John's story as told to Danny McNair for the express purpose of this book, lightly edited by the author.

I was living around the area near Cambridge, Nebraska, when I was inducted into the Army in 1969. I received basic training and advanced infantry training, both at Fort Lewis, Washington. I was at Fort Lewis for three months doing utility work on the barracks after advanced individual training. This would help me later when I would receive an early drop from Vietnam and also the Army.

I finally landed in Cam Rahn Bay, Vietnam, in December of 1969. I was assigned to the 101st Airborne with Bravo Company, 1/506th. I attended SERTS and then was assigned to scout school before going to Bravo Company. The scout school had a class made up of 10 Chieu Hoi scouts and 10 Army personnel. The main purpose of the training was to learn how to communicate with the scout you were assigned. A Chieu Hoi was a former North Vietnamese Army or Viet Cong who had defected to the South Vietnamese to assist in the fight against the North Vietnamese Army. The Chieu Hois were used by American forces to accompany the units in the field to help with reading of enemy signs, reading enemy maps, interrogation of North Vietnamese Army captured, and possible known locations of the enemy.

When the scout school was completed, I reported to Bravo Company with my assigned scout. Scouts received basically the same equipment we carried, including an M16, and my scout and I were sent to the field together sometime in January 1970. When I reported to third platoon, my scout walked point with me following directly behind him. He was very useful in reading enemy signs, especially as it related to trail markers on trees. There was one instance when he prevented us from being surprised by a North Vietnamese attack. The North Vietnamese saw him first walking point and thought he was one of their own and hesitated firing on us. This gave me time to begin firing on the North Vietnamese, along with the other men in my platoon.

During the first couple of months with third platoon we were moving through areas that had increasing amounts of enemy activity and it was good to have the scout with us. There were some firefights and calling-in of support fire, but I do not know the specific dates or details for each one of them. The third platoon was hit hard the first part of February, with one of our men killed and several wounded. This was during the time Sergeant Wannie Cook stepped on a booby trap and lost both of his legs. Sergeant First Class Frank Foronda had been our acting platoon leader in February, until Lieutenant Chuck Choney took over as platoon leader.

We came up on some tunnels and Cecil Dobson volunteered to go down to check them out. Cecil asked that the safety rope we attached to him in case we had to pull him out be tied around his waist instead of the upper part of his body nearer his shoulders. We did end up having to pull him out due to an issue with breathing. When we attempted to pull on the rope his body would double up and he became stuck in the tunnel, making it impossible to get him out. We then tied a rope around the feet of another man and lowered him in to pull Cecil out. This enabled him to be pulled out, but it was too late and Cecil died of asphyxiation. I do not know why Cecil wanted the rope around his waist.

We were finally sent in for a stand-down in March after being out in the field for a very long time. When we arrived at Camp Evans there was time to rest and drink some the first night out of the field. The first night at Evans for our company stand-down, FSB Granite was hit in a major attack. Bravo Company was the reactionary force to be sent out that night. It was the first night in and we were not in any shape to go out that night. We were out the next day for security, and to track the North Vietnamese responsible for the attack. In this same time frame my scout Von Dong was permitted a leave and did not return. I never found out what happened to him.

We would continue the same routine of patrolling, finding the enemy with some firefights and supporting fire as needed. The activity began to pick up, and on April 25 we combat assaulted onto FSB Maureen. My third platoon was not in the area where the major part of this battle happened. We did not have any casualties. The second platoon, however, was pinned down and had many casualties. There were also some casualties from first platoon.

We were around Maureen, very low on ammunition, and began moving down a finger off the mountain. We reached an old landing zone and set up around it, forming a perimeter for the resupply. The second platoon was above us and we (third platoon) covered the next part of the perimeter below the second platoon. First platoon was below us, covering the lower part of the landing zone. The helicopters had resupplied us, and we were surprised by the attack. The North Vietnamese were up the hill above us firing and throwing grenades. Cobra gunships were called in and were firing all around us.

I had taken cover behind a tree with Lieutenant Chuck Choney, my platoon leader, when we were both wounded. I was hit in the helmet with a piece of shrapnel that stuck in my helmet and also hit my ear. I was very fortunate to have my helmet on or probably would have been killed. I was the last one to be medevac'd out that day. There must have been twelve or fifteen wounded placed on a Chinook and flown to a hospital in Da Nang. The weather was bad and the pilot became lost after arriving in Da Nang, so we ended up in a Marine hospital.

I was there for a few weeks and then sent back to Camp Evans. I had been declared unfit for duty in the field due to my hearing. I was then assigned to a sniper team, which to this day makes no sense, if my hearing was not good enough for my previous assignment in the field. I reported to the sniper team that was housed in a nearby hooch that had four sniper teams when at full strength. I carried an M16 and M79 when I was in the field, but was issued a .308 Winchester as the sniper rifle. Each sniper team consisted of three men. We received our orders from battalion for each day. Battalion had to coordinate other sniper teams, ambush teams, and regular units in the field.

We were sometimes assigned to the flatlands near Camp Evans and other times we were out in the mountains close to the A Shau Valley. We walked out of Camp Evans into the lowlands on the assignments close-in and operated at night. We came back in and slept during the day. For the assignments in the mountains, we were taken out by helicopter. We would rappel out of the helicopter when we arrived, sometimes staying a week. We climbed up rope ladders when we were picked up. We made our decisions on what action to take based on the circumstances, mainly determined by the number of North Vietnamese sighted. If there were more than one or two North Vietnamese, we would probably call in airstrikes. The aircraft used would depend on the size of the North Vietnamese unit. There was one occasion a battalion-sized unit was spotted and a B-52 strike was required. We had to move to the other side of a mountain away from that strike.

September 3, 1970, was a date on the sniper team I would never forget. I was on the sniper team with Sammy Daniels and Rod Taylor that night and we were moving towards our position to set up. We found a claymore that had been set up, so we backed off and then unhooked the wire from the claymore when all hell broke loose. Rodney was hit immediately. We started yelling and the firing finally stopped. We called for a medevac and it took over an hour for it to arrive. Rodney was loaded on the chopper and Sam Daniels also got on, with me left standing on the skid of the helicopter. The medic on the chopper said to me, "You don't appear to be wounded," and pushed me off the skid and took off. I had to walk back to Evans and when I arrived at the perimeter the guards would not allow me back on the base. I was in no mood to deal with this, so I took out my .308 and shot a light out behind them. I then asked again if they saw that light shot out and were they now ready to let me in—to which they quickly complied. There was no sleep that night waiting on news about Rodney.

The next day I was not able to find a way to travel to the nearby Quang Tri Surgical Hospital, where Rodney later passed away. Rodney was a country boy from North Carolina who was loved by many and had previously been with first platoon before joining the sniper team. He was a good man you could depend on, and the type of man you had to have on sniper team. Not everyone was cut out for it. We once had a new member on our team who would just light up a cigarette in the middle of the night in the lowlands. You could see the light from the cigarette from a long distance. We called in and reported his issue and told whoever was in charge that something might happen to him if he was not removed from the team. The message was clearly understood, and the guy was removed immediately from the team.

I remember one time I was assigned with another guy to escort a prisoner to the Long Binh Jail (famously known as LBJ), which was not far from Saigon. This was quite a distance, and we were given six days to take the prisoner down and return. The means of transportation in Vietnam was to hitch rides on trucks and aircraft. That way, we were able to get the prisoner there in one day. We went to the officers' club that night and to a nearby airport the second day. It was too foggy to take off, so we spent the night in the airport. The third day someone came in and recognized our unit patch and asked if we were with the 101st Airborne and headed back. He told us he had some pictures from General Abrams that had to be delivered as soon as possible. He asked if we could escort them back to the 101st. He ordered an aircraft for us and we were the only two on the plane as we escorted the pictures and dropped them off at headquarters, arriving back to Camp Evans in three days.

I was able to take R&R in Hawaii and see my wife and son for the first time at eight months old. The 101st was reducing the size of the division as quickly as possible in Vietnam by handing out early drops and immediate separation from the Army where possible. I received a drop due to the extra time spent at Fort Lewis and was able to leave Vietnam and the Army 22 days early. I was sent home in November to Fort Lewis and processed out of the Army. I returned home to the area around Cambridge, Nebraska, and farmed for the next 25 years. My wife and I then decided to open a guest ranch in Colorado, which became a very successful business. We had 75 RV sites, cabins, and a lodge with a total capacity of 125 people. We ran it for a few years, but [in] the area where it was located [it] was difficult to find enough staff. I drove a truck for a few years after that and I also continued to farm some and raise big gardens over the years.

CHAPTER 20

Michael Bookser

In Vietnam December 1969–May 1970

> "I'm never going to be the same. I can tell already and I've only been here for two and a half months."

With permission, the author adapted the following from Mike's written memories, and letters home, during his time in Vietnam.

Mike flew into San Francisco on November 29, 1969. He immediately met a couple of the guys he went through NCO school with and they got hotel rooms together. A taxicab driver took them to the Lafayette Hotel—in a seedy part of town. After a few adventures, the next morning the guys went to the restaurant next door to the hotel for breakfast. The coffee cups looked like they hadn't been washed for years, the food was dry and maybe left over from the day before. To cut a long story short, their day in San Francisco was a time to remember. They got a taxicab to Oakland, where they were to report for debarkation to Vietnam.

Mike left for Vietnam December 2. He remembers asking the other men on the plane "Isn't anyone scared?" One of the guys said, "Are you??" And he replied, "Of course I am, we're a few hours away from war, they're shooting real bullets over there, I'm scared shitless." Mike recalled that "Everyone sort of loosened up and the guy who asked me the question said 'Boy, sarge, you just put us at ease, we thought you were so gung-ho that you didn't realize we could be killed, you had us worried.'"

Upon arriving in Vietnam, Mike wrote home, "Here I am, in scenic Bien Hoa. Last night was fairly eventful.... We traveled in buses with military police [MP] in Jeeps with M60 machine guns mounted on the Jeeps. The buses had heavy screen where windows usually have glass. The MPs told us that this was so hand grenades couldn't be thrown into the bus. That made us feel real good, here we are, every one of us cherries. That wasn't the worst of it, as we were going through the town of Bien Hoa somebody shot at us. The MPs took some sort of action while we got down on the floor of the bus. Yeah, hide on the floor, no gun, no information and we were only in-country for a couple of hours. It's going to be a tough year."

He continued, "When we got off the plane, the first thing I noticed was the smell. I guess the odor is from the dense vegetation or something like that. I should ship out to my unit tomorrow. Pray I get the 1st Cav. One of the guys got the 1st Infantry Division and two other guys got the 101st Airborne Division. I don't know what the temperature got up to today, but it was hot and sticky. The guys who have been in-country for a while must be having fun with us new guys."

Mike would in fact be assigned to the 101st. As he wrote home on December 7, 1969, "Well, I'm at division right now, on my way to a week of in-country training called SERT. I'm now at Phu Bai about twenty miles south of the DMZ. I am with the 101st Airborne Division. I don't have my wings, but I'm with them anyway. The 101st is a rough unit, so they don't have much trouble with 'Charlie,' so you can rest easy. Since I moved so far north, I moved right into the monsoon season. I liked it better when it was dry. They have a saying around here that is used as a response to any complaint about the rear area. When someone complains about the lights going out, a leaky roof or anything else, the response is, 'But Phu Bai is alright.' I guess it's better to be in Phu Bai with any problems than be in the jungle."

Mike moved to Camp Evans for SERT. As he wrote home, "Today we had our first day of training. All we did was learn about the different weapons the enemy is using against us. After that we tore apart the M16, which isn't anything new, but some of the guys around here need the training. Tomorrow we go out to fire. It should be an interesting day. Tonight we have guard duty and I'm one of the commanders of the relief. All the complaining I did during training at Fort McClellan was the truth. All the guys that didn't take their job seriously back in the States, aren't taking it seriously here either. We're in a combat zone and they think guard duty is just for harassment, when are they going to grow up? I don't know what's going to happen tomorrow when we go out in the field to fire our weapons, I don't think they realize that the Viet Cong are real people who are out to get us."

"The company I'm in now has very few infantrymen. Most of the guys are clerks, truck drivers, and other odd jobs. They don't have the infantry training and they don't know what could happen once we leave the safety of our base camp. I guess the training I received was worth it. All I can say is God help them, and me."

"The more I hear from the guys who have been here for a while the more I'm glad I got the 101st. One guy has been here for five months, and only made contact with the enemy once. He said the North Vietnamese Army and Viet Cong stay away from the 101st area of operation because the infantry of the 101st is always in the field. I won't mind staying out in the field if it stays the way it is now. Today we have classes on Viet Cong mines and booby traps. I can tell right now it's going to be a dull day. Oh well, not too many more left, thank God. Yesterday I met one of the guys I went through NCO school with. He's been here for about a month … he's changed, for the worse. I hope I don't change like he did. If I do, please, bear with it until I get home, it can't possibly be a permanent change."

The men were not safe from the enemy just because they were at Camp Evans. As Mike wrote home, "Our perimeter has been under attack.... Patrols are out now trying to repel the force. It's no big thing though, last night we were under a ground attack all night. Things like this happen every night, the Viet Cong just want to see if we're on our toes."

On December 14, Mike wrote home to let his family know he was assigned to Company E, First Battalion, 506th Infantry, 101st Airborne Division, noting "I'm going to be a mortar man. I was worried about having my MOS changed to a regular ground fighter, 11B." In this letter, he noted meeting another soldier he'd known in the States, again noting the ways Vietnam changed a man: "I wish I could say it was great to see him also. He's been in 'Nam for seven months, and this place has changed him. He's having problems talking, he stumbles over words, he can't talk right at all. He looks terrible. As we talked to each other I noticed how nervous he was. He told me about his friends he's seen killed, and he shook like a leaf while he told me. I almost cried while I talked to him, it's a shame to see something like that happen to a guy."

Living conditions at Camp Evans might have been better than in the jungle, but they still weren't great. As Mike wrote home, "I haven't told you what the living conditions are like around this place. To make it short, I will sum it up in one word, BAD. The showers are cold, no hot water. The showers are made from 55-gallon drums with a hose coming out of the bottom. The latrines are at best outhouses, and the barracks are huts. They are made out of wood, but that's all that's good about them. A couple of guys have Christmas trees with lights on them, but somehow they seem out of place. Even though it is the 14th of December, it doesn't seem like Christmas time."

Things were about to get more bleak for Mike. As he wrote home on December 17, "My hope to stay out of the field for a while didn't turn out. I left two days ago on a radar raid. Radar raids are a group of security people (about seven infantry guys) and a couple of radar operators. The team has between 10 and 15 people. We take radar equipment into the field and watch for enemy troop movement at night. Usually the team is extracted each morning and moved to another location. The importance of the move is so the North Vietnamese Army don't know where we are long enough to attack and take the equipment. We should be coming in tomorrow morning. And leave again tomorrow afternoon. I just thought I'd write a small note before the resupply helicopter comes in. I've only been with the company for three days and already I have two days in the field. You've heard the saying 'there aren't any atheists in foxholes'; well it's right. At night when I'm on guard, the only thing I can do is pray, and I'm sure it's that way with everybody. If anybody has been scared to death, it's been me in the past two days."

After another radar raid, Mike wrote, "Sorry I haven't written for a couple of days, but war is hell. I went out on another radar raid which lasted four days. While I was out, I didn't get a chance to write, I know you'll understand. Now I'm at a firebase so I hope to be able to write every night. I should be here for a couple of weeks."

From Firebase Rakkasan, on December 25, Mike wrote, "The [Christmas] ceasefire started last night at 6:00 PM but you never would have known it. At midnight last night we had a 'mad minute.' At exactly 12:00 AM the mortars fired illumination rounds, and when they popped open everyone on the perimeter started firing their weapons. It lasted for 60 seconds. The whole idea was to keep the enemy from trying to sneak up on our position. It looks bad for the guys going to the Bob Hope Show, the clouds are so thick up here the 'birds' can't get up here to pick them up. I hope it clears up."

While the holiday season was sometimes the hardest to endure, being away from home, the smallest gestures provided the men comfort. For example, Mike recalled, "Greek (a guy I went through NCO school with) gave me a Christmas present today. He had two cans of milk he got back in the rear, and he gave me one and said, 'Merry Christmas.' It may not seem like much to you, but we were the only guys with milk. Greek got a Christmas card addressed to, 'A serviceman in Southeast Asia' from a girl at some college. He's going to write her a thank-you note. She wrote a nice note on the card. It's nice that people would take the time to do something like that for someone they don't even know. It takes all kinds."

Still the holidays were no time to allow defenses to slip. As Mike wrote on December 26, "Last night an enemy combatant got through the wire. He didn't do anything but turn and run. It's getting close to Tet, so we're expecting to get hit hard. Tet is the Chinese New Year. I'm safe though because the mortars are in the center of the firebase. In order for us to get it, the perimeter would have to be broken, then he'd have to fight us."

For some, it was especially difficult to bear when their fellow soldiers were wounded in non-combat accidents. Mike wrote home of an instance where a mortar misfired, and "the shrapnel went everywhere. Seven people were hit, our own men. They were all evacuated by helicopter to the hospital. Today was one guy's birthday, he got hit first. One guy got it in the head, he'll probably go to Japan to get fixed up. Nobody was killed, but four of the guys were taken out on stretchers and the other three were able to walk with a little help. I almost cried when I saw them carried away this morning. It didn't even phase the other guys, I guess I'm just not hardcore. It was no fault of the crew, the manufacturer messed up when they made the round. Oh well, I can't do anything about it."

Just as the men found small ways to observe Christmas, New Year's Eve was a time of makeshift celebrations. As Mike wrote, "Last night was a terrific sight here. At midnight everybody let go with flares, star clusters, grenades, machine guns, everything you could possibly imagine. We weren't the only ones either, every military installation did the same. Since we're on top of a hill we could see for miles and it was a beautiful sight to see. The artillery set off illumination rounds that light up the sky like daytime. Last night was one New Years I'll never forget. At 12:00 AM the guy on the radio FSB Rakkasan looking west said 'As we begin another broadcasting day we'll play the national anthem of the Republic of Vietnam.' Instead of the national anthem, the song 'Eleanor Rigby' came on. It was perfect, it started out 'I see all the lonely people.' The GI DJ dedicated it to all the GIs serving in Southeast Asia. I imagine he'll get in trouble for it."

A few weeks into the new year, Mike and his unit prepared to leave FSB Rakkasan for the A Shau Valley, on the Laotian border where the main supply route for the North Vietnamese Army was located (the Ho Chi Minh Trail). After a spell at Camp Evans, it was off to FSB Jack. There, Mike would be transferred to Bravo Company from Echo Company. In fact, as Mike tells it, "Everyone who was on FSB Rakkasan the night the short rounds went out were being transferred to other units. It's something the Army does to eliminate or track possible sabotage. So now I will be a squad leader with B Company, no more mortar or radar raids with E Company. I will have a squad of mortar-qualified troopers. We will work as a regular squad with the ability to provide indirect fire for the company from the field. After being introduced to the squad I jumped on a helicopter and went back to Camp Evans to get my gear transferred from Echo Company to Bravo Company."

Towards the end of January 1970, Mike and Bravo Company prepared to head to the demilitarized zone between South Vietnam and North Vietnam. As he detailed, "Right now plans are for us to be out in the field for 78 days. That will take us into the beginning of April. We'll be going on six-man patrols for a while, then we'll start on platoon-sized patrols. The platoon sergeant just came in and gave me six maps, together they cover the whole DMZ. Last night we were alerted for a combat assault at 11:30 PM. Two regiments of North Vietnamese Army broke through the DMZ and headed for Quang Tri. Our whole battalion leaves tomorrow to stop them. One company left this afternoon for the DMZ as a reactionary force to hold them over until we get there. We shouldn't have any problems with them. Just to give you an idea how safe it will be, I'm carrying four frags, 420 rounds of M16 ammo, 100 rounds of M60 ammo, four smokes, one claymore mine, plus my other gear. Each man carries the same. Our rucksacks weigh about 80 pounds after with our ammo and personal gear."

Armed to the teeth, the men could still sometimes appreciate the beauty of the country. As Mike wrote on January 22, "I wish my whole tour in 'Nam would be like it is now. We're out in the woods and the birds are chirping and the stream is gently flowing by, the sun is bright and all is well. Life is beautiful when one can see all the terrific sights of nature. This country could really make something of itself if it were given the chance. I can't wait to get back to the 'world' and tell everybody just the way it is over here. I don't know when I'll be able to mail this letter, it will probably be a few days before a bird comes in to resupply us. This morning I went fishing with hopes I could get a fish for breakfast, but with the luck I have I didn't get anything. Last night I found an animal trail right in front of our position so I strung a trip flare across the path. I thought maybe something during the night might come by and trip the flare and I could shoot it. My efforts were wasted because nothing came by." In a few days, though, there would be fish to supplement the rations. Mike wrote, "We went out on a patrol and found a beautiful stream, real deep. The fish in it were big too so we threw a hand grenade and POOF, up came a whole bunch of fish. We got about 10, good eating tonight."

Care packages from home, when they could make it to the men, meant the world. As Mike once wrote, "We're going to get resupplied tomorrow. They'll also bring our mail out to us. They don't bring packages out to the field so I won't get your package until after Tet. I hope you sent more Kool-Aid because it goes good in the water from the streams. I have to put purification tablets in the water and the tabs make the water taste funny. I used the cherry drink mix yesterday and it tasted real good."

As January drew to a close, Mike began to see Vietnamization at play. As he wrote on January 24, 1970, "You mentioned about Nixon pulling 50,000 combat troops out of 'Nam. Well, it's true because the South Vietnamese Army are taking over a lot of the fighting. What isn't so nice is that the last two units that will be pulled out are the 1st Air Cavalry and the 101st Airborne Division. The reason is because we're airmobile and we can take care of a large area. So if you're thinking about me being sent home early, forget it. You asked me about censorship over here, and whether or not I think they keep information from us. One must understand that certain news has to be cut out altogether because of the enemy being able to pick it up. The radio stations can't broadcast anything that would be harmful to the Republic of South Vietnam because they (radio stations) are using frequencies allotted to them by the RVN [Republic of Vietnam], and in the best interests of RVN some things are censored, I guess. As for censorship being a major issue I think it would take a deadhead not to see the problems involved in operating a U.S. government radio station in a foreign country."

Vietnamization didn't make all of the men feel better. In fact, it may have made some feel worse. As Vietnam veteran and later Senator John Kerry asked Congress in 1971, "How do you ask a man to be the last man to die for a mistake?"

Mike wrote as January 1970 drew to a close, "I've got three other guys working with me right now, and one of them is trying to get out of the field. He's scared to death and wants me to get him out of the boonies and back to the rear. I'm not going to because this guy has got to learn a few things about life, and this is the time and the place for him to learn. He told me he was a nervous wreck being out here and he can't take it. Frankly, everybody is nervous and scared so there is no reason for him to be different. Anybody who says he isn't scared is a fool. Anyhow, he is causing us a lot of problems and I get very little sleep at night because I have to watch him. One of the other guys sees the problem and he also loses a lot of sleep.

I have a lot of respect for this guy because he worries about everybody, as I do, not just himself. As a matter of fact I'm putting him in for SP/4 next month because he is doing the work of two PFCs which is highly unusual."

Mike spent much of February wandering the jungle. As he wrote, "I have never been so tired in my life. Everything is about the same as it's been since we came out, hump all day and pull guard all night. We've been out here for 39 days now. Who said the infantry goes out for three or four days and come back in? We're cutting a landing zone now, a place large enough for a helicopter to land. A landing zone has to be wide enough for the blades of the helicopter to clear the jungle. We get resupplied today and then start humping late this afternoon. I have to blow a few trees so I might have to drop my letter-writing for a while."

While low morale was certainly an issue for many during the Vietnam War era, Mike remained relatively positive. On March 2, he wrote, "You asked about my feelings about the Army. I'll tell you, as I've said before, I like the Army. It could stand to be a lot harder than it is, but that's just my opinion. I'm just as gung-ho as I was when I enlisted and I doubt if my views will change. I've been lucky with the people I've met in the Army and where it really counts. I've been put with the best unit in Vietnam. Just to show you an example of the spirit this company has, yesterday the first platoon captured an enemy soldier and chased three others. The company commander said over the radio to 'Pat everybody on the back for a job well done.' A reply came back 'That's alright, we're just doing our thing.' The people I'm with out here are not only doing what they have to do, but they're doing what they want to do."

"Our company has a reputation that can't be beat, we're the ones that finally took Hill 996 in May 1969 in the A Shau Valley. With the 'blood and guts' I've seen in men over here, I couldn't say my opinion of the Army has changed. When the time comes for me to step out of my green uniform and put on civilian clothes for good I'm going to lose a part of me, a big part. I'm a Screaming Eagle from head to toe. That's the only way I can describe the way I feel."

Mike realized not everyone felt the way he did, writing his girlfriend, "I'm sorry to hear that your friend and her boyfriend are having problems. I know how he feels and I know what he means by wanting to think. I doubt very much if she knows what he is going through with just being here. Tell her that it's hard on the nerves to write your girlfriend and say 'everything is all right' when you don't know if you'll wake up in the morning. It's hard on him, harder than anyone can imagine unless you've been here. Sometimes I don't know if we're chasing the North Vietnamese Army or if they are chasing us.

One night we set up our night defensive position and as nighttime came the monkeys started making a bunch of noise. Usually the animals stopped making noise when people were around. Those monkeys were really making a lot of noise and none of us liked the idea of not being able to hear the bad guys coming if they were going to try something. After a while, I decided to fire … a little … I used the area the monkeys were in as a good point to have the artillery zero in on. After a round hit the ground I asked for a small fire for effect. A few rounds came in on the target and they 'walked' the rounds up the valley. We had a defensive fire established for the night and the monkeys stopped making noise. Then we got a spooky message from battalion. No one was to take their boots off because 'red eyes' were watching. 'Red eyes' meant that a high-flying airplane would be looking down on us to detect the heat of the feet of the North Vietnamese Army sneaking up on us. The 'red eyes' could tell by heat signature of feet if boots or sandals were being worn. *Oh, this is great, monkeys are making noise and battalion thinks they will be able* to 'see' *the North Vietnamese Army coming up to attack us.* Another night of no sleep. We weren't attacked but we didn't stay there long in the morning."

The heat was an enemy of its own. As Mike wrote, "I hope it doesn't get so hot today as it has been in the past couple of days. The temperature has been above a hundred and the sweat comes rolling down when it gets that hot. We can't hump far when it's hot either, so that messes up our plans of getting to where we're suppose to. It looks like we really will be going to Eagle Beach on the 18th. Plans are being made for a party at the beach and our extraction from the field. I can't believe it, we're really going to the Beach. Our stay at the beach is going to be for two days. After that we're supposed to go to a firebase. I hope we do because then I'll be able to write every day and mail will be going out every day."

Mike wouldn't make it to Eagle Beach, though. Before the unit departed, he got sick and was helicoptered to the hospital to be checked for stomach cramps. As he wrote, "This was the end of my longest stay in the jungle, 54 days, without staying on a firebase or coming back to Camp Evans. I was medevac'd on March 14 and taken to the 85th Evacuation Hospital in Phu Bai. I got sick on the 13th and got real sick on the 14th so I had to be taken out of the field. We didn't have a landing zone for the bird to pick me up so they had to drop a jungle penetrator down and pull me up. I'm all right now, they took tests to find out what happened to me so if anything is wrong with me I'll find out in a few days. I don't like the idea about not going to the Beach, but I can't win 'em all."

Mike would finally make it to Eagle Beach in April. As he wrote home, "We were given three days of in-country R&R at Eagle Beach in April. (Eagle Beach was an island in the South China Sea near Hue operated by the 101st Airborne Division.) There was a Vietnamese village on the island also but the 101st area was fenced in. We were told not to go into the village and the village people weren't allowed near the 101st area. I heard stories of guys going into the village to visit girls, but I never left the beach area."

"We had entertainment at Eagle Beach, along with the beach itself. There was a club for drinking, and doctors and dentists gave everyone physicals while we were there. The dentists were the worst, they made us use 'disclosing' tables that turned the plaque on our teeth red. After turning our teeth red we had to brush them until they weren't red anymore. I think it took all afternoon to get the red off, then they made us chew the tablets again."

"We were given the three days at Eagle Beach because command knew that we were going to FSB Granite. The word was that no unit had stayed on the firebase for more than three days without being overrun by the North Vietnamese. Captain Sullivan knew the history of the firebase and had a pretty ingenious way of handling the possibility of being overrun."

"To begin with he kept the listening posts inside the wire, not in the jungle outside the wire. An 81 mm mortar tube was sent out to my squad, we planted it about five feet from the wire. I told Captain Sullivan that I needed to shoot a round to zero the tube in so I would know where the rounds were going. I picked a hilltop to the north of Granite. He wasn't too hot on the hilltop I picked because another company had patrols out to the north of the hill. I told him that I thought I could hit the hilltop. Lieutenant McCrystal put up a fuss and said that hilltops were the hardest place to hit. He was right but I thought I was that good."

"Captain Sullivan told me to go ahead and try but I was only allowed one round and if I couldn't hit the hilltop I had better be short not long. I calculated the shot and gave the numbers to the crew. After they set everything I checked the charge and gun site and gave the order to hang. We shot a white phosphorus round so we could see the smoke through the canopy. The round hit the hilltop. We bragged for a week about our skills."

"In addition to the mortar tube Captain Sullivan had twice the complement of ammo that a firebase defense called for. His orders were that during the night we would shoot ½ of what we had in each foxhole. That meant that by morning we would still have our normal arsenal, but we would have spent the night keeping the North Vietnamese away from the perimeter. It worked, but we did get a little silly with our firing. We had mad minutes; coordinated hand grenade throws and claymore mine blowing."

"Cal Nolt and I were in the same foxhole and had fun cooking off our hand grenades so we would have the grenade explode in the air. Generally we would cook off for three seconds. An American baseball grenade exploded at five seconds. We would throw the grenade toward the jungle but aim high in the air."

"One night it was raining so we had a poncho rigged above our foxhole. One of the guys in the squad was at our listening post about twenty feet to our right front behind a big rock. Cal and I decided that it was time for a few hand grenades so we cooked a few. I cooked one to three seconds and threw it, but it hit the edge of the poncho and fell right in front of the foxhole. I pushed the grenade down the hill and yelled "GRENADE!" Cal and I ducked into the foxhole just as the grenade exploded right in front of us."

"We were both happy that we were okay as we looked at the smoke in front of our foxhole. Then we remembered that we had a listening post in front of us. We started to yell for the listening post and we didn't get a response. I couldn't believe I wasn't getting a response; I kept yelling. After what seemed to be a lifetime but was probably only seconds the listening post yelled, 'Hey Sarge, can you make the next one a little further out next time?' I was never happier to hear his voice. I asked if he was okay and he said 'It's a little hard to hear you but I'm okay.' The blast must have been so loud to him that it ruined his hearing, at least for a while. Needless to say we didn't cook off any more grenades."

Mike and his unit were on the FSB "for 11 days and were never over run. The best the other units did was three days. Our company commander did a decent job of getting us supplied and we used the ammo all night long to keep the bad guys away. The area around Granite was a hotbed in 1970. Names like FSB Ripcord, Maureen, Kathryn, A Shau Valley, etc. etc. etc. make up a piece of history that really didn't make the news much but was very costly."

After leaving FSB Granite, Mike wrote: "We were on platoon-sized recons during the month of April. During this time we had run out of fresh water. We were in the mountains, so we didn't have access to water like we did when we were in the valleys. To conserve the water we did have, we looked for sources of water. Some of the guys drank out of bomb craters that were filled with water. I didn't like that idea because the water was a terrible green color that looked like every bacteria in the world was living in there. My squad decided to cut banana trees down and suck the moisture out of the trees. Banana trees are like celery, soft and full of moisture. It seemed like a better idea than drinking from the bomb craters, but it wasn't. The next morning several of the guys in the squad, including me, had blisters all over our bodies. I only had the blisters on my arms, the left arm was the worst, but one of the guys had blisters all over his body. We called a medevac for him so he could go to the hospital. We figured that the area had been defoliated with Agent Orange in the past and the trees that grew in were polluted with the chemical and we ended up drinking the contamination. The next morning one of the guys woke up with a centipede on his right upper arm. He didn't like the bugs and animals in the jungle and when he saw it he yelled and brushed it off with his left hand. The centipede dug all its claws into him and opened a gash in his arm from his elbow to his shoulder. Centipedes in the jungle are poisonous and he had to be medevac'd to Da Nang for the antivenom."

In the same letter, Mike continued, "We finally were resupplied and got fresh water, ammo, and mail. Since we had some extra stuff we didn't want to destroy we kept it in a mail bag. We got a supply of M72 LAWs (collapsible rockets like the old bazookas) on this resupply because of what command thought we were going to get into. The mail bag is hard to carry so I decided that I'd be the first to carry it. I asked the medic if he would strap the LAW on his rucksack and he said that he would carry the mail bag. I told him that the bag was harder to carry and I'd carry it. He said 'No, I'll take the bag.' I told him he was nuts because he had to carry the aid bag and the mail bag was hard to carry. He said 'Sarge, can I talk to you?' And he started to move away from the other guys. I followed him. When we got away from the guys in the squad he told me that he was a conscientious objector and didn't want to carry any arms. He said that if I ordered him to carry the LAW he would do so but he would rather not. I apologized to him and told him that I didn't know that he was a conscientious objector and I wouldn't order him to carry any arms. I gave him the mail bag and I took the LAW."

"After we moved out and set up for the night the medic asked if he could talk to me. I said 'Of course,' who wouldn't want to talk? He told me that he didn't believe that men were supposed to kill other men and that's why he was a conscientious objector. I told him that I could understand his point and it was not a problem with me, after all, medics were not in the field to fight, they were in the field to patch up everyone else. He told me that he knows he is correct in his belief and God doesn't want us to hurt other people. He told me a story of what happened to him in another unit."

"The medic said that he was in a battle rendering aid to a GI who had been wounded. As the fighting was going on the North Vietnamese pushed back the GIs and overran his position as he was giving aid. The North Vietnamese soldiers just passed him up and continued to fight the GIs. A North Vietnamese medic passed him and dropped a North Vietnamese aid bag beside him as he continued to follow his troops. As the GIs pushed the North Vietnamese back, the North Vietnamese soldiers passed him again. The North Vietnamese medic picked up the aid bag as he came by again. The American troops regained the land and he was with our troops again. He said the North Vietnamese not only didn't hurt him and the wounded soldier but the medic gave him his aid bag to help the wounded GI. He said that was God telling him he was correct in his beliefs. I couldn't disagree with him."

In late April, Mike wrote, "I began the day thinking that it would be fairly uneventful. Usually we moved in platoon-sized units so I felt a little safer with a whole company making a move. Boy was I wrong. The next week would see B 1/506th just about wiped out along with many others in the 1st Battalion."

"We combat assaulted into an abandoned FSB Maureen. My map had our expected route and distance marked in black grease pencil. We were to go about one and a half klicks along the ridge line toward FSB Kathryn on our first day of the operation. We were on guard as we walked through the jungle. We had been told to expect a regimental-sized unit of North Vietnamese Army regulars in the area. Although the second platoon was the point unit, my squad was the fourth squad in line. We moved approximately 300 meters from FSB Maureen when we made our first contact with the North Vietnamese Army at about 10:00 AM. What we didn't know was we were on top of a North Vietnamese Army stronghold dug underground. The firefight lasted until somewhere around noon. We broke contact and had some lunch."

"After lunch we tried to move again but immediately became involved in a firefight again. Slowly but surely each of the squads became pinned down. The radios were being hit so communications in the area of the firefight turned to yelling at each other. Somewhere around 2:30 PM a second platoon lieutenant told me to try to swing around the right flank of the North Vietnamese and try to break their line. What I didn't know at this time was the lieutenant's radio operator was already killed. He had been my radio operator until that morning. The lieutenant asked him if he wanted to be the platoon radio telephone operator. He jumped at the chance because it was safer operating at the platoon level rather than the squad level."

"I had my squad assembled behind a mound of dirt approximately 50 yards from the rest of the platoon. I was going to try and do a fast movement to our right and then just as fast try to move into the North Vietnamese perimeter. This should draw their attention away from everyone who was pinned down as well as give them a second area to worry about. As I was explaining to the squad what we were going to try to do I told Thomas Kaufman to stay behind the mound of dirt with the radio. I told him not to move out under any circumstances as it appeared the North Vietnamese were looking for the radios to knock them out. I looked around at the other guys in the squad and started to tell them one by one to stay behind the mound. I remember telling one guy to stay behind because I knew he was 'short,' another because he was married, another because he was a cherry, another because he had kids, and my machine gunner, Cal Nolt, because he was the youngest in the squad."

"Cal said, 'Sarge, you're finding reasons for all of us to stay back.' He was right."

"I looked at them all without saying anything, they knew that what we were about to do was not going to be pretty. I finally yelled, 'Fuck it, follow me if you want to.' I got up and started running. I guess I went about 75 yards through the jungle and cut to my left to run into the North Vietnamese positions. I got about 20 yards before a North Vietnamese machine gunner opened up on me. I froze, the bullets were hitting the ground right in front of me just like in cowboy movies, but they weren't getting any closer. Cal opened up on the North Vietnamese gunner and the bullets stopped."

"I jumped behind a big tree to my left for cover. When I hit the ground I bumped into my grenadier, he was right behind me as we ran. As the grenadier and I started to sit up, a sniper's bullet came through the tree. We both jumped back and yelled 'I'm hit.' As we both checked our bodies, he said 'I'm not hit, it was just the bark.' I said 'Oh, maybe I'm not hit either,' and I started to look at my leg. My grenadier said, 'You *were* hit, Sarge.' Still, I said 'No, I think it was the bark too.' He said 'Then what is that sticking out of your boot?' A bullet had entered my right leg on the left side and the bullet was sticking out of my boot on the right side of my leg."

"We were returning fire, the grenadier more than me. I thought he was taking too many risks shooting at the North Vietnamese and I told him to stay behind the cover. He said, 'It didn't help you did it?' He was right but I still didn't feel good about him exposing himself so much. We were pinned down for the next four hours. During that time the lieutenant called artillery in on top of us. He yelled the question to all of us. We all figured it was the only way we were going to get out of there so we all told him to call it in. The first round hit the ground and it was a dud. The ground shook so much we all reconsidered and called off the fire for effect."

"Somewhere around 7:00 PM something happened and my grenadier started moving forward. I found out later that Sergeant First Class Issac, our platoon sergeant, got up with two M16s in his hands and charged the North Vietnamese bunker line to my far left, shooting as he moved. A rocket-propelled grenade blew up in front of him and he slowly turned around to the guys. They said they thought his face would be full of blood when he turned around. As he turned they noticed that there was no blood, he yelled 'The motherfuckers didn't get me,' and continued his assault. He cleared a bunker by throwing a hand grenade into it and went on to the next bunker. A North Vietnamese soldier came out of the first bunker and aimed his rifle at Issac, and pulled the trigger. Issac heard the click and turned around and shot the North Vietnamese sniper."

"Later that evening Issac brought the rifle to me and said, 'Take a look at the gun that got you, I got him.' The gun was inoperable due to a piece of shrapnel from the hand grenade Issac threw into the bunker. The shrapnel had cracked the bolt of the gun and lodged in such a way that the firing pin could not reach the bullet in the chamber. The guys who saw what Issac did said that we would still be pinned down if it wasn't for him."

The day dragged on. The number of killed and wounded rose, and acts of heroism were not uncommon. Mike recalled, "Our medic had been shot four times that day. He was rendering aid to a guy we called 'Sweetmeat,' and a North Vietnamese sniper shot him in the knee; he continued to render aid. The sniper shot him a second time in the other knee. He continued to render aid. The sniper then shot him in his wrist; he continued to render aid. He then was shot for a fourth time in the other wrist. This guy who told me a few days ago that God didn't want us to hurt each other had just been shot four times by a North Vietnamese sniper who shot three other guys square in the head. I think he was right, God was on his side."

A medevac came for Mike and the other wounded men somewhere around 11:00 AM on April 26, 1970. As Mike wrote home, "We were taken to the 18th Surgical Hospital in Quang Tri. When we landed there were litter-bearers on the helipad. I told them I could walk with help. A sergeant from the 101st was standing there and said, 'No one walks here Trooper, let them carry you, your work's done.' It made me feel special."

"The sergeant told me in the emergency room that he was the liaison for the 101st and if we needed anything his job was to get it for us. I had a new nurse because she was looking at my wound and knew she had to debride it but she had never done it before. The liaison was standing there watching. He tried to tell her how to shave the area and cut the dead skin away from the wound but ... it must have been her first day. He looked at me and said, 'Trooper do you mind if I show her how to do it?' I said 'Go ahead, what do I have to lose?' The nurse was going crazy that the sergeant would do something that a nurse should be doing. He gave her some macho response like 'The 101st does everything,' or something like that. The sergeant debrided the wound fast and said to the nurse, 'See, it's not that hard, just do it.' She was a little embarrassed, a little guilty, and a little relieved. I was wheeled to a Quonset hut that was a hospital ward."

On May 6, Mike was flown to Da Nang, because the doctors at the 18th Surgical Hospital had decided that he wasn't going to heal in Vietnam. Mike recalled, "This came as a surprise to me because up until that time I believed I would get patched up and go back to my unit. I felt elated as well as sad because I didn't get to say goodbye to the guys in the squad." Mike would be in a hospital in the States until November. He was discharged from the Army with two years and seven days in service on December 10, 1970.

CHAPTER 21

Danny Mitchell

In Vietnam December 1969–December 1970

"We had very good leaders in Vietnam."

Battlin' Bastard Danny McNair took the initiative to interview several veterans who, quite understandably, were more comfortable speaking with a fellow veteran than an author who is not. What follows is Danny Mitchell's story as told to Danny McNair for the express purpose of this book, lightly edited by the author.

I was living in Martinsville, Indiana when I was drafted into the Army in 1969. I was a country boy who had never traveled outside the State of Indiana. I attended basic training at Fort Knox, Kentucky, and advanced infantry training at Fort Polk, Louisiana. I received orders for Vietnam and my cousin drove me to Indianapolis the end of November 1969 to begin my trip. I met a guy named Cranford at the Chicago Airport, who was with me in training. We were together on the same flight to Fort Lewis, Washington, and were also on the same flight to Cam Rahn Bay, Vietnam. We arrived the first part of December 1969. Cranford and myself received orders at Cam Rahn Bay. I was sent to the 101st Airborne and Cranford was assigned to the Americal Division.

I then took another flight to Camp Eagle, which was the headquarters for the 101st Airborne. I attended Screaming Eagle Replacement Training School before being assigned to Bravo Company, 1/506th Infantry. Bravo Company was located at Camp Evans, which was north of Camp Eagle. I received all of my gear, including an M16, and was sent to the field to join Bravo. Bravo was operating in the lowlands close to Camp Evans near Fire Support Base Jack, the French fort, and Rocket Ridge. It was very wet and sometimes cold in that part of the year. We were assigned to six-man teams setting up ambushes and also blowing landing zones. We were carried by helicopter to the sites for blowing an LZ. The helicopter would hover while we kicked off the cases of C-4 explosives and then we climbed down rope ladders to clear the area of trees for the landing of helicopters. We were also on FSB Rakkasan, which was just being built, and it was very wet and muddy there. Our company commander, Captain Lee Sullivan, did not like firebase duty because he said it was more likely to be attacked, being in a fixed position. We continued to operate all around this area in December 1969 and January 1970. We spent Christmas in and around FSB Jack. I can remember being near FSB Jack looking back towards Rocket Ridge one time and observing a couple of elephants walking along the base of the ridge. We were told that the North Vietnamese sometimes used elephants for carrying their supplies, especially through the A Shau Valley.

We began to move towards the higher mountains west of Rocket Ridge in February and there were many more signs of enemy activity. We had received orders to go to the aid of a downed helicopter during this time around the first part of February. The first day in February the third platoon was attacked, resulting in one killed and several wounded. I had been walking point for first platoon and as I recall we had stopped for a break. Our platoon leader, Lieutenant Falco, decided to train a new man to walk point. The platoon moved out with the new man in the lead with Stahley, West, and Freeman following. They began to move out and there was a large explosion. Stahley and West both lost a leg in the booby trap explosion. Platoon Sergeant Freeman was also wounded and would be medevac'd out with Stahley and West. Stahley and West would not return to the field and were sent home. Freeman would eventually return to first platoon.

Another event that I remember very well occurred on February 1, 1970. We had found four graves and were ordered by battalion to dig them up to identify how they had been killed. This was one of my worst experiences because the smell was so bad. The bodies had been wrapped in ponchos and we determined they were killed by artillery. The remainder of February and March I do not really remember much that stands out. We did begin to find more enemy bunker complexes and enemy equipment. I do remember the Chieu Hoi scouts during that time, who found some of the North Vietnamese bunkers and soldiers. Sam Brown, who was a friend of mine, had a scout. Later in March I do remember FSB Granite being attacked and going out to provide security after many of the men in that battle were wounded or killed. I remember we used a starlight scope while there on Granite. I do not remember anything else of significance while on Granite.

I fell and infected my knee in March or April and was sent to Camp Evans until it could heal. I was not in the field for the major battles of April 25 or May 1. I returned to the field after May 1 while the company was back around the FSB Maureen area. We would continue to find enemy bunker complexes and [continue to have] sighting[s] of the enemy. There was support fire at various times with air support and artillery from the firebases. This support fire could be while humping or around a perimeter of a night defensive position. I also remember the North Vietnamese firing mortars, but none that hit us. I do remember seeing a B-52 strike at some point, but cannot recall the date. There was one attack on FSB Rakkasan where the North Vietnamese fired rocket-propelled grenades. There was another night when we heard North Vietnamese mortar tubes being fired while we were set up in nighttime defense position. I remember we could see flashlights in the area where the North Vietnamese were located the night of May 23, where the mortars were being fired from. Captain Sullivan directed fire that night to the mortar positions which stopped the mortar fire.

We were sent into Camp Evans June 1 for a three-day standdown and received some training. After the three days at Evans, we were back to the Maureen area to resume the same type of operations. We eventually ended up around the top of the mountain where FSB Maureen was located. We were near an old landing zone one day taking a break when second platoon got into contact not far from where I was located with first platoon and headquarters platoon. Word came back to us that some enemy intelligence had been taken after the contact and that it was to be picked for the intelligence by helicopter and taken back to the rear area. We remained in position until the helicopter picked up the intelligence and then set up a nighttime defense position with headquarters platoon. The second platoon set up a night defensive position not far from us.

We were on high alert that night for a possible attack. A little after midnight the second platoon did come under heavy attack. We were ordered to prepare to move out in support of second platoon. It was dark and we began to proceed very cautiously towards their positions. By the time we were getting close to them, the heavy fighting was almost over. We made it into their perimeter and immediately took up positions. Staff Sergeant Turner, Bob Haberle, and I took cover in a bomb crater made by a B-52 strike. During this time, we were throwing some grenades and actually engaged a wounded attacker, killing him. I threw one grenade that hit a tree, as sometimes happens, and it exploded. The men in my position latter gave me the nickname of "Marshmallow Arm." The next morning as it became light, we could see the results of the attack. Everyone that was able began to do what was required to move casualties to be medevac'd and to police up the discarded equipment to be taken out. I helped stack all the enemy dead together in one pile in the same bomb crater we had used as a defensive position. Much of second platoon had either been killed or wounded. The remainder of second platoon combined with the rest of the company and we all moved out of the area of the attack. We were around the immediate area for a few days and at some point, began to move off the mountain down a ridgeline. This all happened June 25 and 26, according to official records.

We soon picked up some dog teams and continued to move on down the mountain. I recall this was during the beginning of July, because my birthday was on July 3, 1970. My good friend Hank Bow ("Hound Dog") also had the same birthday. We were finding increasing amounts of enemy bunkers, ammunition, supplies, and graves. On July 3, the dogs were sent out and alerted. We called in artillery to the area where the dogs alerted. On July 4, the rear part of the company, which was higher up on the ridge behind us, was attacked by rocket-propelled grenades, wounding four of our men in first platoon. On July 5, we spotted the enemy not far away from us. Sergeant Keck, who was an excellent leader, called in artillery with great accuracy and the explosions were right on top of them.

That night, as it came time to set up in a night defensive position, we convinced our platoon leader, Lieutenant Lucas, to set up on a higher point because the weather was bad. This meant moving back up the hill some distance. I was having some trouble getting up the hill and I ran into Sergeant Borusiewich from third platoon. Borusiewich was a very sturdily built man and he reached out a hand and pulled me on up and said, "I bet I looked like God to you." (Borusiewich would be wounded the next day.) The rest of our company, made up of third platoon, headquarters platoon, and what was left of second platoon, set up some distance away from us.

We received a call near daybreak the morning of July 6 that the other night defensive position had been hit and we were ordered out in their support. We quickly grabbed our gear and moved out, with most men not having time for any breakfast. Our regular platoon sergeant, Mike Turner, had gone into the rear a couple of days earlier for medical reasons so our staff sergeant, Sandy Porter, led the platoon out that morning towards the area of the attack. When we were approaching the perimeter of their night defensive position, shots were fired by someone on their perimeter, fatally wounding Staff Sergeant Porter by friendly fire. We were eventually able to proceed on into their perimeter and take up positions. We were all in a state of shock and depressed by the loss of Porter, who was a great leader loved by all of us. The medevac finally was able to get all the casualties out. We moved out and patrolled for the next few days in the general area. Everyone thought we would be attacked again, but we were finally picked up by choppers and flown to FSB Bastogne where we worked on ambush teams and truck security before being sent to a firebase.

I had been a radio telephone operator at squad or platoon level and sometime in the next couple of months was moved up to the company operator. My memory of where we were is not clear during this time because we were moving from one area to another all the time. Someone gave me the nickname "Mad Dog," which became my call sign on the radio. I picked up the name probably because I was from Indiana and loved hunting dogs and hunting. There are some events I remember that have stuck with me. There was one time that our Battalion Commander Lieutenant Colonel Porter ("Razorback") came out to the field to spend some time with Bravo Company. I knew his call sign because I was on the radio. He came over to introduce himself to me and asked me if there was anything I needed. I explained to the Colonel that I had needed some boots and no one could ever find my size. He asked me for my size and he left in his helicopter. Probably two to three hours later his helicopter returned, landed, and someone jumped off and handed me a pair of boots my exact size.

We had very good leaders in Vietnam and I give a lot of credit to Lieutenant Falco and Staff Sergeant Mike Turner for getting me back home, because they made good decisions. We also had many good troopers I fought with, medics and all other support. I am still great friends with many of the men I served with. One funny story that stands out concerns Doc Lohm, who is still a friend of mine. Medics took great care of us in so many ways that included [treating] the infections we received in the field that caused boils, cellulitis, and other infections. Doc Lohm was from New York, but he talked with a "John Wayne" drawl. I had a very bad boil on my buttocks that really needed some attention. Doc came over to take care of it. In his John Wayne drawl he said, "Drop your pants, Pilgrim! And would you like for me to get you a bullet to bite down on while I take care of this?" He has not changed much and still has his same voice after all these years.

I was still in the field November 1970 and was getting close to leaving Vietnam in December. I was the Bravo Company radio telephone operator by that time and kept in touch with my good friend Bob Haberle ("Ragman"). Ragman had been the first platoon radio man in the field with me the first few months I was in Bravo. He eventually received a job in battalion and left first platoon. Bob always joked with me that he came to Vietnam one day before me and would leave before me. Ragman called for me one night on the radio in late November. The guy on the radio watch at that time woke me up and said that Ragman wanted to speak to me. I got on the radio and told Ragman that because he woke me up that it better be something important. Ragman started the same joke and asked me if I knew when I was going home. I responded back that yes, I guess it would be one day after him. Ragman then responded that both of us had just received a twenty-two-day drop and would be leaving in six days to go home! He told me to get back to Camp Evans immediately. The weather was bad and I did not know how I was going to get to Camp Evans. I came up with a plan. I went to the captain and told him that with all the wet weather that if the men didn't get some dry socks, they would begin to have issues with their feet. The captain ordered some socks. The weather was still very poor all the next day. Late in the day the sky just opened up and a chopper with the dry socks the captain ordered showed up. I jumped on the chopper waving to everyone and headed back to Evans just in time to leave.

When I arrived in Cam Rahn Bay to go home, I met my friend Cranford again, who came over with me in 1969. Cranford had served his time in the Americal Division while I had served mine in the 101st Airborne Division with Bravo Company. On the flight home we had a delay in Japan and were to remain there for 36 hours. I bought two fifths of bourbon to take home with me. We ended up in a motel and decided it was time to celebrate going home. I gathered together maybe four or five men and we drank all the bourbon. I bought two more fifths to take home. Cranford and I arrived at Fort Lewis to be reprocessed back and left on the same flight back to Chicago. Cranford then flew to Detroit and my flight was back to Indianapolis. When I arrived at the airport, I called my mother to pick me up. My mother and great aunt arrived, and we were driving back home from the airport. On the way home a police car that was parked by the side of the road pulled out in front of us and we were following. My mother joked that I was receiving a police escort! I reported to duty at Fort Knox, Kentucky, and met Cranford again. We served the remainder of our five months together. I returned to the job I had prior to the Army, at a nearby brickyard.

CHAPTER 22

Robert Harasick

In Vietnam January 1970–December 1970

> "In the BUSH there ain't no whites, Blacks, browns, Catholics, Jews or Protestants, just GRUNTS!"

For his contribution to this book, Robert chose to share some "short yarns" about events he experienced during his tour in Vietnam. These have been lightly edited by the author with his permission.

Impressions play an important part in being a leader and when I was assigned as the commander of Bravo Company one of the things I was worried about was being fashionably correct. *Do I wear a flak jacket or not? Is my camouflage helmet cover too new? Wear rank and name tags, and are they too new? Jungle fatigues too new?* Well, after being airlifted to the company, I was the combat fashion model of the company. On my first day upon leaving the Huey, I heard a call I thought was directed to me. It sounded like "F—you." I quickly looked around to see who said that, when I heard it again. I thought to myself, *What kind of unit is this telling the company commander "F—you?!"* Well, the outgoing commander greeted me when the call came again, and as he looked at my facial expression, he said, "Don't worry, it's a lizard that makes that 'f—k you' noise."

Apparently, the company was being resupplied that day, so I decided to walk around the perimeter introducing myself, trying to get to know the troops. The Huey was just above me when I looked up to see a tree branch come falling directly onto me. The branch hit me in the face, knocking me back a few yards. As I was falling back, I thought to myself, *The troops must think I am a complete f—up.* Luckily, I did not get injured and I just got up and walked around like nothing happened. The next day the company split into platoon-sized units and moved out to go on patrol. On the fourth day we set up an early night defensive position. Well, after four days I had not had any bowel movements, so I went into the jungle to take care of my biological needs. Upon my return I was greeted by an extremely upset non-commissioned officer who chewed the heck out of me. Apparently, I walked out of the perimeter and was subjected to [risk of] being killed by friendly troops or captured by the enemy. That was the last time I ever did that, and as a footnote I can't recall ever moving my bowels during my entire time in the field. While on patrol we came across a small river that had a large pool and was very inviting. After setting up a defensive position and searching the area for bad guys, we rotated men to bathe and swim for a while. This is after patrolling for three weeks without a bath or a shave. I remember how happy the troops looked forgetting about the war and just enjoying having fun and a little relaxation. These were combat soldiers acting like teenage kids. Even the fish biting the troopers' bodies didn't create a problem!

Patrolling during the monsoons, you learned that you could sleep with water runoff as a mattress. Nothing is dry and trying to climb a hill with a ninety-pound ruck is almost impossible. The clay is very slippery, it is cold, and lightning was constant and dangerous. One time, we established a night defensive position on the top of a mountain in the middle of a monsoon thunderstorm when lightning struck a short distance away, electrifying the area around us. Those soldiers in direct contact with the ground received a shock, and I had a six-foot earthworm or snake crawling between my legs. I really don't know what it was except it was BIG and moving fast.

A technique we used to try and stay safe was to set up a claymore ambush. A claymore ambush consists of several claymores pointed in the direction of an approaching enemy. One night we were told that the enemy was angry that we were in their area, and "they were going to destroy us." Well, that night we set up an ambush and it was initiated around three in the morning. Naturally the entire perimeter was awake waiting for the attack. Sunrise came and no attack. A squad was sent to check the area of the ambush and [they] were to count the bodies they found there. The count was zero because the ambush was initiated by one huge python! No bad guys.

Combat troops travel either by foot or on Hueys. While travelling by helicopter, soldiers have a fear of falling out of the bird because the pilots love to bank very steep and fast. Soldiers look for something to hang on to so they will not fall out. You be surprised how much leverage a screwhead has to hold on to. And for your feet—a pair of dry socks is worth a million dollars!

After spending time in the jungle (three–five weeks), the company would be given the mission to secure and defend a firebase. Roughly, a firebase is on the top of a mountain that has artillery pieces and a command structure. The infantry is used as manual laborers, filling sandbags, digging foxholes, patrolling, etc. We live in bunkers that may or may not be dry, share a residence with bugs and three-foot rats that love to chew on ears and toes. An unauthorized sport is how many rats one can kill in one's sleeping area. However, there is usually mail and hot food.

Every so often the company receives a stand-down. A stand-down is usually time in the rear, in which the unit goes to Eagle Beach for rest and relaxation. Eagle Beach is a beautiful ocean beach that offers hot food, beer, massage parlors, swimming, and just the good old times. After the beach, soldiers can get clean uniforms, boots, fighting equipment, a haircut, and a shower in their respective areas. One can also use a unique public restroom facility called a "piss tube." A piss tube is a six-inch-wide tube drilled in the ground that you can use to relieve yourself while traveling in camp. *Playboy* magazines very rarely were received in the mail, beer isn't that bad warm, care packages are shared, hot sauce is invaluable, round eyes (American females) are perfect, you don't use drugs in the bush. In the BUSH there ain't no whites, Blacks, browns, Catholics, Jews, or Protestants, just GRUNTS!

CHAPTER 23

Don Rollings

In Vietnam April 1970–April 1971

> "I looked up to where my ruck and M16 were located and could see the ruck had been hit and was burning."

Battlin' Bastard Danny McNair took the initiative to interview several veterans who, quite understandably, were more comfortable speaking with a fellow veteran than an author who is not. What follows is Don's story as told to Danny for the express purpose of this book, lightly edited by the author.

I was living in Washington State with my parents while working for the railroad before I was inducted into the Army. I received basic training and advanced infantry training, both at Fort Ord, California. I then received orders for Vietnam and my brother took me to the airport to report to Oakland, California, to be processed to Vietnam. I arrived in Cam Rahn Bay in April 1970 and then received orders to the 101st Airborne. I attended Screaming Eagle Replacement Training School, which was required for all incoming replacements, and was assigned to Bravo Company to receive my equipment and supplies required in the field. We were told the rucksack with all the equipment we received would weigh about eighty pounds or more. I carried an M16 rifle, four bandoliers of M16 ammunition, one hundred rounds of M60 ammunition for the M60 machine gun, two claymore mines with detcord, blasting caps, detonators and wire, two pounds of C-4 explosives, an M72 LAW, six days of C-rations, eight quarts of water, seven frag grenades (one in my web for easy access and six on my rucksack), two smoke grenades, an entrenching tool, machete, poncho, poncho liner, a personal waterproof box that was used to carry my toilet tissue, personal hygiene items, extra socks, maybe an extra shirt, letter and writing materials, a steel pot, body armor, and insect repellent. There were veterans in the rear who provided help in what was needed and what to expect. The company had just been attacked a few days before I went out to the field, with many wounded and killed.

I was to be a replacement for the heavy losses in second platoon. I was flown out by helicopter to the platoon in the field about the end of April 1970. The company was located up on a ridgeline, which I would later learn was near FSB Maureen. We began moving down that ridgeline, and on my third day in the field we had stopped at an old landing zone to be resupplied. The resupply began and helicopters were coming and going for some time. I was located on the top edge of the landing zone with second platoon facing the direction we had just come from. Second platoon was assigned that part of the perimeter responsibility.

A squad leader had directed me to police up the area around us so that the trash could be burned. I had placed my rucksack down and leaned my M16 up against the ruck and began policing the area as ordered. The squad leader stopped me and wanted to introduce me to another sergeant, since I was a replacement and had only been in the field about three days. I was standing with the sergeants when an AK-47 opened up. I immediately hit the ground and began crawling for cover, thinking the two sergeants may have both been wounded. We were receiving heavy fire, and grenades were being thrown down towards us from higher positions above the landing zone. I looked up to where my ruck and M16 were located and could see the ruck had been hit and was burning. Lieutenant Falco from first platoon had come up to my position and told me to get my M16. I told him that my ruck with my equipment had been hit and was burning along with my M16. Cobras were called in for support and firing all around our positions.

Finally, the North Vietnamese attack was stopped. I was able to reach my ruck to salvage some food and personal items. I realized a claymore on my ruck had been hit by enemy fire, thus starting the fire on my ruck. I was able to find enough equipment and another M16 from all of the equipment left behind by our casualties. When the battle was over there were only three men left in our second platoon. I did not know if the sergeants I thought were hit were OK until many years later. The third platoon also had killed and wounded that day.

We finally were able to medevac out all of our killed and wounded along with the equipment and weapons they had been carrying. Our second platoon was combined with the rest of the company, and we moved out of the area where we were attacked. I would not remember all of the names of the men I served with. I know that by May 1, 1970, I had met Sergeant Doug Turner, who was one of the squad leaders who arrived almost the same time as me. John Garza was another of the first men I would meet, who also arrived about the same time as me. There were others like Duane Day, Wylie Glover, and Roger Fitch, to name a few, who would all end up in second platoon with me. We were all on high alert, believing there was a good possibility of being attacked again that same night of May 1. We did not get hit that night.

We continued to move all around that same general area over the next few weeks. I can't recall the exact timing of where we were and when, but there were events that became part of a routine of humping most of the time, finding signs of the enemy such as bunker complexes, markings on trails, comma wire, and enemy supplies.

There were also the times of calling in artillery or air support to destroy enemy positions or sightings. We were on a couple of firebases during this time in May to provide security in and around them. We were on FSB Rakkasan when it was attacked by rocket-propelled grenades. We were near FSB Kathryn when we heard mortar tubes firing. We later found out the North Vietnamese were firing at Kathryn, the same base we had just left, that same night. Our company called in artillery and air support on the area where the North Vietnamese mortars were firing from. Most of us would not find out until many years later that the attack resulted in many American personnel wounded and killed on Kathryn that night.

We were airlifted to Camp Evans for training and then sent back out after a mere three-day stand-down. We combat assaulted back to the area around the Rau Trang River and FSB Maureen. We were on patrols in June finding a lot of signs of the enemy and experiencing some minor contact. On June 25, 1970, we were near FSB Maureen on a landing zone near a trail when two to three North Vietnamese moved down the trail and were engaged by some of our men from second platoon with a frag grenade. The men who engaged the North Vietnamese thought that maybe one of them had been hit by the grenade, and a patrol was sent out to follow them. The patrol found a blood trail and a rucksack. The rucksack was inspected and was full of intelligence. The rucksack contained satchel charges, also an indication that they were sappers. There were also maps with plans to attack nearby firebases. This information was reported, and second platoon was ordered to wait on a chopper to come out and pick up the rucksack.

By this time, we were well aware the enemy had our exact location and everyone was beginning to get nervous. We had been at that same location for a period of time before a light observation helicopter picked up the North Vietnamese rucksack. It was getting late and it was decided to set up a night defensive position, which made me more uneasy. It was decided the night defensive position would be set up on a lower part of the old landing zone. I remember the lower part could be measured [so] when standing up that the upper part was a head high above us. The lower portion, when walking off down from the landing zone, off to the right there were some trees. We were set up in three-man positions with nine total men on my side of the night defensive position and nine men on the other side. I think there were three men in the middle of the night defensive position for a total of twenty-one men. I felt very uneasy, with a strong feeling we were going to be attacked that night. I told the other two newer men in my position with me to stay alert.

I was waiting until dark to set out my claymores as I always tried to carry two of them when available. Sergeant First Class Reid, who was a Green Beret attached to Bravo, earlier had instructed me about setting out the claymores in front of our positions as close to dark as possible for better concealment from the North Vietnamese Army. The acting platoon leader, a sergeant first class, came by while it was still daylight and asked me if I had set out my claymores. I told him no because

I thought it was better to wait until dark so I would not be seen by the North Vietnamese setting them out. He told me to set them out and I again responded, no, I was not going to set them out because it was a bad idea. He gave me another order and I obeyed by setting them out against my better judgment.

We were prepared to have one man awake at every position, taking turns all night on watch. I was in my position with two fairly new replacements and I took the first watch. I was not awakened later for my next turn on watch. Instead, we were attacked and I was awakened by the first explosion. I rolled over a log and spotted a North Vietnamese soldier almost even within our perimeter and shot him. I then spotted another further up the landing zone and tried to fire again, but my weapon jammed. I was attempting to fix the jammed M16 when an explosive charge was thrown at my position and landed right under my chest. I dropped the M16, stood up, and dived away from the explosion. I could feel the blast on my legs and feet as I dove.

I was wounded in the arm and the explosive charge landed on my M16, causing it to be inoperable. I did not know what had happened to the other two men at my position. I was without a weapon and told some men on my side, which had been hit the worst, that I was going to get to the other side of the perimeter and try to find another M16. The men on the other side told me to get in a foxhole. I refused, telling them I needed an M16. No one had an extra M16, so I returned to my side of the perimeter. There was a tremendous amount of support fire and illumination fire coming in all around us. The nearby night defensive position with first platoon made their way to our night defensive position in support.

When daylight finally arrived, we could see our dead as well as the North Vietnamese dead all around the night defensive position. There were also satchel charges that had not been detonated by the North Vietnamese Army lying all around. We had to get all of our killed and wounded out. I also went out to take down our claymores so that none of our men would set any of them off by accident. My ears were ringing and I could not hear. I also had the arm wound, so I was flown out to the USS *Sanctuary*. The doctors on the hospital ship told me in order to remove the shrapnel they would have to cut some muscle out of my arm. I told them I would not allow them to damage the muscles in my arm. I explained that my job back home was with the railroad, and the possible permanent loss of those muscles would end my career when I returned home.

I was returned back to Camp Evans and my major concern was that I had lost my hearing. Being sent back to the field with no hearing would put me in a very bad position to defend myself. My hearing had to be improved before I was fit for duty in the field as an infantryman. For the time, I would serve as a night guard on the perimeter of Camp Evans most nights. The perimeter was set up and defended to the point that the hearing loss was not as much of a concern as in the field.

This went on for months, with my perforated ear drums being constantly tested. There was gradual improvement.

Finally, I was assigned to a facility I believe was called OP [outpost] Phantom. It was designed with some type of radar scope to scan and detect enemy movement. There was no concertina wire around the hilltop where the radar was located. When movement was detected, it was reported so that airstrikes could be called in on the movement. I provided security and cleared brush from around the perimeter. I was assigned to a two-man position on alert all night until morning, when the men from patrols in the area around the facility returned.

There was a small landing strip at the bottom of the hilltop for helicopters to bring in supplies. Chinook helicopters would bring in bladders of fuel to run the radar equipment on top of the hill. I was informed that Bravo Company could be assigned to OP Phantom to rotate platoons in and out for security. The 101st was reducing troop strength in Vietnam at a greater rate and anyone with less than three months' remaining in the military was able to receive an early drop out of Vietnam and the Army. I tried to extend my tour and was denied. I eventually traveled to Australia for an R&R. On the way back from Australia I was able to visit a friend of mine assigned to transportation. My departure date came up in April of 1971 and I returned home.

I was then assigned to Fort Sill, Oklahoma with about five months left in the Army. I applied for the honor guard at Fort Sill and was accepted. I was involved in military funerals and also met other Vietnam veterans. It was actually good for me at Fort Sill to be able to talk to others who had been to Vietnam. It was a great therapy versus just going back home with no one to talk about my experiences who would understand. I returned back home to Washington and was blessed to retire from the railroad after 39 years of service.

CHAPTER 24

Danny McNair

In Vietnam April 1970–March 1971

> "When I look back at the situation of constant replacements for the casualties incurred as well as those who were about to DEROS, it was amazing that Bravo did as well as it did under such difficult circumstances."

The following was submitted in writing and lightly edited by the author with Danny's permission.

I was inducted in to the Army in 1969 with basic training at Fort Bragg and advanced individual training at Fort McClellan, Alabama. I was living in North Carolina with my parents in between attending college when I was drafted. My father had been a career Marine who had joined in 1940 and fought in the bloody Pacific amphibious battles/landings across the islands. He was seriously wounded on Peleliu. He made the famous Inchon Landing in Korea and was also surrounded at the Chosin Reservoir. He continued to be on ships and deployed to other countries. My mother had been through too many deployments already, worrying and taking care of my brother and me. I said goodbye to my mother on the front porch and my father took me to the airport.

I left for Vietnam in April 1970 to be processed from Fort Lewis, Washington. I landed in Cam Rahn Bay, Vietnam. The wait for orders was relatively short at Cam Rahn. I received my orders to go to the 101st Airborne based about four hundred miles north of Cam Rahn Bay. This would be my first stop for processing before going another twenty-five miles north of Camp Eagle to Bravo Company, 1/506th, at Camp Evans. Army units no longer came over and left as a unit, but were assigned as needed replacements based on MOS, which for me was the infantry. There seemed to be a lot of men going to the 101st. The 3rd Brigade Headquarters was in Phu Bai where Camp Eagle was located. We were assigned to long wooden sleeping quarters with tin roofs at Camp Eagle for processing. This was my first real experience with the heat, humidity, and mosquitos, which we would become acclimated to in time.

I would attend SERTS before actually reporting to Bravo Company. This would be our air assault training for combat assaults from helicopters. We would also be trained in patrolling, the use of equipment like starlight scopes, and pull actual guard duty on the perimeter. We became familiar with the method of air assault on a Bell UH-1 Iroquois (Huey) helicopter that usually carried six fully equipped infantry. The helicopter crew would consist of a pilot, co-pilot, and a door gunner on each side with M60 machine guns mounted on a swivel pedestal. The infantry would usually fly with two outside men dangling their feet out each side of the chopper above the skids and with two others in the middle. The plan was to unload the infantry as quickly as possible as the chopper came into the landing zone for a combat assault, which meant sometimes the chopper would hover slightly above the ground, never landing for unloading. The training required several days to complete. Many people in the United States at that time thought that the Vietnam War was winding down, and it was for the most part, but the 101st Airborne seemed to be pretty active

I arrived at Bravo Company at Camp Evans and was assigned to similar barracks (hooches) like those at Camp Eagle. We received the remainder of our equipment and would prepare to be taken out to the field. The 1/506th Infantry Battalion and the 2/506th Infantry Battalion were both located at Camp Evans as part of the 3rd Brigade. I met other replacements at Bravo Company and would meet many more in the days ahead, all arriving about the same time. It was obvious that Bravo Company had recently sustained many casualties.

Final preparations were being made for me to be taken out on a supply chopper to join up with Bravo Company in the field. There were always men in the rear area from Bravo Company at Camp Evans. Some were on light duty recovering from all the infections or injuries that can occur in the field, some coming off R&R, some preparing to end their Vietnam tour of duty, or rear personnel such as clerks, supply, etc. These men were a source of information on what was going on in the field or just of helpful information for the replacement cherries preparing to go out.

Some of the veterans' suggestions were to carry more than three of the 1-quart canteens that you were issued. It was suggested by someone that eight 1-quart canteens were a good number to carry and that there were a lot of discarded rucksacks and equipment in a hooch behind the Bravo CP [so] that I might be able to pick up extra canteens. I was directed to that hooch, but I was not prepared for what I saw when I entered that hooch of discarded equipment. The hooch was full of the equipment from the recent wounded and killed over particularly the last two to three weeks. I began going through the equipment trying to find five additional canteens. Much of the equipment had been riddled by bullets, shrapnel, and stained with blood. It ended up being difficult to find canteens that did not have holes. This immediately instilled the reality of what I would soon face. The discarded equipment almost had a smell of death. This was something I would remember for the rest of my life.

I would finally load up my eighty-pound rucksack and my M16, and proceed to the helipad for transport to the field on or around May 14, 1970. I flew out on a Huey resupply chopper with another replacement named David Sanchez, who would be part of my squad in second platoon. There were many thoughts going through my head as we flew out over the jungle and mountainous terrain of what was actually a beautiful country covered by a thick jungle canopy. We were coming up on our final ascent to the company location. We circled and as the chopper came closer to the ground, I could finally see a river through the thick canopy. This was a river I would become familiar with in the coming months, named the Rao Trang River, located below the abandoned FSB Maureen.

I would also become quite familiar with the nearby area where the abandoned FSB Maureen was located on Hill 980. There was a break in the canopy right over a very shallow place in the Rao Trang River with exposed rocks. The chopper hovered just above the rocks as David Sanchez and myself hopped off and headed towards a perimeter of men that had been concealed in the thick vegetation. This was also always an opportunity to bring out supplies, water, etc., that were also offloaded. I was immediately placed with an experienced trooper named MacArthur Reid to learn some of the ropes of being in the field with the company. We were only in the field for a couple of days before we were airlifted to defend FSB Rakkasan on May 17, 1970.

May 18, 1970, we would be hit at night by a rocket-propelled grenade attack on FSB Rakkasan, with David Sanchez and MacArthur Reid both wounded. Sanchez had a very slight wound and MacArthur was sent to Da Nang for wounds that required more care. While on Rakkasan I would become more familiar with two very good squad leaders in Sergeant Doug Turner and Sergeant Vic Cambas, both in second platoon. Both NCOs had already been through some very tough combat before I arrived. It was obvious these two NCOs cared about their men and had a tough task of receiving in a great number of replacements, because second platoon had been in the worst of the action with most of the losses.

Sergeants Turner from Nebraska and Cambas from Louisiana had an air about them that instilled confidence in the men in their squads, and I greatly respected both of them. I began training as a radio telephone operator and I would end up walking point for Sergeant Turner later. There was not much time to turn all of us cherries into a team if we were to survive in this FSB Maureen area of Vietnam. When I look back at the situation of constant replacements for the casualties incurred as well as those who were about to go back to the States, it was amazing that Bravo did as well as it did under such difficult circumstances.

We were airlifted again on May 21, 1970, to FSB Kathryn for a couple of days in defense of the perimeter. I would become more familiar with Sergeant Turner, Sergeant Cambas, Staff Sergeant Gist, and Sergeant First Class Reid because I was training as a radio telephone operator and was around the senior NCOs as well. Reid was actually a Green Beret attached to Bravo to complete his tour of duty and would be leaving for home soon, but he was another NCO that instilled confidence in the new men. I remember when we were attacked on May 18, Sergeant First Class Reid was running up and down the perimeter line directing fire as the rocket-propelled grenades had just been fired at us.

Our squad would consist of probably eighty percent new men. The NCOs had to quickly evaluate each man and put them in positions based on their evaluations. Wylie Glover was a strong guy from Kentucky who could hump those mountains better than anyone I knew and was assigned to the M-60 machine gun. Wylie was also one of the most dependable and could really put down some fire power. I would end up walking point, Roger Fitch from Ohio would walk right behind me in the slack position, and David Sanchez would carry the M40 grenade launcher, which we referred to as a Thumper. Brian Allen from New Hampshire was a good trooper, and so was Duane Day from Illinois. These were the men in our squad that would all depend on one another.

The squad leaders, like Doug Turner and Vic Cambas, would find out who kept their weapons clean, who would dig in adequately at night on the night defensive positions, who took care of themselves and their equipment, who followed orders well, and basically who could be trusted to do their job to the best of their ability. The squad leaders would then place groups of men at positions around the perimeter. The squad leaders also directed placement of mines out in front of the positions that were connected by wire and a detonator to be remotely detonated in the case of movement or an actual attack. The M60 machine guns were also strategically placed around the night defensive position as well because they provided the heaviest firepower. The night defensive position was manned with someone awake all night at each dug-in position taking turns awake on guard while the others at that position slept. This required a lot of trust and teamwork.

On May 23, 1970, Captain Sullivan would lead Bravo Company off of FSB Kathryn to conduct the daily routine search and destroy that took place when we were not on a firebase or a three-day stand down at Camp Evans for training, etc. The firebases were a prime target for the North Vietnamese because most of our infantry fire support originated from the large artillery and mortars. These fire support bases were strategically located around the A Shau Valley with the purpose of blocking North Vietnamese troops and supplies coming from North Vietnam.

The first night off the firebase, we could hear the distinct and deadly sound of enemy mortar tubes being fired near our position. This was something we would hear more of with Bravo, and we would always wait in anticipation of what was being targeted. Captain Sullivan called in air support, directing all the firepower possible at the estimated sound and point of origin of the firing. The North Vietnamese Army mortar attack was directed at the artillery on FSB Kathryn, which we had just left, resulting in three killed and twenty-five wounded. The remainder of May resulted in finding bunker complexes destroyed by air strikes. It was also very obvious that Bravo Company was in an area with great numbers of North Vietnamese present. Heavy-gauge commo wire was found on wide trails, in addition to the bunker complexes indicating the large units of North Vietnamese. We did not realize how many North Vietnamese units we were up against until many years later, through reading the after-action and intelligence reports.

We were airlifted back to Camp Evans the first of June for training and a change of command ceremony for our company commander, Captain Lee Sullivan, who would be replaced by Captain Bob Harasick. Captain Sullivan had completed his six months in the field and was being reassigned. There had recently been several officers wounded in the area around the former FSB Maureen. Chuck Choney, the third platoon leader, was wounded on May 1, 1970; Lieutenant Ed McCrystal, the second platoon leader, was wounded on April 25 and May 1. Lieutenant Pete Falco, the first platoon leader, was assigned duties with the South Vietnamese Army troops around this time and then to a FSB as he completed his six-month tour in the field. We were flown back out, after the three days at Camp Evans, to our usual area of operations around the Rao Trang River, Maureen, Kathryn, and other firebases. We had been on the same day in, day out routine. We then heard we were going to be flown to an area near FSB Ripcord.

We were near the area of FSB Maureen and FSB Kathryn until June 13, 1970, when we combat assaulted to the area northwest of FSB Ripcord. When I jumped off the helicopter I was coming in on, there was another company we relieved. That company had been defending the FSB Ripcord area and they jumped back on the same helicopters to leave the area that we came in on. I knew this was Charlie Company 2/506th because a friend of mine named Don Williams was with Charlie Company 2/506th, and this was a one-in-a-million-chance happening: he jumped back on the same helicopter I had just exited. We had seconds to exchange greetings. Don Williams and I met at the bus station on the way to basic training at Fort Bragg in 1969 and stayed together in training until we were both sent to Vietnam. My parents kept in touch, and I knew he was with our sister battalion the 2/506th with Charlie Company. This is the only time we would see each other in Vietnam because he was later seriously wounded in defense of FSB Ripcord on July 7, 1970, near Hill 1,000, and sent to Japan for major medical attention. We have stayed together as friends and have discussed this chance encounter for over fifty-three years, always wondering how it occurred.

On June 15, 1970, we were airlifted on a CA from the Ripcord area of operations back to our own area of operations near the Rao Trang River, which was at the base of FSB Maureen. There were more minor encounters with the North Vietnamese, with mortars and AK-47 rounds. More bunkers were destroyed by artillery. Infantry companies routinely set up landing zones landing zones at strategic areas within their assigned areas of operation. These were areas that were cleared of all trees using C-4, which was a plastic explosive to allow for immediate or future use to bring in helicopter for a CA, supply, or medevac chopper. I can remember going on at least one detail to blow a landing zone in this area. You never knew when a landing zone might be needed, but the disadvantage is the North Vietnamese also knew the purpose and could booby-trap the landing zone or zero it in with mortars if it was used.

We resumed our search and destroy and employed the best practice of avoiding the old, well-maintained trails by making our own trails through very thick vegetation. I can remember walking point and using a machete to make new trails in very hot and humid conditions that required a lot of water and breaks to prevent heat exhaustion. These old, well-maintained trails were a prime target area for the North Vietnamese ambushes and booby traps. This is where the good leadership of the officers and squad leaders [gained] through their experience probably prevented ambushes. My experience while in the field was that we were never ambushed on a trail. The routine each day was always pretty much the same, with the exception of major engagements. [It's] almost impossible to remember when and where something happened unless detailed years later with after-action reports. The same was true for the air support.

I was taken out of the field about June 20–22 for a medical test in Phu Bai and would not return for about a week. I was therefore not involved in the action of June 25/26 which resulted in major losses. With only about six men left in second platoon after the action of June 26, 1970, we were combined with headquarters platoon and third platoon. We received tracking dogs near the end of June, which were the first I had seen.

We continued moving in the same general area near FSB Maureen on into July. We began to move down from the higher ground towards the valley in pursuit of the enemy. We found many bunkers as we moved cautiously down the mountain using grenades or gas in some bunkers to ensure no enemy personnel inside. We found two unmarked enemy graves that we dug up to gain possible intelligence. There were also enemy grenades found. It was obvious this was a very big North Vietnamese Army unit with trail markings all along a large trail at times. It began raining the next couple of days as we were moving down the mountain.

On July 5, 1970, we set up a night defensive position on the side of the mountain and dug in for the night. I was with what remained of second platoon, along with headquarters platoon and third platoon. Early on the morning of July 6, I got up and prepared for moving out. I was positioned at the bottom side of the mountain in the six o'clock position. We were hit by rocket-propelled grenades and satchel charges which came from the upper side of the night defensive position near the 12 o'clock position. Gus McDonough, who was in third platoon at the 12 o'clock, responded immediately, returning fire and killing two North Vietnamese very close to the perimeter of our position.

There were a lot of men hit very quickly. Barry Mechbach ran immediately to my position, wounded very badly. I could see that he had been hit multiple times by the holes in his shirt in the chest area. I took his shirt off and used all my medical dressings to apply [them] to the worst wounds. There was no way I had enough to cover all the wounds. I did what I could and tried to keep him calm. The two medics were both wounded and had their hands full at the time attending to others, but made their way to Mechbach. I looked up towards the command post area of the night defensive position and could see that Captain Harasick had been hit in the head, and his whitish-blond hair was red with blood. Lieutenant Chuck Choney, who had been in the command post and directing fire, also had been hit. Chuck had been hit in two places and told me years later that a wound in the mouth was the hardest to heal. Lieutenant Wintermute and his radio telephone operator were wounded in the command post area. The dog handler, Bruce Bond, and his dog were also wounded. Bruces' scout dog Jim Dandy alerted that morning and started growling right before the attack.

We were still all on high alert as the wounded were being attended. Medevacs were called, as well as aerial support from a light observation helicopter. The North Vietnamese had employed the use of rocket-propelled grenades to cause maximum casualties, firing the RPGs into the trees over the middle of the night defensive position where the command post was located, resulting in a great deal of shrapnel that caused most of the wounds. First platoon began moving from their own night defensive position towards our position to reinforce. I went to the middle of the night defensive position with my machete to help clear out some small trees. We began clearing an area to drop a jungle penetrator. We were under a very thick canopy and had to remove some trees in order to take the wounded out by the penetrator into the medevac. We were only thinking about cutting the trees down as quickly as possible, leaving some of the trees with some sharp ends.

The medevac came in and dropped the penetrator down through the opening in the canopy to the ground to take out the two worst wounded men. Barry Mechbach and Bruce Hosier, both from third platoon, were the first two men put on the penetrator. The penetrator slowly began to lift the two men up, and after getting up fairly high, the penetrator was dropped. It seemed surreal and almost in slow motion to me as I could not believe what was happening. I could see that both men hit some of the sharp ends of what was left of the trees we had just cut. Bruce hit his leg on one tree, and I think Barry may have hit his mouth too. Bruce Hosier would later lose the leg that hit the tree stump. Barry Mechbach would have both lungs collapse, but would survive his terrible injuries.

Our first thoughts were that the chopper was receiving enemy fire because, between the medevac and the light observation helicopter on site, there was a tremendous amount of noise. Most of us did not find out until 40 years later that the high winds that sometimes hit the mountains were in danger of causing the Huey to crash on top of the entire company. The pilot had radioed to our Captain Harasick and told him he would have to drop the penetrator or incur a tremendous number of casualties from a crash. There was no other choice, therefore the pilot dropped the penetrator. Bruce Hosier later told me he had no regrets or hard feelings about what took place that day.

Captain Harasick at some point gave the order to Sergeant Doug Turner to take out a reconnaissance patrol. Doug basically assembled most of the men in our squad from second platoon, and we walked out of the perimeter and headed back up via a ridge and circled back in the direction the attack originated [from]. We walked in our normal order with me at point, Roger Fitch at slack with Doug Turner, Brian Allen—and I don't remember who else was on that patrol. We reached the top of the ridge with no enemy sightings or contact. Doug radioed back to Captain Harasick, who ordered us to return to the night defensive position.

We started back down the mountain with a light observation helicopter flying all around the area creating a lot of noise. We were not too far from the perimeter when I walked up on a North Vietnamese soldier watching the medevac lift out the wounded. He never heard me or saw me as I fired my M16. My first thought was he was part of at least a squad, and I yelled for everyone to get down after I hit him. A few more shots were fired in that direction and when we saw nothing else, we went to his body and found he was wearing a belt buckle with a star on it, indicating he was probably at least an NCO. We also looked in his wallet and found pictures of what may have been his wife or girlfriend. The rest of the company inside the perimeter did not know what was happening at that point, but Captain Harasick then ordered us to move back into the perimeter. I picked up the North Vietnamese AK-47 and carried it back with me and dropped it in the middle of the perimeter to be taken out.

When we were attacked that morning of July 6, the first platoon, who was set up at a nearby defensive position, was radioed and told to immediately move towards our defensive position to reinforce. The worst part of the day was the friendly fire that killed Staff Sergeant Sandy Porter when he was leading the first platoon support towards our perimeter. A trooper who had not been with us long from the Big Red One Division on our perimeter opened up with his M16 on some movement. The trooper did not identify the friendly before firing towards the movement, shooting Porter. Sandy was another great non-commissioned officer liked by everyone. It was another huge loss for Bravo. We were really blessed by great officers, NCOs, and troopers in Bravo, or none of us would have made it home from Vietnam.

We were finally able to remove all the wounded by the jungle penetrator. I did not know until later that we only had 45 total men and were actually no longer a combat-effective company at the end of the day on July 6, 1970. I remember leaving that night defensive position later in the day and not seeing any officers left in the field. I understood later that first platoon still had Lieutenant Nichols, who was the platoon leader. I only remember Sergeant Turner and other E-5s, maybe an E-6, as we walked off the defensive position. E-5 and E-6 became platoon leaders and senior NCOs very quickly.

In the end, good decisions were made from Captain Harasick on down through the company chain of command, in my opinion. We had NCOs and troopers who now had been through enough that they stuck together and knew what they were doing as a more seasoned *team*. I remember that first night after the attack, going out on a listening post and thinking, *I may not make it.* I knew from all the contact and the signs of large numbers of North Vietnamese we had found that we were well outnumbered and could be easily overrun, and to this day do not understand why the North Vietnamese did not take advantage of the situation.

We were in that general area until July 10, 1970, and then airlifted to FSB Bastogne. I was put on a small team along a river to set up ambushes. This area had minimal enemy activity and was chosen purposely in order to bring in enough replacements to bring the company back up to combat effectiveness. Lieutenant McCrystal was brought to FSB Bastogne to act as company commander. We were then airlifted on July 20, 1970, in defense of FSB Kathryn. Then on July 28, we were airlifted to Eagle Beach for a much-deserved break. A great number of officers and enlisted personnel would be required to fill our ranks, including senior NCOs for replacements in the field.

We spent most of August being moved from one firebase to another as the company was being replaced in the field and the rear areas. The responsibility for gathering and moving supplies to the helipad fell to William Shue, who was leaving at the end of August. The responsibility for the Bravo mail fell to Dickie Dills, who was also leaving at the end of August. Needless to say, taking care of the mail was probably one of the most important duties that has to be performed for many reasons for any military unit away from home.

Acting First Sergeant Dunn came to me one day in August to offer me the job Dickie Dills was vacating at the end of August 1970. This was not normal, because the rear positions usually were offered to those near the end of their tour. I never knew why I was offered the job and have thought about it often, somewhat surprised I was even asked. I did not even know Dunn, and I did not know he knew I existed. I thought about the offer and made the assumption that I was offered it because someone recommended me and felt honored. I took the offer seriously and performed the job like I feel I did everything else in Vietnam—to the best of my ability.

There was another tragic friendly fire accident right after I came into the rear area. Rodney Taylor, who was from North Carolina, was killed by friendly fire while out on a sniper team with John Brown and Sammy Daniels. Taylor was approaching the end of his tour on September 3, 1970, when he was assigned out that night with his two team members. The friendly fire was caused by confusion between Bravo and an ambush team from the 3/187th, all caused by mistakes made about information coordinating those two units between Camp Evans and FSB Jack. The night Rodney was hit, the news spread quickly, and some of us were up all night waiting for information from Quang Tri Surgical Hospital. The sad information finally came through the next day, September 4, 1970. I believe his injuries were so severe he died from loss of blood.

We were finally assigned a new commanding officer named Captain James Warden in August 1970, who was a good leader in the field by all accounts. He also did an excellent job coming into such a challenging change of command. The platoon leaders came in at different times, and first platoon had a couple over the next few months. It's all a bit of a blur to me as so many replacements were flowing into Bravo, as officers had the six-months' time in field and then were sent back in. The company had been technically built back up to 103 men in November 1970, but foxhole strength was only 69 due to many other reasons such as: permanently rear-assigned personnel; injuries; leaves; temporary duty; and there were also three men on the sniper team from Bravo, who worked out of Camp Evans.

The state of the operations was changing fast in the 101st Airborne in the field. After July 1970, there was still some contact, but the intensity and number of casualties had decreased to minimal in comparison. Rumors continued to increase about the 101st being sent home. President Nixon had met with President Nguyen Van Thieu on June 8, 1969, on Midway Island less than a month after Hamburger Hill. Nixon kept his campaign promise from 1968 and announced the withdrawal of the first twenty-five thousand combat troops. There just seemed to be a disconnect with the leadership in I Corps/101st, with one operation after another. Little did anyone know then that another Hamburger Hill would happen in July 1970 on Ripcord, with the same results.

But back to my time in the rear as a mail clerk, a mule driver moving supplies, and a jack-of-all-trades. I know that some in the field did not like men working in rear jobs, but I could not let that bother me. I knew it was a natural feeling when they were out there humping and busting their butts most days. I had my friends that I was in the field with that never seemed to waver in their friendships with me. It did bother me that my friends in the field were continuing to battle the elements they faced each day. It was especially tough during the wet months of monsoon. But there were incidents to deal with in the rear that could be dangerous, and it required staying aware and on alert at all times.

There are always the troublemakers and instigators from every group who can cause conditions to worsen. Many did not hear about the serious rear incidents in Vietnam and especially back home, but sometimes information did surface to the news. My mother, for example, sent me an article from *Newsweek* about "The Evans Nine." The article was dated June 29, 1970. It was about our own sister company Alpha Company, 1/506th, right there under my nose! It was about a racial confrontation between Black and white [soldiers] that quickly exploded to weapons drawn, and Black soldiers refusing to go back to the field. The Alpha Company Commander was also Black, and did his best to handle the situation, but it had to finally be handled by the battalion commander, Lieutenant Colonel Holt.

This was an extremely explosive time of racial issues back in the States, and the military was not exempt from that. Some of the Black soldiers in the military referred to Vietnam as a "white man's war." There were some soldiers, Black and white, who purposely wounded themselves with weapons to prevent being in the field. There were instances at this time of fragging in other units. I did also personally observe an enlisted man hit an officer during this time.

I remember one instance in which a new replacement had been dragged out of his hooch and beaten by a gang. He ran to where I was sleeping for protection. I ran out unarmed in my underwear to confront the entire group who was in hot pursuit. [I did so] to protect the young soldier from further harm. It was all [through] my sheer bluffing of what I might do if they didn't back down. Thank goodness they didn't follow up on my tough talk. Basically, there was always someone waiting to go to the Long Binh Jail (LBJ) located near Saigon for getting in trouble—and that's just part of the total story of the war.

A new First Sergeant arrived in November of 1970 and brought leadership, discipline, and professionalism to Bravo. He had been an aide to General Westmoreland and had an air of professionalism about him. He was tall, in good shape, and his uniform was always in perfect order. He did not hang out in the rear all the time, and went to the field to check on the company. I enjoyed working closely with him because he was trying to make Bravo what it should be. I was privileged to spend some time talking to him and enjoyed getting assignments done for him. I left Vietnam months before this First Sergeant, but found out years later through one of our officers that he had lost a leg in Vietnam. One of the men in the rear obtained a weapon and began to threaten others. The First Sergeant reportedly attempted to intervene and was shot, which resulted in him losing the leg. He remained in the military even after the loss of the leg. I was not surprised at all about his attempt to handle the situation, or that he continued to serve.

I was selected from the 3rd Brigade at Camp Eagle to serve as a security guard for the Bob Hope at the 1970 Christmas Show. I was specifically assigned to Bob Hope, which was a very memorable event. I was able to take an up-close picture of Bob Hope who happened to be talking to maybe the most decorated military member in Vietnam. His name was Joe Hooper, and he was a member of the 101st Airborne serving more than one tour. He had earned the Medal of Honor in 1968 as a staff sergeant.

Hooper went on to be awarded two Silver Stars, six Bronze Stars with the V Device, eight Purple Hearts, and five Air Medals. He had somehow talked his way back to Vietnam and also managed to "sneak" back into the field at some point in 1970. He had a difficult time staying out of trouble, but finally received a field commission and rose to the rank of captain before being mustered out of the military during the huge downsizing. He began drinking heavily and in 1979 died at the age of 40. I have looked at that picture over the years and thought about the loss of such a warrior, and the wasted life.

I was able to travel to Australia in February 1971. I returned home at the very end of March, completed college at North Carolina State University, and got married. We had one girl (who in turn had three sons, now aged 18, 21, and 24). I completed 47 years in the textile industry, retiring four years ago. I power walk/ do light jogging, exercise, and am an avid hiker, including backpacking. I travel and spend time with my brothers, whom I served with in Vietnam, quite often. They have become major lifelong friends. I have no regrets about Vietnam. I am proud of my service!

CHAPTER 25

Brian Allen

In Vietnam April 1970–March 1971

"I still find it amazing that one year of my life … can occupy so much space in my mind!"

For his contribution to this book, Brian Allen chose to share several short vignettes from his service with the author. As he notes, "Some are funny, some are sad, and some are heartbreaking, at least to me." These accounts have been lightly edited with Brian's permission.

I reported to the Battlin' Bastards of Bravo after a week at SERTS. Bravo was in the field seeing plenty of action, so we would join them when they got to Rakkasan for firebase duty. I spent three days in the company area preparing for war. I met a man from Georgia who got there the same time as me. He was a big old country boy, a slow talker, and we were instant friends. We went to the PX and bought matching cassette tape players to record on and send home tapes to family. We also went to a USO show and drank quite a few beers together. It is amazing how much you can learn about somebody in such a short time—especially when you know how short life might be.

His name was Gerald McDowell and we were both FNGs (fucking new guys). We had no idea how to prepare our rucks for the jungle and fortunately a couple of guys helped us. We both went to the firebase on a Chinook, and when we got there an officer sent Gerry one way to first platoon and me a different way to second platoon to learn the ropes. This was early May. On June 27, the day after second platoon was overrun, Gerry was killed by small arms fire. To this day I often wonder what the outcome would have been if I got off the chopper first. Guess you would call that classic survivor's guilt. Rest in peace Gerry, you are never forgotten.

So after a few days on Rakkasan we humped down into the jungle. My sixty-five-pound ruck was killing me. Though probably in the best shape of my life, I was still barely keeping up. About the third day out we got resupply and some warm beer. I pounded mine down and someone smarter offered me theirs, which I also drank quickly. We rucked up and my knees wobbled. Then I guess it rained, because we started uphill on a sharp incline! Being about fifteenth or twentieth in line, the path we followed turned very muddy and very slippery. I couldn't make it up, even dragging myself by vines and bushes, and kept sliding back down. Our lieutenant started screaming at me to get my ass up that hill! I thought I was going to pass out!

An experienced trooper, Alvin Nohorse (who was 100% Native American), came back down the hill, threw my ruck on top of his, and headed back up. I followed him, barely keeping up with nothing but my rifle and ammo. Our lieutenant—call sign Bluechip—hated me for the rest of time we were together, even when I was his radio telephone operator late in my tour. When we got to the top of the hill, Doc pulled me aside gave me some salt tablets and water and told me not to be stupid anymore. Lesson learned—no beer, especially warm beer, when you're humping!

A sampling of what you carried in your rucksack might include four days of food, four to six canteens of water, extra socks, maybe a jungle T-shirt, a poncho and poncho liner, probably your third bandolier of ammo. Our standard ammo carry was 27 magazines of 18 rounds, plus 1 in your weapon (504 rounds). We would also carry four to six grenades, four smoke grenades, two claymore mines, an entrenching tool, a machete, some C-4 with detonation cord and blasting caps, two hundred rounds of M60 ammo, all your personal items, cigarettes, candy, books, writing paper and envelopes—in a dry ammo can strapped to the bottom of your ruck. And sometimes extra stuff like LAWs and starlight scopes and myriad other items for where you were heading. One interesting item that we carried for a while were thermite grenades with a 35-meter blast pattern. Somebody finally decided that might be dangerous in triple-canopy jungle—you think!? Later when I was a radio telephone operator, I would add 18 pounds for an AN/PRC-25 radio, plus three extra batteries and two antennas, to the load (but subtract two hundred rounds of M60 ammo).

When I first went into the jungle and was clueless, the first guy to help me out was Big Daddy Wright. Wright was a Black man from Connecticut, I believe, and he was near the end of his tour. He had been on Hamburger Hill with his buddy McClain, another Black guy. Of course, their reasoning to help me and set me straight was also for their survival. I remember McClain saying, "Keep your eyes on that trail, cherry, I didn't survive Hamburger Hill to have some FNG get me killed when I'm short." But they were both very helpful to this untested soldier. Nobody in an infantry unit saw colors, or race, as a problem. We were brothers with the same objective, to survive and return home! In 1970/71 there may have been some racial problems in Vietnam, but most of these were in the rear where guys had too much time on their hands. When *we* got to the rear, all we did was party and enjoy the camaraderie of guys who had faced the worst, and enjoyed partying with each other.

We were issued machetes for multipurpose uses. When cutting bamboo, they got dull and your arms tired rapidly. For other uses they were not good. So I sent home for a knife and my dad sent me a beauty. About a nine-inch-long buck knife and sheath. At the time I had a Kit Carson scout and he would sharpen it every night for me; you could shave with it. I was sure he would slit my throat one night; we weren't getting along. Anyway, at that time, whenever we had to blow a landing zone, the job would be mine, which I loved! So we had a fairly large open area with large trees all around. We called for a lot of C-4 and blasting caps. I was using my buck knife to tie the C-4 to the tree with it and stick the open end of the cord into a manual blasting cap, as I had been taught. We decided to daisy chain about six trees together and were excited to see the damage.

We backed off, and as we mashed the clacker, I realized my knife was still in the last tree where I stuck it. I figure it came down somewhere in North Vietnam! Another time we had just finished a large landing zone when a sergeant came towards us and a large piece of tree came down and hit him on the head and knocked him unconscious. This was a few minutes after our last blast, and I thought it was like in the cartoons and the tree branch must have flown up about a thousand feet to come down so long later! Many years later while conversing by phone with one of my brothers, I found out that what really happened was that an inbound chopper was coming in low and the rotor wash caused the branch that was hanging in a nearby tree to get shook loose and take Steve out.

One night, a guy named Wylie Glover grabs me by the leg and says, "Get up, were being hit!" This is how the first and worst major firefight of my tour began. Within probably a few seconds of him alerting me, at least one major explosion just behind my head made me roll and crawl down to our water-filled foxhole as I, waking up, realized my M16 was still where I was sleeping. Crawling back, it was gone, and satchel charges were going off all around; guys were screaming. I had no way to help the platoon except to feed Wylie's M60.

Our position was, I believe, wrongly off the trail and kind of overlooking a steep drop. That is probably what saved us. That and the rate of fire of an M60. We were also spending our second straight night in the same night defensive position, which everybody knows is a no-no. The battle raged for god knows how long; you could actually hear the satchel charges that were landing and NOT going off! Sergeant Doug Turner got to the command post and probably saved us all by taking over and calling in all kinds of support.

The battle flagged and morning came. The scene was devastating. As the medevacs came in, we loaded the wounded and dead. Our command post had been wiped out at the very start of the battle, as the North Vietnamese always try to do. Grady Norris, our platoon leader, was mortally wounded and died a month later. Rodney Koerner, our conscientious objector medic, was dead, as were others. Their position was less than three feet from where we were sleeping, and I believe it sustained the first blasts as Wylie was waking me up.

I found my rifle; it was destroyed by a satchel charge. While policing up bodies and equipment, I came across a good friend of mine, John Angel Garza, dead with a bullet hole through his head. His weapon was lying beside him, so I took it and used it for the rest of my tour. Also killed two positions over from ours was my squad leader Victor Cambas; he was hit in the face and was barely recognizable. For the rest of my tour, my M16 remained attached to me and I vowed to do much better next time, which I did. Besides our dead we had about a dozen wounded, leaving only (to the best of my memory) six men in the platoon. Sergeant Turner was awarded the Silver Star for his efforts that night; he is definitely one of many heroes I served with. We had a good body count but as you can see, "It don't mean nothin'," because we had lost men of our own.

You should realize that only a small percentage, I think they say ten to fifteen percent, of the men in Vietnam were infantry. All the rest supported us. We were not crazy about anyone who was not infantry and had a name for them: REMFs (rear-echelon motherfuckers). They did not like that, and we did not care! We often spent thirty to forty days straight in the mountainous jungles of northern I Corps, and when we would get to the rear there would be nothing for us to buy from the PXs 'cause every time a new truckload of anything came to Camp Evans, the REMFs would buy up everything for themselves, or to ship home. So we would definitely want to get even, and it was not appreciated. When we got off the helicopters, sometimes they would take most of our ammo, grenades, and C-4 away from us, just to be safe.

From our radio telephone operator sleeping quarters behind the dayroom, you could look out over a small valley and see the MP headquarters, which could easily be reached by a round of gas from an M79 grenade launcher. Did I mention we did not like MPs? They were always ruining all the fun when we were on stand-down. It was often difficult getting any sleep on stand-downs because you never knew when a smoke grenade would be popped in your hooch during the night, or when the next drunk would fall down trying to maneuver the stairs. The USO shows were really exciting, there were usually a few fights between drunks from different battalions over who was better, or drunker! For these reasons, we were kept in the field as long as possible. In a book written by Benjamin L. Harrison, *Hell on a Hilltop*, he writes, "Unlike most of the infantry units in the rest of Vietnam it was common in the 101st to spend months in the field with the only break being rotated on to a firebase to provide security. I noted this to General Hennessey soon after my arrival in the division. He responded that if he brought them back to the base camps or to Eagle Beach, they would just get into trouble." *Boy was he right!*

One time, we were out of food after four days and were waiting for resupply. The weather was turning bad and the fog was lowering the visibility in the mountains. They said they would move us and then resupply us. We had the battalion chaplain with us, and he was due to go home. He was to go to the rear when our resupply took place. Well, you guessed it, they got us where they wanted and then told us they could not bring us food 'cause of the low ceiling. We did not know right away that we were on a previous night defensive position just below Firebase Ripcord. I found out when their 155 battery started firing a mission. The battery was almost straight above us, and every once in a while they were visible through a break in the fog.

As soon as our company was completely on the ground, one platoon was in contact. Luckily it was light and let up pretty quickly. I say luckily because we were constantly using all kinds of air support to keep the North Vietnamese at bay, and there was no way for air support with the low ceiling, we were virtually socked in. Also, we were so close to Ripcord it would be difficult to support us, except maybe with mortars. The old night defensive position we were in had that smell of death that you recognized when going through areas that had been contested before. Then it started raining heavily for three days and we were on our own.

The second day with no food, I emptied my ketchup into my canteen cup, added water, and made a delightful bowl of tomato soup. The next day I ate my toothpaste, it was minty and good. The next day I didn't eat. It rained continually night and day, and it was pretty cold at night. To sleep, I put my legs on each side of a tree trunk that was facing downhill and leaned over with my poncho liner and my shelter half over my head and caught a few ZZZs. One of the guys who was actually more inept than I had been, dropped a grenade in one of our important foxholes that was chest deep and small in circumference. He had either pulled the pin or removed the safety, I can't remember which. So you did not want to jump into this narrow hole feet first for fear of having your legs removed. So two guys held my ankles and lowered me face first into the hole to retrieve it. It went well, as my ability to tell this story indicates.

Finally, the weather broke and they got us out of there to FB Katherine, I believe. We were once again *damn* lucky because the weather was so bad that contact in that area was extremely minimal for what was going on at that time. I like to think having the chaplain with us at the time had something to do with it. After we left, the entire area exploded in combat, any book about Ripcord will tell you what was happening there.

A couple of weeks before Christmas 1970, I think it was, one of our platoons came upon a huge cache, many small weapons and an awful lot of ammunition. I remember seeing the story in *Stars and Stripes* many years later in some type of archive. It showed a couple of REMF officers holding some of the weapons and smiling for the camera. That certainly pissed me off! What happened was, we were in platoon-sized elements patrolling on the back side of Rocket Ridge, if my memory is correct, almost due west of Camp Evans. When the platoon that found the cache called the command post, it was decided for all the platoon to get together and get help extract all the captured goods. I was with the command post, not the platoon that found the cache. There were enough weapons that everyone in the platoon that found them got one, and there were still some in decent shape for anyone who wanted one.

I took one, which I later found out (to my detriment) was a 1912 Russian sniper rifle with attached bayonet. It had a cracked stock but was still functional. When the news got to the rear, a bunch of high-up officers took a chopper to check things out and said they would send choppers to backhaul all the goodies and then extract our company for a big celebration. Well, the choppers kept coming and we kept loading them until everything was loaded and gone. It then got quiet and we realized we did not hear anymore choppers inbound. We called headquarters and were told it was getting too late and they would extract us the next day. I screamed "bullshit!" and got ahold of the captain, whose name I do remember but won't mention. He was screaming at them that they were not going to have a party for us, without *us* being there, and they had better get those ships out to bring us in. Amazingly, they listened, and I can remember it almost being dark when I loaded up with the rest of the command post and there were still troops behind us.

Well, we started at our party pretty late, and our rear guys were way ahead of us at drinking, but we were able to catch up. The outcome was that the colonel in charge bought everybody in the company Zippo lighters, which he personally handed out. They had our Eagle on one side and Psalm 23 (I believe) on the other side. I lost mine of course, and I lost my rifle on the way home because the paperwork was allegedly wrong. I held it over my head in Phu Bai, I think it was, and said, "Who wants to buy it for twenty bucks?" I sold it to some REMF, and he's probably still telling war stories over it!

Then a few days before Christmas 1970, we went to a small hilltop named LP Longshot in a fairly quiet area. We renamed the hill FB Noel. I was the company radio telephone operator, and I got a call from the rear to get five guys ready, as a chopper is coming to take them to the Bob Hope Christmas Show. I go to my captain—I can't remember his name because the leadership was changing quite often as the war was winding down, and every rear-duty officer was trying to get his records to show he led an infantry unit in the field for a while. But I tell the captain we need to get four guys and me ready for the chopper. I don't know if he knew I was lying or not, but we picked four guys and off we went when the chopper came. We were fairly filthy, we been out for a few weeks, and we took our weapons with us. That may or may not be why we got such good seats! We picked them out ourselves, right behind Vietnam's Vice Air Marshal Nguyen Cao Ky, and no one complained.

While clearing our weapons, some clown chambered a round in his .45 and then dropped the magazine and pulled the trigger. *Blam!* It hit the asphalt by my feet and sent a piece of it to the corner of my eye. Unbelievably, this was the second time this had happened to me! So anyway, Bob comes out to start the show, and a gunship a couple clicks outside the wire opens up with his minigun which sounds like a buzz saw and sends a solid line of tracers into the ground. I realize that this probably happens at every show, with the gunship boys trying to impress Bob.

It's a great show: Bob, Johnny Bench, Lola Falana, and others. We leave right after the show, and back to FB Noel we go. Not sure if it was that day or the next, but one of our guys had had enough and decided to shoot himself in the foot.

I was either still at the show or somewhere else on the perimeter because I don't remember hearing the shot. I go back to the command post and there is this guy laying on my poncho liner bleeding profusely. He foolishly put his foot on a rock, then pulled the trigger, and the bullet went through his foot, hit the rock, and came out up at his knee. All I could think of was, *Who laid this guy on MY poncho liner?!* I was pissed! He healed up eventually and was sent to LBJ (Long Bien Jail). We never saw him again.

July 6, 1970, is one date seared into my memory. I'm talking to a lieutenant and holding my rucksack in front of me to get my canteen cup for coffee, because it's early morning. A rocket-propelled grenade, the first of many, explodes close to us, and he and my ruck catch most of the shrapnel. I'm blown backwards by the concussion right into my foxhole and feel a burning in my chest. I grab at it, and pull out a small piece of burning metal which burns my fingers. I toss it. I found another the next day in my shin, when I went to lace up my boots.

Then we were facing down a trail with our M60 when we saw movement in a tree maybe a hundred meters away. Wylie wasn't firing, because we lost the butt plate. I told him I knew from somewhere you could still fire it without it, so I tried it. Put a few hundred rounds into the tree and gave it back to him. We had been caught by surprise because the North Vietnamese do not usually attack in the daytime, especially early morning. Things let up after awhile, and some of us were called to secure the other side of the perimeter where most of the wounded were. I was sent and took up a position with another man who had just come to us as a replacement, I did not know him at all. I was handed a radio, which I was completely unfamiliar with, and told to keep contact with the command post.

Second platoon had joined third platoon because we had lost almost our whole platoon on June 26. The company command post was also with third platoon, and while we had no one killed, we had 19 wounded plus the tracker dog that was with us. Almost all the officers and the two medics were wounded, and a lot of guys didn't know each other, so that added to the confusion. There was a dead enemy soldier with his brain exposed right in front of my new position, and this was really bothering the guy with me. We had movement, and while trying to establish where reinforcements were coming from by radio with the command post, there was much confusion. One of our own was killed by friendly fire.

You encounter some strange natural phenomena in Vietnam. One time we were humping the boonies, with me barely keeping up and my ruck kicking my ass again. We were in the lowlands when this happened, on the ocean side of Highway 1. We were pretty beat as usual when we came upon an area of quicksand and decided to take the long way around. Only having seen quicksand in Tarzan movies, I had to check it out. Bad idea! Thank God the guys weren't too pissed at me, and pulled me out. You don't go down as slow as they show in the movies, especially with a sixty-five-pound ruck. Another time in the mountains we were eating breakfast,

I think I was having cold beans-and-weenies C-rats, when we heard this strange rumbling. We had just traversed this valley and were sitting on the side of the hill. The rumbling got really loud and all of a sudden a wall of water came through the valley basically at our feet. First and last time I ever saw a flash flood! Luckily we didn't lose anybody that time. But another time we did.

We often would use rivers as trails to get where we were going, 'cause 99 percent of the time, there were no booby traps and you could make good time not cutting jungle. We did lose two guys one time crossing a deep river. You're crossing with a sixty- to eighty-pound ruck while trying to keep you rifle or the radio dry. I can't remember if we found the bodies or not, but I was with the company command post at the time and I do remember laughing with my fellow radio telephone operator about something that had nothing to do with the drowning, and having our new captain come up and start chewing us out for laughing. He actually said, "You think it's funny, now I have to write two letters to the men's families, you think that's funny?!" I thought it *was funny* that he was more upset that he had to write the two letters than he was about two guys drowning!

I have a picture that says underneath it, "January 21, 1971, last firefight, six wounded." It shows a medevac leaving our position in a small opening in the jungle. I am assuming that within the next couple of days I was sent to the rear to finish my tour. I had been out about ten months, whining to whoever would listen that was too long, and the odds were stacking up against me not being wounded or killed. It was easy to complain as I was the captain's radio telephone operator, and he had probably been out there less than two months.

We had had a chaplain come out and travel with us for about a week, and he was by himself. They usually traveled with an assistant, but he had no one. I talked to him about this and by the time he left, he told me he would be sending for me to replace his assistant who was staying in the rear 'cause he was short and I was a good choice. He left, and I never heard from him again! This is probably one of the reasons I'm not a religious sort (but believe me, there are no atheists in foxholes).

I guess my whining was working because the captain said I would be going in soon, and he kept his word. I was assigned with a buddy of mine to the Post Office, a great job. The first night I invited a few close friends, ones that I always got in trouble with, to celebrate, and we drank the night away. We were so obnoxious, I'm pretty sure someone in the Post Office put in a word and I lost that job! I was sent to take a driving test, the international one, with mostly pictures with lines through them, which was pretty self-explanatory. I passed, and with no road test they gave me a license to drive anything up to a deuce and a half! Well, that did not go too well.

The first day I was assigned a ¾-ton truck, which I drove into a ditch and could not get out. A guy came along and said he could get it out and he did. The next day I was assigned a deuce and a half and sent down the road to Phu Bai to pick up some supplies. On the way back I crossed a narrow bridge at a fairly decent speed with another deuce and a half coming the other way. His tailgate chain was swinging, and removed my driver's side mirror. The next morning I was called to some officer's Quonset hut—he actually had air conditioning! And I was told that they needed a good radio telephone operator out at Rakkasan, and asked, would I be interested? Of course, it was not really a question of whether or not I was interested.... The chopper took me out there the next day and I finished my tour there!

Brian came home, married his wonderful wife Charlene, and spent 25 years as a professional firefighter in Connecticut. Over the years, the Allens lost both of their sons to muscular dystrophy. Today, they are retired and living in Wolfeboro, New Hampshire.

CHAPTER 26

Doug Turner

In Vietnam April 1970–March 1971

> "I had only been with the platoon for three days, not long enough to get to know many of the men who were casualties."

Battlin' Bastard Danny McNair took the initiative to interview several veterans who, quite understandably, were more comfortable speaking with a fellow veteran than an author who is not. What follows is Doug's story as told to Danny for the express purpose of this book, lightly edited by the author.

I was living in North Platte, Nebraska, which is in the central-west part of the state, in 1969 when I was inducted into the Army. My father had served in the United States Marine Corps prior to WWII and later worked for the federal government as an air traffic controller. We moved quite often, living in Hawaii, Alaska, Utah, Nevada, and other states before settling back in my parents' home state of Nebraska. I attended high school in North Platte and worked for the Union Pacific Railroad during the summers. After that came an unsuccessful stint in college, and receiving my draft notice. I met a guy named Rich Smets from northern Nebraska on the way to the induction center. We attended basic training and advanced infantry training, both at Fort Lewis, Washington. We were then selected for non-commissioned officer school and went on to Fort Benning, Georgia, to complete training to become a sergeant, E-5. I graduated from NCO school and was selected to be part of the cadre at Fort Lewis, as an instructor for an advanced infantry training class. I then received my orders for Vietnam, along with my friend Rich Smets.

We flew to Bien Hoa Air Force Base, which was a large air base just north of Saigon, arriving about the middle of April 1970. We were processed in about a day to the 101st Airborne Division located in Phu Bai. We arrived at Camp Evans and attended SERTS before actually reporting to Bravo Company, l/506th. (I was assigned to Bravo Company and Rich Smetz was assigned to Charlie Company, 1/506th, which were both in the same battalion located at Camp Evans.) I was issued my M16 and the long list of equipment [I was] required to carry to the field, to include four bandoliers of M16 ammunition. Two of the bandoliers crisscrossed my chest, one bandolier around my waist, and one bandolier in my rucksack. Each bandolier held seven magazines with eighteen rounds per magazine, which in total was about five hundred rounds.

I was issued a rucksack in order to carry the following: about eight quarts of water, a canteen cup, a week's worth of C-rations, a poncho liner, a poncho, body armor, a steel pot helmet with helmet liner, a protective gas mask, an entrenching tool, basic first aid supplies, insect repellent, fragmentation grenades, smoke grenades, one hundred rounds of M60 machine-gun ammunition, an M72 LAW, a claymore mine with detonator and wire, one pound of C-4 explosives, a machete, a utility knife, a waterproof ammo box to carry dry socks, a T-shirt, toilet tissue, writing materials, and personal hygiene items. There was certainly a lot going through my mind before leaving Camp Evans to join my company in the field, especially with the added responsibility of leading others as an NCO.

My training at NCO school had emphasized how to be respected by those you lead, but not to become so close that it could interfere with being an effective leader. There was no doubt that being firm but fair was very important to maintain the discipline in order for all of us to survive the combat in Vietnam and return home. The lack of discipline and alertness at all times could result in many casualties. We were taught how to read maps and also how to read the compass during the day or night in NCO school. Land navigation was taught and it was extremely important to know your location at all times. We spent a lot of time learning how to operate the radios. Land navigation and operation of the radio were two of the most important aspects of training required for an infantry unit in Vietnam. The training emphasized the use of the main weapons used in combat such as the M16, M79, M60, and M72. The responsibilities of an E-5 squad leader were taught, along with tactics that would be used in combat.

There were various other aspects of the training that were important to weed out weak candidates, such as physical conditioning, rappelling, sneak and evade, and ranger week. Training at Fort Benning versus actual conditions in Vietnam would prove much more difficult based on the extreme terrain of the mountains and jungle in Vietnam. I would soon experience this firsthand as I was sent to the field as a very green NCO the last part of April 1970. One thought I had later was that much more should have been taught to us about what to really expect in Vietnam to better prepare us.

As I was preparing to go out to the field to meet with Bravo Company, I already knew the company had been in some major combat the last couple of days in April, with heavy losses just as I had arrived as a replacement. I saw the equipment from the casualties as it was sent back to the rear area of Bravo Company, before I was sent out. I did not know until later that there had been five killed and seven wounded on FSB Maureen on April 25, 1970. I was flown out to meet up with my company and introduced to the officers and men who were still operating near that same area of Maureen. Lieutenant McCrystal was the platoon leader for second platoon, where I was placed due to the second platoon casualties of April 25. Lieutenant McCrystal assigned me to follow Sergeant Jimmie Hill, who was a squad leader in second platoon, to orient me as a new squad leader.

I had been in the field for just three days on May 1, 1970. We were moving along a ridge line of FSB Maureen. The company was low on food, ammunition, and other supplies, which required a resupply. We reached a finger off of the ridge line that led down to an old landing zone that was chosen as the location to bring the helicopters in for the resupply. Sergeant Hill set up security on the upper side of the finger next to the ridge line we had just come down, with a couple of other troopers. Hill did not place me with him that day. I was settled in a position down the finger from Hill. The rest of second platoon was on that upper part of the old landing zone toward the ridge line and Hill. Third platoon was placed right below second platoon and first platoon, with the headquarters platoon on the bottom side of the old landing zone below third platoon.

There was a lot of activity that day as resupply choppers came in and out. Some high-ranking officers from battalion also came in that day. We had been there for some time before all the resupply had been completed when Hill and his security team were attacked. I picked up my M16 and I remember kicking my steel pot downhill. We took cover behind some very large boulders and began firing at the point of attack above me. I was limited at how much I could fire due to the proximity of Hill and the other rear-guard trooper above me. I could hear the wounded men above me screaming for help. The North Vietnamese had surprised Hill and taken the high ground above us, and were firing down with AK-47s and tossing grenades taken from our wounded troopers.

Maybe an hour into the firefight, McCrystal ordered me to take three men and try to outflank the North Vietnamese position above us. I moved out with the three men. We were about halfway up the right-hand side of the finger and were fired on by one of our own Cobra gunships, wounding the other men with me. We were in the open without cover and I had no other choice but to move the wounded troopers back to a more secure area. The Cobras were firing all around and in some cases right into us, trying to break up the attack. I found out later that third platoon was also sent out to outflank the enemy from another direction, and was also hit by the Cobras. The attack was finally repelled, and the enemy withdrew. As I recall we recovered only one dead North Vietnamese soldier. Sergeant Jimmie Hill, along with his security team, had been killed. Lieutenant McCrystal had been wounded and his radio telephone operator was killed. Several other men were killed and wounded. I had only been with the platoon for three days, not long enough to get to know many of the men who were casualties.

The rest of the day we loaded the killed and wounded on the choppers to be taken out. The discarded equipment was collected and placed in a large pile. There were only three men left in second platoon, including me as the only non-commissioned officer remaining. The three of us remaining from second platoon were assigned to remain with all the equipment until a chopper could be sent to pick it up and return it to Camp Evans the next morning. It was a little uncomfortable for me to think about remaining with this large stack of gear overnight. We would later join up with the rest of the company the next day. Second platoon was no longer combat effective and therefore was combined with the rest of the company. Captain Sullivan was the only officer remaining in the field after the action on May 1, 1970. Lieutenant Choney of third platoon had been wounded and Lieutenant Falco of first platoon left the field that day for a rear job after serving his required six months in the field as an officer.

The evening of May 1, we thought the company could be attacked again. Security was greatly increased. The company dug extra-deep fighting positions around the perimeter preparing for an attack which luckily did not occur. I had been in Vietnam a little over two weeks and went into that battle of May 1, 1970, as "green as green" as a sergeant E-5 could be. I was fortunate to have had the NCO training, but I learned about the reality of actual combat in Vietnam. That would help prepare me more as an effective squad leader. It was apparent that the size of a platoon in Vietnam was only two squads at best, which was well short of what was taught in NCO school. But May 1, 1970, would quickly teach me the importance of the many details that must be taken care of on a daily basis and at all times.

The company moved away from the area of the May 1 attack that day, but we were still in the same general area around FSB Maureen. We began receiving many replacements to build Bravo back up to an effective combat unit. This added to my responsibilities the training of so many new men, and placing them in the best-suited positions within the squad. There was the basic maintenance of weapons and ammunition, which meant keeping both clean at all times. The men already had a great deal to do on a daily basis and keeping the ammunition clean was one of the most difficult.

Teaching and enforcing discipline 24/7 was critical to surviving, with everyone remaining alert at all times being most important. The North Vietnamese knew most of the time where we were located and would choose the most opportune times to attack, trying to find any time we might not be alert. I was the only NCO in the second platoon, though new ones would be added very soon from other platoons or as replacements. For example, Sergeant Vic Cambas was a very good and well-respected squad leader in third platoon who would be moved to second; Sergeant First Class Reid would also be added to second platoon as the platoon sergeant. Vic Cambas was from New Orleans and Reid, who was actually a Green Beret finishing out his Vietnam tour, was, I believe, from Massachusetts. Lieutenant Ed McCrystal from New Jersey returned to second as our platoon leader after being wounded on May 1.

There were quite a few enlisted replacements in the coming weeks, from all across the country. Heavy replacements in Bravo over the next months would become the norm. We were basically a newly formed platoon that had to become a team very quickly. This process began immediately after May 1 as we continued to remain around the same area of Maureen and the Rao Trang River. There were always daily signs of enemy presence and activity, such as trails and markings, bunkers, and supplies. On May 17 we were airlifted to defend FSB Rakkasan and continued to pick up replacements.

The night of May 18 on FSB Rakkasan we received RPG rounds, wounding two men in second platoon by shrapnel. There was some additional probing of the Rakkasan perimeter, in which second platoon responded by fire from the perimeter. May 21 the company combat assaulted to defend FSB Kathryn. We remained at FSB Kathryn until May 23, when Captain Sullivan led Bravo off the firebase back into the general area around Kathryn. I remember that same night we observed enemy flashlights and flashes from mortar tubes. We could hear the sound of the mortars firing and Captain Sullivan called in air support on the mortar positions, which stopped the firing. Men were wounded constantly.

The remainder of May, going forward, there was more time to form a unit that would become familiar with one another and would also experience combat together. Knowledge passed from man to man about his responsibility to be an effective member of the squad and to follow the best possible practices on a 24/7 basis. A trust was developed between the squad leaders, who would find out who needed to be pushed to keep weapons and ammunition clean, those who were not always alert or were careless, those who did not always prepare the best defensive position within a perimeter. There were other times when men had to be reminded or disciplined.

A typical day in the field with Bravo began early each morning when leaving a nighttime position. The objective was to not set up a defensive position too early the day before, and to leave as early as possible the following morning. It had been proven over time that remaining too long in a night defensive position was more likely to result in a well-planned attack by the North Vietnamese. The day began by preparing some breakfast, taking care of bodily functions, taking care of personal hygiene, gathering up the items to pack the rucksack, and retrieving the hundred rounds of M60 ammo that was carried for the M60 gun crew. You'd have to go outside of the perimeter and bring in the claymores set up the night before.

It was very important that everyone remained on high alert during this time of preparing to move out, by keeping weapons ready and within reach at all times. The North Vietnamese always chose times to attack when they observed units not being alert due to a lot of activity going on at a very fast pace. The platoon- or company-sized unit would then form up in the order of march and move out of their overnight defensive position with the heavy rucksacks, while always on high alert with weapons ready. It was important to reduce noise as much as possible, even though the North Vietnamese may [already] know the general or exact area we were located much of the time. The squad would have a point man in the lead with another trooper at the second position referred to as the slack position. Each man in the formation would maintain a predetermined distance based on the terrain or type trail, which might be anywhere from ten to fifteen meters separation.

It was the responsibility of the point and slack man to move at a rate that allowed observing the 180 degrees in the direction of travel, be alert for trip wires, snipers in trees, movement in front or [from] each side, bunkers, trail signs, or any other signs that should halt the unit and be reported back down to the squad leader, who was typically near the front of the formation. Each squad would have an M60 gunner with his assistant maybe about the middle of the squad, an M79 "thumper man," and typically four other troopers rounding out a squad of about ten men total.

The best practice was to always make your own trails and not to use existing trails, because existing trails might have booby traps or snipers. Cutting new trails was very exhausting in the tropical climate of Vietnam, requiring a lot of water intake and possible heat exhaustion, not to mention the noise it could make. Movement might be affected by the rainfall causing muddy conditions. The elevation changes in the mountains were another challenge to contend with, even more so combined with the rainy and wet conditions.

Camp Evans was in the Lowlands and farther west of Evans the elevations increased after reaching the first ridge lines. Many of the FSBs were two thousand five hundred to three thousand feet. FSB Maureen, which was referred to as Hill 980, was about three thousand two hundred feet. It also has to be considered that the difficulty increases going up and down multiple hills. These heights may not seem that high, but with heavy rucksacks combined with other difficult conditions, it can be extremely tough. The higher elevations combined with the rainy seasons could cause resupply to be more difficult and sometimes impossible. Resupply, when it did happen, required time and activity with helicopters in and out, which also drew enemy attention. The attack on May 1, with so many causatives, could have been due to a breakdown in alertness.

There was not always an available LZ for a resupply. Some days included blowing new landing zones with C-4 explosives or dynamite, which also used up time and energy in the process. The exhaustion during the course of the day, combined with the heat, required taking breaks. These breaks were another time that being fully alert was difficult. Lack of sleep also impacted how alert you were. Setting up a new night defensive position after a long, exhausting day was a major endeavor. First of all, the fighting positions around the perimeter had to be prepared. The fighting positions were dug with an entrenching tool that we all carried in our rucksacks. The small shovels had a collapsible head that folded out to approximately thirty inches when being used. We later also began carrying one full-sized shovel in each squad. The deeper and larger the better, because the positions were typically manned by three men. The soil conditions varied, from hard, or wet, or sometimes rocky, which could make it extremely difficult to dig the best fighting positions.

Letters were extremely important to receive from home, and it was important to write home and let your family know how you were doing. Writing letters could be hard, though, due to combat, weather, or just lack of time. Eating something at the end of the day was important, and of course taking care of bodily functions. Weapons had to be maintained and that required good lighting, before the end of the day, when there was still some daylight. Some troopers did a good job cleaning weapons and some not so good. The squad leaders usually knew who had the dirtiest weapons that required attention. There were times men required attention from the medic to attend to infections such as boils or cellulitis caused by the wet and dirty environment. Medics also distributed salt tablets and malaria pills each day.

Patrols were sometimes done for reconnaissance of the area, and sometimes men were placed *outside* of the main perimeter at night in a listening post to detect a possible attack. The work just continued on, 24/7. Every night required that someone remained awake at all times for every position working their shift as a team. The long and grueling days made it very tough to remain awake much of every night. There were sometimes costly failures when men went to sleep while supposedly securing their assigned position on the perimeter. Hopefully the man on the next shift would wake and realize no one was awake and take over before it was too late. Too many times the North Vietnamese detected that men were asleep and they could penetrate the perimeter through a position with no one awake. This was usually done by North Vietnamese sappers, who were trained in extreme stealth, causing extensive casualties using satchel charges and grenades.

The sappers were probably the most feared North Vietnamese unit in Vietnam, as they were capable of this type of attack. They would choose the early morning hours, maybe around 2:00 AM, when men were most likely to fall asleep. I think that every man had the fear he or someone else was susceptible to falling asleep while on guard. This may be one reason why men have stated that they never felt like they received a full night's sleep during their entire tour in Vietnam. A unit in the field had to work together as a team and know the habits of their fellow troopers, which was my responsibility as a squad leader. The known weaker team members required constant monitoring and reinforcement of their responsibilities.

I mentioned the terrain, the elements, and constant stress on the men [which we had] to deal with on a daily basis. There were also all kinds of insects such as mosquitos, leeches, poisonous spiders, and poisonous centipedes. The spiders and centipedes were some of the largest and most poisonous in the world. The centipedes could be six- to seven-inches long and were known to be aggressive. Then there were the snakes, such as the bamboo viper. They were a beautiful green color—and very poisonous. They were sometimes killed while cutting trails through thick vegetation. Elephants or their trails were seen in various areas from the lowlands to the Laotian border, and could indicate use by the North Vietnamese to carry heavy loads of supplies and/or ammunition. Tigers were also in Vietnam and could sometimes be heard growling during the night.

We were airlifted back to Camp Evans on June 1st for training and a change of company commander for Bravo Company. Captain Lee Sullivan had completed his six-month tour as an officer in the field and was being sent to an administrative position. Captain Sullivan would be replaced by Captain Bob Harasick. We would combat assault back to the same area of operations near FSB Kathryn, Maureen, and Granite. The same routine of men leaving and new men arriving in the company, beginning with a new company commander, continued. Our second platoon leader, Lieutenant McCrystal, was at the end of his six-month tour as an officer in the field and would also be reassigned to a new job in the rear area. He was replaced by Sergeant First Class Grady Norris as acting platoon leader after we went back to the field in June. We also received a new medic named Rodney Koerner, who I believe may have replaced the medic wounded April 25, 1970. It was like a revolving door of personnel in many ways, while it was at the same time so important we operated as a team. Many of the men in the second platoon were still relatively new, as replacements were being received all the time.

We generally operated in this area close to the Rao Trang River, which flowed past Maureen and Kathryn. There were sightings of small groups of the enemy, bunkers, and signs of the enemy during this time, with the same fire support being directed by artillery or all types of air support at various targets. We also conducted a CA into the area around FSB Ripcord for a few days where our sister battalion, the 2/506th, was in a major defense of FSB Ripcord. We then CA'd back to the same area we had just left after a brief period of time. Then, we were conducting operations on Maureen on June 25.

I was the acting platoon sergeant. We humped to the small landing zone below FSB Maureen by midafternoon and sat down to rest while circled around the landing zone. There were fighting holes partially dug on the perimeter. While resting, I and two other troopers were facing a small trail that led up to the landing zone. We were just sitting there, not talking, just sitting there, and all of a sudden two or three North Vietnamese Army regulars came walking up the trail to the landing zone. We were as shocked to see them as they were to see us. One of the guys sitting next to me, maybe Wayne Pratt, plucked a grenade from his web gear and threw it at them as they turned and ran. It seems like it hit one of them in the steel pot.

After advising the sergeant first class what had happened, a couple of us walked down the trail to see if the grenade caused any damage. We found a blood trail and a rucksack. No sign of the North Vietnamese. We moved back to the landing zone and opened the rucksack to find personal information, satchel charges, and maps of FSB Kathryn showing routes in and routes out with movement arrows. It was clear to us that the North Vietnamese we had engaged were sappers that intended to attack FSB Kathryn in the near future. We felt the entire platoon was sure that we would be hit that night, as we had drawn blood that afternoon.

We were all very active in preparing for the night. Our holes were extra deep, we placed our two M60s to cover the higher landing zone and the trail area, and we spotted our claymore mines with care. The squad leaders went from hole to hole preparing the guys for what we knew was going to be a long night. Probably at 2:00 AM, all hell broke loose with satchel charges coming inside of our night defensive position like rain. They were small explosive charges with metal wired to the outside. I recall that many did not explode. Our M60 machine gunners were working hard on effective fire, we were blowing claymore mines but hesitated to toss grenades as there were so many trees in front of us. Sergeant First Class Norris was wounded early on and I took over the radios to contact first platoon, where I believed our commanding officer was, to give him an update and warn them of a similar attack.

We called in illumination and medevac ships as we had many wounded. I can remember telling the guys to shoot any North Vietnamese that could be seen in the head to make sure they were dead. First platoon managed to link up with us as things quieted down, and we were all very happy to see them as our platoon was in bad shape. When the smoke cleared, we had four dead, I believe, and six to eight wounded. We had also done a job on the attackers. I don't remember how many we killed but the pile of their bodies was very large. As the sun came up, we were able to kill another North Vietnamese soldier that we found crawling away from the area. The battalion commanding officer came out that morning and I gave him a tour of our defensive position and reviewed the firefight. My most vivid memory of the firefight was the bravery of the troopers in my platoon. I can't say enough about how they fought. I'm sure the North Vietnamese had a new opinion of American troopers after that night.

And on and on it went. It sometimes seemed a blur of movement from one firebase to another as we received replacements. I developed a medical issue from coming into contact with liquid gas on my arm/elbow. I remember spreading gas inside North Vietnamese bunkers to make them unusable and some was spilled on my arm, causing irritation and blistering that required medical attention. I was sent to a hospital to be treated and was gone for maybe a couple of weeks. Bravo Company and the entire third brigade was in a state of reorganizing from all the casualties.

I was offered several options when I returned to the company sometime in August or September. The options were: promotion to staff sergeant E-6 or as a legal clerk in the rear. I chose the legal clerk option. The war in Vietnam and the 101st was coming to an end as far as major combat. The rumors of the 101st going home continued for the rest of my tour. Many were sent home early over the remaining months. I was able to go to Hawaii on R&R with Rich Smets before my tour was up.

I served as the battalion legal clerk at Camp Evans the remainder of my tour in Vietnam, which included security duty on the Camp Evans perimeter from time to time. There were no real attacks on Camp Evans, with the exception of the occasional rockets fired on holidays, such as January 1. I received an early drop from Vietnam and the Army. I returned to the States in March of 1971 and was released from active duty at Fort Lewis. I went back home to finish college and worked briefly for the Union Pacific Railroad. I was presented another opportunity with a private company that offered the possibility of eventual ownership. I opted for the job with the best long-term potential, with the small private company. I made that decision in 1974 and it led to my eventual ownership of Anderson Industrial Engines (AIE) based in Omaha, Nebraska. The company has grown into a medium-sized company over the last fifty years, with offices in Omaha, Kansas City, Las Vegas and Modesto. We now have 100 employees serving 15 states. We deal mostly with industrial engines and are the largest engine distributor in the States. We sell many brands and have a large engineering department that can customize our product lines based on our customer requirements.

I have been blessed with three talented children who have worked very hard over the years in many positions within the company. My children also blessed me with seven grandchildren, who I now have more time to spend with in my retirement. My wife and I travel a great deal, which has also included my children and grandchildren on some very special occasions.

My military experience from basic training to Vietnam actually saved my life. I came from the darkest time in my life to a position in life that has allowed me to find great success in family and profession. But, looking back, there are many things that leave me cold when thinking about our individual preparedness as an infantry trooper. Basic training was primarily directed to physical training, an introduction to military life, and some weapons training. Basic took eight to nine weeks. Advanced infantry training was simply an extension of basic training. There was no mention of the conditions we might face in Vietnam. NCO school concentrated on physical training and some advanced training on land navigation, radio, weapons, and how to be a leader of men. It was twelve weeks or so. Bottom line, I feel—and so do most men I know—that our training was inadequate for the mission that lay before us.

The experience for eighteen- or nineteen-year-old young men was extremely difficult. In Vietnam we didn't receive the support expected: new troopers were sent to the field with wool blankets as the supply was always short of poncho liners. We ate C-rations exclusively. These meals in a can were barely edible. Hot food might be available on the FSB or on stand-down at Camp Evans, but never in the field. We were issued green fatigues and seldom received clean sets. We might be thirty or more days in the same set of clothes. The men at Camp Evans wore camo fatigues which were never offered to the guys in the field.

Our M16 was supplied with a 20-round magazine and we only filled it to 18 rounds. The guys in the rear were sporting M16s with a 30-round magazine. We would have loved to have more capacity. We all carried a machete for cutting trails.

It was nearly impossible to get our hands on a file or sharpening stone, so we found ourselves chopping trails rather than cutting. Chopping made a lot more noise. A dull machete isn't much use. When we would blow a landing zone for resupply, we normally use C-4, detcord, and blasting caps to cut down trees. The blasting cap fits over the detcord and is secured with a crimping tool. We could never get our hands on the crimping tool, so in order to secure the blasting cap to the detcord, we would put the blasting cap in our mouth and clamp it down with our teeth.

We constantly ran out of water, forcing us to drink out of the mountain rivers and streams. We all were transported to Vietnam as individuals rather than as units. After arriving in Vietnam, we were given orders to report to units all over the country, alone, one-off. I personally would have expected much better from the military, and I am not being critical here, just making the reader aware.

CHAPTER 27

Gordon Roberts

In Vietnam May 1969–June 1970

Gordon expressed support for this book but was unable to participate for personal reasons. His brothers were adamant his "Medal of Honor" citation be included here.

"For conspicuous gallantry and intrepidity in action at the risk of his life above and beyond the call of duty. Sergeant Roberts distinguished himself while serving as a rifleman with Company B, during combat operations. Sergeant Roberts' platoon was maneuvering along a ridge to attack heavily fortified enemy bunker positions which had pinned down an adjoining friendly company. As the platoon approached the enemy positions, it was suddenly pinned down by heavy automatic-weapons and grenade fire from camouflaged enemy fortifications atop the overlooking hill. Seeing his platoon immobilized and in danger of failing in its mission, Sergeant Roberts crawled rapidly toward the closest enemy bunker. With complete disregard for his safety, he leaped to his feet and charged the bunker, firing as he ran. Despite the intense enemy fire directed at him, Sergeant Roberts silenced the two-man bunker. Without hesitation, Sergeant Roberts continued his one-man assault on a second bunker. As he neared the second bunker, a burst of enemy fire knocked his rifle from his hands. Sergeant Roberts picked up a rifle dropped by a comrade and continued his assault, silencing the bunker. He continued his charge against a third bunker and destroyed it with well-thrown hand grenades. Although Sergeant Roberts was now cut off from his platoon, he continued his assault against a fourth enemy emplacement. He fought through a heavy hail of fire to join elements of an adjoining company which had been pinned down by the enemy fire. Although continually exposed to hostile fire, he assisted in moving wounded personnel from exposed positions on the hilltop to an evacuation area before returning to his unit. By his gallant and selfless actions, Sergeant Roberts contributed directly in saving the lives of his comrades and served as an inspiration to his fellow soldiers in the defeat of the enemy force. Sergeant Roberts' extraordinary heroism in action at the risk of his life were in keeping with the highest traditions of the military service and reflect great credit upon himself, his unit, and the U.S. Army."[1]

As Warren Sutton recalled, "How he got through the North Vietnamese Army fire and our cover fire without getting hit is beyond me."

CHAPTER 28

Michael "Doc" Flood

In Vietnam September 1968–April 1969

> "There is nothing worse for a Gold-Star family than to have people forget those who gave their all for our great nation."

Thus far, you have been reading the stories of some of the Battlin' Bastards who are still with us, in their own words. In sharing their stories, they give you, the reader, an idea of the trials, tribulations, and sometimes, triumphs, of the combat soldier in Vietnam. But as you've seen, Bravo Company suffered heavy losses. In this last story, we hear from Marlene Van Matre, whose brother, Michael, did not make it home. While those of us who have never had a loved one killed in combat can never truly understand the pain of a Gold-Star family, Marlene's account goes a long way towards relaying the lifelong grief that comes with such a loss. It has been lightly edited with Marlene's permission.

On Wednesday, April 9, 1969, our family changed forever. I was 12 years old and was on spring break for Easter. We always looked forward to Easter because we always had the week off for the religious holiday back then. That day, the Cumberland County sheriff, Pat Thomas, brought an Army lieutenant from Fort Sheridan to our farm in rural Toledo, Illinois.

That morning I had gotten up before 6:00 AM to eat a farmer's breakfast and do my chores. Once I had completed them, I hopped on my bike before noticing that the sheriff and another man were talking to my dad. I wasn't alarmed because periodically the sheriff would make his rounds in the rural areas to check in and shoot the shit with the farmers. I rode my bike up north to an elderly couple who lived a quarter of a mile from us. I sat on a swing and visited with Harry for a while. He had dementia and always asked me, "Who mows the lawn down at your place?" and "When did you move in down the road from us?" Each time I visited with him, I answered the same and learned tolerance for the aging mind. Once Harry ran out of conversation and fell asleep, I went into the house and visited in the kitchen with his wife, Beula. She was always busy with her vegetables from the garden and with baking.

When I went back home to watch some TV, the sheriff, my dad, and the other man were still there, and my brother Dan had joined them. Again, I didn't approach them. I went in the house and turned on the TV. I always liked watching Lucille Ball. The episode airing that day was the one where Lucy was in the candy factory stuffing her mouth with chocolate due to the conveyer belt going too fast for her to put the candy in the boxes. I suddenly heard the back door open and my dad calling out, "Charlene!" I could tell by his tone that he was upset about something. My mom was washing dishes and just said back, "What is it?" and continued washing the dishes. By this time I was in the kitchen with my hands braced on the back of a chair. My dad said, "Come here! I need to talk to you!" She sighed then grabbed a dishcloth and started drying her hands as she walked to the back door. (Dad had not walked in because his boots were muddy and probably had manure on them, and no one was allowed to enter the house with dirty shoes!) Dad looked at my mom when she got to the back door as she was saying, "What is it?" He said, "Mike's missing!"

My mother fell apart. She started hitting my dad in the chest saying loudly, "No! No! I knew something was wrong!" Friday before the notification, she had been awakened by a tap on her shoulder. Mike had always gone into their bedroom and tapped her on her shoulder to let them know he was home when he had been out late with his friends. She cried, "Oh, it can't be true! No! No!" My dad was hugging her as tight as he could and trying to console her. At that point I could not stand to watch and hear my mother's inconsolable crying, so I ran out the front door and got my bike and took off for Harry and Beula's again, sobbing all the way. I kept saying, "Mike's missing! I won't see him again! He never said goodbye!" When I got to Beula's back door, I hit the screen door with my fist then barged into her kitchen without waiting for a response. She ran around the table to greet me and saw that I had been crying. She grabbed me into a bear hug and asked, "What has got you so upset?" All I could get out was, "Mike's missing and I don't know what to do!" She hugged me tighter, trying to console me. She asked, "What happened?" I told her I didn't know anything else, then I broke away and ran out of the house, hopped on my bike, and that is last thing I can remember of that day.

We received three telegrams. The first came April 9, confirming Mike was missing in action on April 4. The second came on April 10, saying Mike was killed in action. A third also came on April 10, saying he was killed by land mine. We received very little info about the circumstances of Mike's death in these short messages, or in the years to come. I remember people coming with food (especially his girlfriend Polly Thomas, who was the sheriff's daughter). I remember the closed casket with a stainless-steel cover bolted over where you would normally see the person. We placed Mike's rosary on that, then closed the casket. We were told that the government seal could not be removed by anyone.

I remember that a couple whose son (Otis Cathers) had graduated with Mike showed up. Their son was in basic training with Mike, then went AWOL when they were on a two-week leave. He claimed he was a conscientious objector. Mike called him a coward and wanted nothing to do with any of them. Some of my friends came to the wake. One asked, "How do you know he is in there?" They meant in the casket. I just shrugged my shoulders because I just believed the government story. The person then said, "You know that it might not be him at all. They get the dead people mixed up all the time. You might be burying someone else's brother." Another one piped in, "I heard they may have transported drugs in his body. They take everything out and replace it with the drugs, then when the body gets to San Francisco, they remove the drugs and sew them back up."

When I went back to school someone said that he deserved to die because all they did was kill babies over there. After hearing those horrifying things, I found that I really had no one to talk to. Hearing those things from my friends made me go silent on the subject of my brother. We didn't discuss anything as a family either. Our parents were so upset, and mother would cry so much, she didn't need us kids crying or asking questions—so we just never verbalized anything. We didn't want to upset them. We just silently thought about things and kept to ourselves.

One of my fears was that protestors would show up at Mike's funeral like they did in some communities all over the States. I remember the 21-gun salute at the cemetery and a couple of guys playing taps. A childhood friend's brother picked up some of the shell casings. My dad had to go to their house and have the father get them from his little boy so they could be mounted with his medals in the shadow box. I never cried once through it all. Someone came to our house and was talking to my mother about me not crying or talking much. My mom told the person to leave me alone, and that she thought I would talk when I was ready. Who would have thought that I would never discuss anything till 2003?

We received Mike's Purple Heart, Bronze Star, and Silver Star all at different times. They were presented by a lieutenant from the University of Illinois ROTC program. Each time there was another wave of tears from our parents. Mother wrote a lot of letters to the government and many of the men who served with Mike because there were inconsistencies about where and how he died, as well as who was there. We had three guys visit that knew Mike. One fabricated stories. He came three times and embellished the story each time. My parents [initially] grasped on to it all but were very mad and devastated when they found out the guy was not in the field that day and had fabricated everything.

We searched for the truth for a long time. The pain and sorrow never ended, but was accepted daily as something we just had to try to put in the back of our minds and live with. Holidays were never the same because we were no longer whole. Easter is still the worst. Even though the date changes every year, that memory of Holy Week and the days to follow can never be forgotten. They are always there.

I never had anyone to talk to at home or school. I didn't want to hear any more things that would cause more pain. I never said anything when the kids said those things to me. I forgave those kids long ago because I know they were only repeating what they had heard at home. I truthfully don't even remember who specifically said those horrific things to me. I guess I was in such a fog and my mind protected me from certain facts.

Vietnam was so controversial, and I avoided speaking about it to protect myself from the pain of the hateful things people said back then. I felt ostracized when I told people that my brother was a medic and was killed there. They never knew what to say and avoided me after that. That is one thing that still happens today. Some say they are sorry for our loss, but some just say "oh," then either walk away or change the subject. People don't realize that we Gold-Star families need to talk about it, since we never did back then and we never had any professional help, either.

When the guys from Company B, 1/506th, 101st Airborne contacted us, I was the only one in the family who would meet with them. My parents had asked me in 2003 to take over the search for the truth. I decided that if my parents could handle it for 34 years, I should continue their quest. I was very cautious and was really rather rude to Jerry Hoffman. I let him know up-front that our family had been hurt by the lies of the government and one man, and I was not going to let that happen again. I almost had him in tears. He couldn't talk for a while because he was trying not to cry.

When he got home that night, he emailed me a message that clearly came from his heart, and I knew he indeed knew Mike and really cared about him. He never bragged about himself and confessed that he was still haunted by the fact that they let both Mike and Walter lay out there before recovering their bodies. He felt they should have been able to do something about it. He put me in contact with Pete Falco, who was researching Bravo's history. I gradually fed him information that my parents and I had obtained. He was able to find almost everyone involved that Good Friday, get an account of what each remembered, and match it with the official archived records. I was able to tell mother the final truth of what happened to Mike 10 days before she died on Holy Saturday, April 7, 2012. These Bravo men took me under their wings, elaborated on their experiences with Mike, and told me what they could about his death and the recovery of his body.

I had never had any closure. I never got to say goodbye to Mike. The night before he left, I refused to go to bed till he promised me that he would wake me before he left for his plane in St. Louis. The next thing I remember was waking up after hearing the shifting of the gear shift of our '62 Chevy. I bolted from the bed and ran downstairs and ran outside. All I saw were the red taillights. I was so mad, I just stood out there and cried, yelled at him, then went back to bed and cried till it was time to get up for school. I asked my mom why she didn't wake us. She said that Mike didn't want to wake us but he did come upstairs and watch us sleep for a while.

The day before he left, he walked the entire farm by himself. We found out after he died that he had told one of his friends that he had a feeling he was not going to make it back home. Anyway, my being involved with these veterans has helped me finally go through the mourning process. Repressed grief is like post-traumatic stress disorder. Until you face grief through all the stages, you can never have closure. Talking and writing about the experiences all those years ago has been the only thing that has helped me. Meeting these Bravo men has been a godsend for me.

I decided to get Gold-Star license plates in July 2014. The lady was initially telling me that I was not eligible to receive them. I showed her a copy of the DMV website and she clammed up real quick. I received the Gold-Star plates on September 9. About two weeks later, one of my less respectful supervisors hollered across the parking lot at me, "What the heck does Gold Star mean anyway!?" I replied, "I had a brother killed in Vietnam and got them to honor his memory." She just said "Oh," and walked away as quick as she could. Her response shows that even now, so many years after our country's unrest over a war that was so controversial, the subject of Vietnam is a very touchy subject.

I decided to visit the Vietnam Veterans Memorial in Springfield, Illinois, on the 46th anniversary of our family's loss, on April 4, 2015. It was very emotional for me to see and feel Mike's name on that wall. It was a rather overwhelming experience, but I think I healed a little by going. I remember back in 1988 when they were going to dedicate the memorial. They invited all the families of the fallen from the state of Illinois. My mother had not contacted me soon enough and I was unable to get the time off from the hospital where I worked. I have always regretted not being there with my parents to support them during this most sad but proud moment in all our family's life.

In 2014 I went to the Memorial Day celebration in Mahomet. I had not been to one since 1976. I only went to those before I moved to Champaign, out of respect for my parents for they were active in the VFW and American Legion. I cried through the entire ceremony because they had a speaker who told the story of learning what a Gold-Star family was from a neighbor who had lost a son in the Vietnam War. That day was a big breakthrough for me in the grieving process. Back in the early '70s, my mother had gotten both myself and one of my sisters into the women's auxiliary at the VFW, but I never was an active member because I never wanted to talk to anyone about our loss. I have now been to see the wall in Springfield three times. Each time I stayed a little longer.

I went to the Vietnam Veterans Memorial in Washington, D.C., in May 2015 during Memorial Day weekend. Rolling Thunder was the most awesome show of respect for the losses our nation suffered that I have ever seen. We went to the wall seven times before we left DC. It was a very sad but healing experience. I felt like I was walking on hallowed ground. You could have heard a pin drop, it was so quiet. A park ranger was reverently picking up mementos that had been left behind at the wall. He respectfully placed each item into large Ziplock bags. All the items are cataloged and stored. Eventually they will be rotated in displays at the Vietnam Education Center that will be built in the future.

My husband, Dave, has been very supportive, and now understands what I went through as a young adolescent. I had never told him about anything, except that Mike was killed in Vietnam. I never felt comfortable talking about it with anyone, for most can never understand what I went through. I just revealed a few years ago to my oldest sister what some of the kids said to me back then. She was appalled that I had never told our parents. The pain was just too great for all of us who still lived at home. We didn't want to cause more pain for each other. The only thing she has ever told me was that Mike had helped her move from home to her apartment just before he left for Vietnam, and she regrets not hugging him and telling him that she loved him. I think that about hits the nail on the head for each of us left behind.

I now know that a lot of these men who served with my brother also feel regret over not being able to prevent the deaths of their fallen brothers. Some feel it was their fault that the others were killed. Nearly every single one of them has survivor's guilt and cannot understand why they were spared death and have been able to live out their lives, to live futures they only dreamed about when in combat. When they get together for reunions, they talk about their experiences and discuss specifics about their fallen comrades. They want to talk to the families of the fallen so each family will learn the truth of what type of soldier their loved one was, and how much all these men loved them as brothers. It is the best healing process I could ever hope for after so many years of unspoken thoughts and feelings of tragic loss. I am indebted to all these men and their wives for bringing Dave and I into their family.

My brother, Michael Harold Flood, was born on October 1, 1948, and was the oldest of seven children of Harold and Charlene Flood. I am his youngest sister. We lived on a farm northeast of Toledo, Illinois. Mike always helped take care of his siblings; always entertaining the young ones. He used to take a handkerchief, roll it behind his head, and pull it back and forth to make it look like he was cleaning out his ears. They would try to mimic him.

Mike, at a young age, also started working with dad, caring for the cattle and pigs, and working on farm equipment. He started assisting with getting the crops in the fields, cultivating and harvesting as soon as his feet could touch the pedals on the equipment. One time he wore a sombrero while cultivating, winning a bet with our doubting mother that he wouldn't wear it all day in the field. He also helped mother and dad clean chickens. His job was to chop the head off. The younger kids were not allowed to be around to watch this because they didn't want them to have nightmares. One time Mike coaxed the three youngest to sneak behind the outhouse and told them to peek around the corner when he whistled so they could watch the chicken run without its head. They didn't believe that could ever happen but decided they wanted him to prove it. They watched and mother started screaming at him because blood was flying everywhere until the chicken finally collapsed. Just one of many things learned from Mike.

Mike used to gig frogs when the population was too high at our two ponds. We all thought it was so cool to help fry the legs because they looked like they were hopping in the skillet. They would also go out and shoot the muskrats that tore holes around the pond and caused problems with the pump. They developed good marksmanship with the .22 rifle.

Mike was very active in Future Farmers of America throughout high school. He found that his favorite class was building and trades. He took it all four years. He loved building so much that he decided after graduation from Cumberland High School in 1966, he wanted to work full-time at the builder's supply store in Toledo. Mother and daddy were not happy but they made a deal with him and his employer that they would let him off when needed for planting and harvesting. Then, though, he received his draft notice in January 1968. He took his basic training at Fort Leonard Wood, MO, and advanced individual training/combat medic training at Fort Sam Houston, TX. Mike was deployed to Vietnam on September 7, 1968. He was attached to Company B, 1st Battalion, 506th Infantry, 101st Airborne. Mike always carried his M16, unlike some of the medics who were conscientious objectors. He believed in what his country called him to do and assisted the infantryman until his medical expertise was needed. Mike quickly earned the name "Doc" from his Band of Brothers. He gave aid and saved many lives during his seven-month tour.

There is nothing worse for a Gold-Star family than to have people forget those who gave their all for our great nation. I will see to it that combat medic Michael Flood is honored to the day I die. He didn't receive a welcome home from his home community; there were no lines of people holding flags and saluting to honor him as the hearse brought him home or to his burial site. That is what occurs today, because of our Vietnam veterans. They never want anyone who has served our nation and did what our country asked them to do to be treated the way they were when they came back to "the world." Our veterans must be treated with honor and respect without fail.

PART III

Postscript: Reunions and Requiems

CHAPTER 29

Postscript

Just as the men introduced in this book *arrived in* Vietnam at different times, due to the Army's Vietnam-era replacement system, those who survived their combat experience *came home* at different times—generally whenever they were wounded, or their tour was up. As we have seen, sometimes, due to circumstances beyond their control, the men didn't even get to say goodbye to their brothers. Some came home and immediately wanted (or needed) to put the war behind them. They had been asked to witness and to do the unthinkable, and came home to a country where most people either didn't want to hear about it, or actively protested the war. For myriad complex reasons, many of the men had no interest in keeping in touch with anyone who might remind them of what they had just endured. They just wanted to move on with their lives. Even if one *wanted* to keep in touch, it wasn't necessarily easy to do so unless you'd shared contact information in advance. Remember that, in the pre-internet age, you couldn't Google a name, or search for people on social media. And yet, today, many of the remaining members of the Battlin' Bastards of Bravo are closer than ever. How is that?

In 2007, former Bravo Company commander Lee "Baron" Sullivan set out to try to gather the men who served in the Company in Vietnam from October 1969–October 1970. He advertised in veterans' publications. He also harnessed the power of the internet, which of course hadn't existed when the men first came home, establishing a Bravo Company website as a way to connect and share information. Eventually, an in-person reunion followed in Washington, D.C. Of course, it included a visit to the Vietnam Veterans Memorial Wall, which had been dedicated in November 1982 to honor the over fifty-eight thousand American servicemen and women killed during the conflict. Bravo Company reunions became annual, held in different cities across the country. More and more men came, sometimes bringing wives and other family members. Gold-Star family members began to join, as well.

Jim Hartman remembered how he became involved, sharing:

> Back home in Roseville, which is a suburb of St. Paul, Minnesota, I had been talked into running a VFW. If somebody didn't take over and run it, it was going to disappear. So I did that. And it's supposed to be—they call you the commander, you get a new commander every

> year. Well, that didn't quite work out. So I told my wife, I said, "If I take this thing, it's going to be the dumbest thing I ever did." And she says to me, "You're going to do it, aren't you?" I said, "Yeah," and I did it for 12 years. I ran the post. And in the process—they have a *VFW* magazine and every month, in the back, it has reunions. And I'm reading this reunion section, and it said, "B Company—Bravo Company—1/506th, 101st Airborne." And it caught my eye and my wife—I'm computer illiterate and quite proud of it—I had her look it up, on the website that they gave. And I'm watching football one cold winter day down in Minnesota, down my man cave. And she come down and she says to me, "Did you have a nickname when you were over in Vietnam?" I said, "Yeah." She says, "Was it 'so-and-so'?" And I said, "Yeah." I said, "How the hell did you find out!?" She said, "Well, your name's on this roster, and you got the nickname right in parentheses alongside your nickname." They called me "Sergeant Rock."
>
> So I thought about it, and I made a couple calls to some of the guys that were on the list that I knew; one to a kid from New York. So I call this gentleman named Mike Liano, who was in the third platoon, my squad, New Yorker. Good guy. He said, yeah, he's gone to a couple. So I told my wife, I says, "I think we'll go to this." And she said, "Well, you go to the first one, see what you think, and if you want to continue, then the next year I'll go with you." First one I went to was in Biloxi, Mississippi. And I've gone to five or six of 'em now.[1]

More and more men were "found" and invited to the reunions every year. As Jim Tarleton recalled:

> I got a phone call from Pete Falco in 2014. I did not know him, but he told me he had been in B Company, 1/506th in 1969–70. He had gotten my name from "someone" who had also served around then. The unit was holding a "reunion"—would I join them? Pete was visiting family near where I lived and we met for lunch. Pete was an affable guy and convincing—I reluctantly agreed to attend the next reunion, attending one held that summer in Myrtle Beach, South Carolina. It was amazing—over thirty men who had served together, in combat, forty-five years earlier, and who had survived. Some of the men I had known—many I did not, as our time did not overlap. Nonetheless, it was an extraordinary gathering of extraordinary men—now aging, able to remember the past with laser focus. Far from maudlin, any tears were from either the laughter or a momentary and fleeting memory of a comrade lost. It was cathartic for me—and I've since attended five more reunions.[2]

Sadly, even as many of the men were re-connecting for the first time, they were continuing to lose brothers—from age, from illness, and from the scourge of chemical defoliants like Agent Orange, in particular.[3] Jim Tarleton lamented, "Since I attended my first B Company reunion in 2014, *at least* fifteen former B Company soldiers have passed, among them Viking [Harold Ericksen], Pete Falco, Bob Caloud, and Sergeant Major Frank Foronda."[4] Similarly, Terry Taylor recalled:

> Many have died. Many from diseases that are attributed to Agent Orange. I don't recall ever being sprayed with Agent Orange but there were many defoliated areas in and around the A Shau Valley. Often we drank water and filled our canteens with water from bomb craters in those areas. I feel sure we drank Agent Orange.[5]

And the reunions just aren't for everyone. As Terry continued:

> All these years later, some people who have been found, but there are also a number of folks who have been located but have no desire to attend a reunion or relive any memories of Vietnam. I know how they feel. It was really hard for me to attend the first one I went to, but it was a healing experience. I now try not to miss one. A lot of the guys who come to the reunions did what I

> did. They came home, went to college on the GI Bill, and went about living their lives. A lot of the guys who didn't do college became police officers. And then some others didn't fare well.[6]

For those who *do* attend the reunions, a highlight is the "Missing Man Table." A senior sergeant oversees the lighting of candles for the killed and missing in action by comrades, family, and friends. A "Currahee" toast is then made. That toast is led by the senior officer present. The table is small and set for one, symbolizing the frailty of human life. The chair is empty, in honor of those not present. The tablecloth is white, symbolizing the purity of purpose of those who answered the nation's call to arms. A black POW flag covers the table to symbolize the somber mood. The table holds: a bible, representing the strength gained through faith to sustain those lost for the country founded as one nation under God; a black candle for those from Bravo Company who have died since coming home; a single rose, in honor of the families and loved ones of the fallen; a slice of lemon on a plate to represent their bitter fate; salt on the plate to symbolize the tears of families and loved ones; and an inverted glass, as those gone cannot join in the toast.

In addition to the reunions, the reconvened Battlin' Bastards embarked on the writing of the Bravo Company journal, mentioned in the Acknowledgements of this book and cited by several of the Battlin' Bastards in their testimonials and oral histories. Its primary compilers, Lee Sullivan and Pete Falco, sought to document, sometimes day-to-day and minute-to-minute, the movements of the company at key moments in 1969 and 1970, and, especially, the circumstances surrounding each casualty the company suffered while in-country. This involved recording firsthand accounts from the men of the company and painstaking research at places such as the National Archives. It was hoped that this effort would create a fuller picture of the efforts of Bravo Company for the historical record, honor those who died, and help provide some closure to the men who survived—and, perhaps especially, to the families of the men who did not survive. As Lee and Pete wrote in the Foreword to the journal:

> This journal tells the stories of some of the men who served in Bravo Company of the 1st Battalion of the 506th Infantry during their service in the Republic of Vietnam from 1969–70. Bravo Company was known as the "Battling Bastards of Bravo" and the 506th Infantry were known as the CURRAHEES with the slogan "We Stand Alone."
>
> The journal begins with the movement of Bravo Company into the battle for the hilltop that would become known as "Hamburger Hill" and ends with the last major battle between an American Infantry Division and Divisions of the North Vietnamese Army during the war. This battle is known as "Ripcord," taking the name from Fire Support Base Ripcord which was the center point of the battle.
>
> All of these events happened a long time ago, in a place far away from where these Troopers had ever imagined they would be. The events happened during a time when America had begun a disengagement from Vietnam and when the new President, Richard Nixon, had pledged that we would have "Peace with Honor" in Vietnam. Almost half of the total casualties in Vietnam would occur after President Nixon's pledge for achieving "Peace with Honor." The Troopers of Bravo Company would become engaged in some of the last major battles of the war and many of them would make the ultimate sacrifice in a pursuit of the "Peace with Honor" that never came.

> Warfare is sometimes described as unimaginable boredom interrupted by moments of stark terror. The troopers of Bravo Company would have more than their share of stark terror and this would lead to strong bonds between those who endured terror together. Outsiders cannot imagine the emotions that bind together those who become "Brothers in Arms" by the shared terror they experience. The Troopers of Bravo Company would become a "Band of Brothers" from Vietnam in a way that men of "Easy Company," 2nd Battalion of the 506th Parachute Infantry Regiment (PIR), 101st Airborne Division described in the book and television series *Band of Brothers*, did during their service in World War II. All men who fight in small infantry units in warfare achieve a mutual dependence and "love" for each other as they bond together in a fight for mutual survival. Some of them will die during these brutal firefights with the enemy. When you are in a firefight you do not fight for your Country or for your Division, you fight for the "Brothers in Arms" standing beside you because at that moment they are the only thing that matters.

For the "Brothers in Arms" of Bravo Company who were participating in the reunions and then the journal, both went a long way towards honoring the dead, reigniting comradery, and healing old wounds. Some of the men of Bravo Company wanted to take things a step further. They began organizing a return trip to Vietnam for 2017. The men who made the journey ventured right back into the heart of the A Shau Valley, using the Bravo Company journal as a guide. They visited many of the very sites where they lost their brothers-in-arms, letting them know that, all of these years later, they had not been forgotten. As Steve Conroy recalled, this was all part of Lee Sullivan and Pete Falco's original vision:

> The mission Pete Falco laid out, and Lee Sullivan—basically, they wanted to have a reunion, the journal, and the third piece of the triangle was to have a trip back to Vietnam....
>
> Pete basically organized this whole thing. And he first reached out and says, "Who wants to go?" And strangely enough, a lot of the guys didn't want to go.[7] It ended up being Pete and I, Jerry Hoffman, Terry Ostendorf, who was a recon platoon leader, and Mike Smith, Pete's friend ... who was an artillery guy. So the five of us decided to do it.[8]

The men prepped for months, getting their travel paperwork and insurance in order, and researching in advance the exact locations in Vietnam they wanted to visit. They visited cities like Saigon (now known as Ho Chi Minh City), and restaurants and museums. They were shocked by how different the country looked, how thriving the economy seemed, and how welcome they were by the Vietnamese. They visited their old base camp, Camp Evans—now farmland. Their top priority, however, was pinpointing the sites where they had lost men, in order to physically go there and honor those killed in action. They visited these often remote locations, and left behind personal items—things like apple seeds, dog tags, family photographs, rosary beads. At each site, the five veterans also took a photograph with a "Never Forget" banner.

That 2017 return trip surely deserves a book of its own but, suffice to say, from the reunions to the Bravo Company journal to the return trip to this new book, the surviving Battlin' Bastards are tireless in their efforts to honor their dead and to document what they did themselves, in honor of all combat veterans, and in the hopes that we might as a society learn lessons that lead to a better tomorrow.

Appendix

Lineage and Honors Information

Headquarters and Headquarters Battalion, 101st Airborne Division, (Screaming Eagles)[1]

Constituted 23 July 1918 in the National Army as Headquarters, 101st Division
Organized 2 November 1918 at Camp Shelby, Mississippi
Demobilized 11 December 1918 at Camp Shelby, Mississippi
Reconstituted 24 June 1921 in the Organized Reserves as Headquarters, 101st Division
Organized 10 September 1921 at Milwaukee, Wisconsin
Redesignated 31 March 1942 as Division Headquarters, 101st Division
Disbanded 15 August 1942; concurrently reconstituted in the Army of the United States as Headquarters, 101st Airborne Division, and activated at Camp Claiborne, Louisiana
Inactivated 30 November 1945 in France
Allotted 25 June 1948 to the Regular Army
Activated 6 July 1948 at Camp Breckinridge, Kentucky
Inactivated 27 May 1949 at Camp Breckinridge, Kentucky
Activated 25 August 1950 at Camp Breckinridge, Kentucky
Inactivated 1 December 1953 at Camp Breckinridge, Kentucky
Activated 15 May 1954 at Fort Jackson, South Carolina
Reorganized and redesignated 3 February 1964 as Headquarters and Headquarters Company, 101st Airborne Division
Reorganized and redesignated 16 September 2004 as Headquarters and Tactical Command Posts, 101st Airborne Division
Reorganized and redesignated 16 October 2009 as Headquarters and Headquarters Battalion, 101st Airborne Division (organic elements of Headquarters Battalion concurrently constituted and activated)

Campaign Participation Credit

World War II

Normandy (with arrowhead)
Rhineland (with arrowhead)
Ardennes-Alsace
Central Europe

Vietnam

Counteroffensive, Phase III
Tet Counteroffensive

Counteroffensive, Phase IV
Counteroffensive, Phase V
Counteroffensive, Phase VI
Tet 69/Counteroffensive
Summer-Fall 1969
Winter-Spring 1970
Sanctuary Counteroffensive
Counteroffensive, Phase VII
Consolidation I
Consolidation II

Southwest Asia

Defense of Saudi Arabia
Liberation and Defense of Kuwait

War on Terrorism

Iraq
Liberation of Iraq
Transition of Iraq
Iraqi Governance
National Resolution

Afghanistan
Consolidation II
Consolidation III

(Additional campaigns to be determined)

Decorations

Presidential Unit Citation (Army), Streamer embroidered NORMANDY
Presidential Unit Citation (Army), Streamer embroidered BASTOGNE
Meritorious Unit Commendation (Army), Streamer embroidered SOUTHWEST ASIA 1990–1991
Meritorious Unit Commendation (Army), Streamer embroidered IRAQ 2003
Meritorious Unit Commendation (Army), Streamer embroidered IRAQ 2005–2006
Army Superior Unit Award, Streamer embroidered 2014–2015
French Croix de Guerre with Palm, World War II, Streamer embroidered NORMANDY
Belgian Croix de Guerre 1940 with Palm, Streamer embroidered BASTOGNE; cited in the Order of the Day of the Belgian Army for action at Bastogne
Belgian Fourragere 1940
Cited in the Order of the Day of the Belgian Army for action in France and Belgium
Netherlands Orange Lanyard
Republic of Vietnam Cross of Gallantry with Palm, Streamer embroidered VIETNAM 1968–1969
Republic of Vietnam Cross of Gallantry with Palm, Streamer embroidered VIETNAM 1971
Republic of Vietnam Civil Action Honor Medal, First Class, Streamer embroidered VIETNAM 1968–1970

Headquarters Battalion additionally entitled to:
Meritorious Unit Commendation (Army), Streamer embroidered AFGHANISTAN 2013–2014

By Order of the Secretary of the Army:

CHARLES R. BOWERY, JR.
Chief of Military History

1st Battalion, 506th Infantry Regiment (Currahee)[2]

Constituted 1 July 1942 in the Army of the United States as Company A, 506th Parachute Infantry
Activated 20 July 1942 at Camp Toccoa, Georgia
(506th Parachute Infantry assigned 1 March 1945 to the 101st Airborne Division)
Inactivated 30 November 1945 in France
Redesignated 18 June 1948 as Company A, 506th Airborne Infantry
Allotted 25 June 1948 to the Regular Army
Activated 6 July 1948 at Camp Breckinridge, Kentucky
Inactivated 1 April 1949 at Camp Breckinridge, Kentucky
Activated 25 August 1950 at Camp Breckinridge, Kentucky
Inactivated 1 December 1953 at Camp Breckinridge, Kentucky
Activated 15 May 1954 at Fort Jackson, South Carolina
Reorganized and redesignated 25 April 1957 as Headquarters and Headquarters Company, 1st Airborne Battle Group, 506th Infantry, and remained assigned to the 101st Airborne Division (organic elements concurrently constituted and activated)
Reorganized and redesignated 3 February 1964 as the 1st Battalion, 506th Infantry
Inactivated 5 June 1984 at Fort Campbell, Kentucky, and relieved from assignment to the 101st Airborne Division
Assigned 16 March 1987 to the 2d Infantry Division and activated in Korea
Relieved 30 September 2005 from assignment to the 2d Infantry Division and assigned to the 4th Brigade Combat Team, 101st Airborne Division
Redesignated 1 October 2005 as the 1st Battalion, 506th Infantry Regiment
Relieved 17 April 2014 from assignment to the 4th Brigade Combat Team, 101st Airborne Division and assigned to the 1st Brigade Combat Team, 101st Airborne Division

Campaign Participation Credit

World War I

Normandy (with arrowhead)
Rhineland (with arrowhead)
Ardennes-Alsace
Central Europe

Vietnam

Counteroffensive, Phase III
Tet Counteroffensive
Counteroffensive, Phase IV

Counteroffensive, Phase V
Counteroffensive, Phase VI
Tet 69/Counteroffensive
Summer-Fall 1969
Winter-Spring 1970
Sanctuary Counteroffensive
Counteroffensive, Phase VII
Consolidation I
Consolidation II

War on Terrorism

Iraq
Iraqi Governance
National Resolution

Afghanistan
Consolidation II
Consolidation III

(Additional campaigns to be determined)

Decorations

Presidential Unit Citation (Army), Streamer embroidered NORMANDY
Presidential Unit Citation (Army), Streamer embroidered BASTOGNE
Presidential Unit Citation (Army), Streamer embroidered DONG AP BIA MOUNTAIN
Valorous Unit Award, Streamer embroidered DEFENSE OF SAIGON
Valorous Unit Award, Streamer embroidered PAKTIKA PROVINCE 2010–2011
Meritorious Unit Commendation (Army), Streamer embroidered VIETNAM 1968
Meritorious Unit Commendation (Army), Streamer embroidered AFGHANISTAN 2008–2009
Meritorious Unit Commendation (Army), Streamer embroidered AFGHANISTAN 2013
Meritorious Unit Commendation (Army), Streamer embroidered SOUTHWEST ASIA 2018–2019
Navy Unit Commendation, Streamer embroidered ANBAR PROVINCE 2006–2007
French Croix de Guerre with Palm, World War II, Streamer embroidered NORMANDY
Netherlands Orange Lanyard
Belgian Croix de Guerre 1940 with Palm, Streamer embroidered BASTOGNE; cited in the order of the Day of the Belgian Army for action at Bastogne
Belgian Fourragere 1940
*Cited in the Order of the Day of the Belgian Army for action in France and Belgium
Republic of Vietnam Cross of Gallantry with Palm, Streamer embroidered VIETNAM 1968–1969
Republic of Vietnam Cross of Gallantry with Palm, Streamer embroidered VIETNAM 1971
Republic of Vietnam Civil Action Honor Medal, First Class, Streamer embroidered VIETNAM 1968–1970

By Order of the Secretary of the Army:

CHARLES R. BOWERY, JR.
Chief of Military History

Endnotes

Preface and Acknowledgements

1. For more on the history of Fort Monmouth, see Melissa Ziobro, *Fort Monmouth: The US Army's House of Magic* (Havertown, Pennsylvania: Brookline Books, 2024).
2. For more on the "dollar princesses" of New Jersey, see Melissa Ziobro, "'The almighty dollar will buy you, you bet / A superior class of coronet': Biographical Sketches of NJ's Gilded Age 'Dollar Princesses,'" *New Jersey Studies: An Interdisciplinary Journal*, Volume 4, Number 2 (2018), 230–62.
3. Jim Hartman interviewed by George Bogdanich, September 2023.

Introduction

1. Jerry Hoffman interviewed by the author, May 2024.
2. "Troops count cost of Vietnam's Hamburger Hill—archive, 1969," *The Guardian*, https://www.theguardian.com/world/2017/may/24/troops-count-cost-vietnam-hamburger-hill-archive-1969. Accessed November 3, 2024.
3. Jim Tarleton email to the author, May 2024.
4. Terry Taylor email to the author, March 2023.
5. Jerry Hoffman interview.

Part I: The Screaming Eagles and the War in Southeast Asia

1. Mark Bando, *101st Airborne: The Screaming Eagles in World War II* (Minnesota: Zenith Press, 2011).
2. United States National Archives, "Screaming Eagles," https://www.archivesfoundation.org/newsletter/the-screaming-eagles/. Accessed November 3, 2024.
3. Russ and Susan Bryant, *Screaming Eagles: 101st Airborne Division* (Minnesota: Zenith Press, 2007).
4. U.S. Army Center for Military History, "Headquarters and Headquarters Battalion, 101st Airborne Division (Screaming Eagles) Unit Lineage and Honors," https://history.army.mil/html/forcestruc/lineages/branches/div/101abdb.htm; U.S. National Archives, "Screaming Eagles." Accessed November 3, 2024.
5. Gordon L. Rottman, *US World War II Parachute Infantry Regiments* (London: Bloomsbury Publishing, 2014), 1.
6. U.S. Army Center for Military History, "Headquarters and Headquarters Battalion, 101st Airborne Division (Screaming Eagles) Unit Lineage and Honors"; U.S. National Archives, "Screaming Eagles."
7. Kurt Gabel, *The Making of a Paratrooper: Airborne Training and Combat in World War II* (Kansas: University Press of Kansas, 1990), 37.
8. U.S. Army Center for Military History, "Headquarters and Headquarters Battalion, 101st Airborne Division (Screaming Eagles) Unit Lineage and Honors"; U.S. National Archives, "Screaming Eagles."
9. U.S. National Archives, "Screaming Eagles."

10. The Japanese surrender was announced on August 15 in Japan; because of the time zone difference, it was announced August 14 in America.
11. U.S. Army Center for Military History, "Headquarters and Headquarters Battalion, 101st Airborne Division (Screaming Eagles) Unit Lineage and Honors."
12. Continue reading for an explanation of the domino theory if needed.
13. Note that "the rest of the division deployed" means on paper. Individual personnel rotated in and out of theater based on their own contracts with the Army. This is a simplification, but, during the Vietnam War, most soldiers served one-year deployments. This meant a much quicker turnover than during World War II, where many soldiers served for years—from their enlistment through the duration, whatever that might be.
14. U.S. National Archives, "Screaming Eagles."
15. U.S. Army Center for Military History, "Headquarters and Headquarters Battalion, 101st Airborne Division (Screaming Eagles) Unit Lineage and Honors."
16. United States National Archives, "Screaming Eagles."
17. James A. Page, "The Story of 'Old Abe,' famous Wisconsin War Eagle on 101st Airborne Division patch," U.S. Army, November 15, 2012, https://www.army.mil/article/91178/the_story_of_old_abe_famous_wisconsin_war_eagle_on_101st_airborne_division_patch. Accessed November 3, 2024.
18. Kelly Eads and Daniel S. Morgan, *Black Hearts and Painted Guns* (Pennsylvania: Casemate Publishers, 2023), 7–8; James Frederick, *Black Hearts: One Platoon's Descent Into Madness in Iraq's Triangle of Death* (New York: Crown, 2010), 19; U.S. National Archives, "Screaming Eagles."
19. Christina Knight, "U.S. Army Units Explained: From Squads to Brigades to Corps," PBS, https://www.thirteen.org/blog-post/u-s-army-units-explained-from-squads-to-brigades-to-corps/. Accessed October 31, 2024.
20. Philip A. Russell interviewed by Alan Thompson, March 8, 2001. Courtesy Library of Congress.
21. Earl McClung interviewed by Sheralan Marrott, December 2, 2003. Courtesy Library of Congress.
22. Philip A. Russell interviewed by Alan Thompson, March 8, 2001. Courtesy Library of Congress.
23. U.S. Army Center for Military History, "506th Infantry Regiment (Currahee) Unit Lineage and Honors."
24. Earl McClung interviewed by Sheralan Marrott, December 2, 2003. Courtesy Library of Congress.
25. U.S. Army Center for Military History, "506th Infantry Regiment (Currahee) Unit Lineage and Honors."
26. Ibid.
27. Ibid.
28. Ibid.
29. On April 2, 1917, President Wilson asked Congress to declare war on Germany. He condemned German submarine attacks on U.S. and other neutral shipping. He also argued that autocratic governments, such as the German regime, with their habitual intrigue, unrestrained by the will of their people, were a threat to free and self-governing nations. The president asserted, "The world must be made safe for democracy. Its peace must be planted upon the tested foundations of political liberty. We have no selfish ends to serve. We desire no conquest, no dominion. We see no indemnities for ourselves, no material compensation for the sacrifices we shall freely make."
30. George C. Herring, *America's Longest War: The United States and Vietnam, 1950–1975* (New York: McGraw Hill, 2013), 25.
31. Ibid., 8.

Terry Taylor

1. As Terry notes, "… we called them 'gooks' and 'slants' in order to dehumanize them and make killing them easier than killing a human being." Those terms are used in this book only when

the veterans are relaying things they said in the field, to remind readers of the dehumanization that takes place during war.

Gordon Roberts

1. "Gordon Ray Roberts," Congressional Medal of Honor Society, www.cmohs.org. Accessed December 12, 2024.

Part III: Postscript: Reunions and Requiems

1. Jim Hartman interviewed by George Bogdanich, September 2023.
2. Jim Tarleton email to the author, May 2024.
3. According to the Vietnam Veterans Memorial Fund, "Agent Orange was first sprayed in August 1961. President Kennedy had authorized the use of herbicides in December 1961, and the U.S. Air Force began flying Operation *Ranch Hand* missions the following month. Operation *Ranch Hand* (part of a larger program known as *Trail Dust*) was designed to defoliate areas used by the enemy as cover for ambushes, as well as to destroy enemy subsistence crops. The chemical weapons used were known as 'Rainbow Herbicides'—Agent White, Agent Purple, Agent Blue, Agent Pink, Agent Green, and Agent Orange—named for the colored bands painted on their respective storage drums. Between 1962 and 1971, the U.S. sprayed an estimated 20 million gallons of these herbicides in Vietnam, eastern Laos, and parts of Cambodia, usually from helicopters or low-flying aircraft, but sometimes from backpacks, boats, and trucks. Agent Orange alone accounted for more than half of the total volume of herbicides deployed. One of its key ingredients, dioxin, is highly toxic even in tiny quantities. Operation *Ranch Hand* deployed about 375 pounds of dioxin over an area about the size of Massachusetts, contaminating the entire ecosystem and exposing millions of people—on both sides of the conflict—to horrifying long-term effects, including skin diseases and cancers among those exposed, and birth defects in their children. The ecological, health, and legal issues created by the use of chemical defoliants during the Vietnam War are complex, internationally debated, and continue to the present day. U.S. military personnel who were exposed to Agent Orange while serving in Vietnam have litigated the issue for decades, seeking compensation for medical care resulting from Agent Orange exposure. They have sued both the U.S. government and the corporations who manufactured the chemical compounds." The Vietnam Veterans Memorial Fund, "Agent Orange," https://www.vvmf.org. Accessed October 31, 2024.
4. Ibid.
5. Terry Taylor email to the author, March 2023.
6. Ibid.
7. Recall that Jim Hartman, in his story in Part II, shared, "I've been asked if I wanted about going back to Vietnam, for these tours. I would never do that. It has nothing to do with the people. The country was so ungodly, hot, humid. It was not my favorite place, so I would never go back."
8. Steven Conroy interviewed by the West Point Center for Oral History, July 2019.

Appendix

1. U.S. Army Center for Military History, "Headquarters and Headquarters Battalion, 101st Airborne Division (Screaming Eagles) Unit Lineage and Honors."
2. U.S. Army Center for Military History, "506th Infantry Regiment (Currahee) Unit Lineage and Honors."

Author's Suggestions for Further Reading

The Screaming Eagles

Ambrose, Stephen. *Band of Brothers: E Company, 506th Regiment, 101st Airborne from Normandy to Hitler's Eagle's Nest.* New York: Simon and Schuster, 2001.

Bowen, Robert. *Fighting with the Screaming Eagles: With the 101st Airborne from Normandy to Bastogne.* Pennsylvania: Casemate Publishers, 2010.

Eads, Kelly, and Daniel S. Morgan. *Black Hearts and Painted Guns.* Pennsylvania: Casemate Publishers, 2023.

Hughes, Christopher. *War on Two Fronts: An Infantry Commander's War in Iraq and the Pentagon.* Pennsylvania: Casemate Publishers, 2016.

Jones, Robert E. *History of the 101st Airborne Division Screaming Eagles: The First 50 Years.* Tennessee: Turner Press, 2010.

Sherwood, Ed. *Courage Under Fire: The 101st Airborne's Hidden Battle at Tam Ky.* Pennsylvania: Casemate Publishers, 2023.

Theotokis, Nikolaos. *Airborne Landing to Air Assault: A History of Military Parachuting.* Pennsylvania: Casemate Publishers, 2023.

Wiknik, Arthur. *Nam Sense: Surviving Vietnam with the 101st Airborne Division.* Pennsylvania: Casemate Publishers, 2018.

The War in Southeast Asia

Bahnsen, John C. *American Warrior: A Combat Memoir of Vietnam.* New York: Citadel, 2007.

Boccia, Frank. *The Crouching Beast: A United States Army Lieutenant's Account of the Battle for Hamburger Hill, May 1969.* New York: McFarland, 2013.

Carver, Ron, et al. *Waging Peace in Vietnam: U.S. Soldiers and Veterans Who Opposed the War.* New York: New Village Press, 2019.

Doyle, David. *U.S. Aviation and Naval Weapons in the Vietnam War.* Pennsylvania: Casemate Publishers, 2024.

Herring, George C. *America's Longest War: The United States and Vietnam, 1950–1975.* New York: McGraw Hill, 2020.

Kotcher, Joann Puffer. *Donut Dolly: An American Red Cross Girl's War In Vietnam.* Texas: University of North Texas Press, 2017.

Lemire, Elise. *Battle Green Vietnam: The 1971 March on Concord, Lexington, and Boston.* Pennsylvania: University of Pennsylvania Press, 2021.

MacDonald, Charles B. *The U.S. Army in Vietnam.* Washington, D.C.: Government Printing Office, 1972.

Moore, Harold G., and Joseph L. Galloway. *We Were Soldiers Once … and Young: Ia Drang—The Battle that Changed Vietnam.* California: Presidio Press, 2004.

Moore, Harold G., and Joseph L. Galloway. *We Are Soldiers Still: A Journey Back to the Battlefields of Vietnam*. New York: Harper, 2008.

Nash, N. S. *Logistics in the War in Vietnam Wars, 1945–1975*. Pennsylvania: Casemate Publishers, 2022.

Nguyen, Lien-Hang T. *Hanoi's War: An International History of the War for Peace in Vietnam*. New York: Blackstone Publishing, 2013.

Perrett, Bryan, and Walter Walker. *A History of Jungle Warfare: From the Earliest Days to the Battlefields of Vietnam*. Pennsylvania: Casemate Publishers, 2023.

Pike, John. *Vietnam and the Cold War 1945—1954: French Imperial Decline and Defeat at Dien Bien Phu*. Pennsylvania: Casemate Publishers, 2024.

Scott, Wilbur J. *Vietnam Veterans Since the War: The Politics of PTSD, Agent Orange, and the National Memorial*. Oklahoma: University of Oklahoma Press, 2004.

Smoyer, Nancy. *Donut Dollies in Vietnam: Baby-Blue Dresses and OD Green*. New York: Chopper Books, 2017.

Terry, Wallace. *Bloods: An Oral History of the Vietnam War by Black Veterans, 1984*. New York: Presidio Press, 1985.

Zaffiri, Samuel. *Hamburger Hill: The Brutal Battle for Dong Ap Bia, May 11–20, 1969*. New York: Random House, 2000.